The

RESILIENCE

BREAK-

THR UGH

Advance Praise for *The Resilience Breakthrough*

"Christian Moore has written a handbook based on his personal and professional experience that will have universal appeal for people who want concrete, workable tools to develop resilience. His passion for helping those who most need resilience shines through this work, and his 'ask and task' directions for building resilience skills one step at a time make the process clear and manageable."

> —Dr. Margaret Wehrenberg, author of *The 10 Best-Ever Anxiety Management Techniques*

"Christian's book was arresting and engaging from the first page. Resilience is a topic I care a great deal about, and he offers an authenticity, humility, and vulnerability that is deeply moving to me. There is not a topic of greater urgency for the future than resilience. And there is not an author more qualified to teach it than Christian Moore. This book is an important contribution to global well-being. It is also an intimately vulnerable invitation into the soul of one of the world's most promising influencers."

> —Joseph Grenny, *New York Times* bestselling coauthor of *Crucial Conversations* and *Influencer: The New Science of Leading Change*

"This book had me heart and soul from the beginning. Christian's powerful storytelling, the weaving of other thought-leaders' insights, questions for the reader to ponder and act on, made this one of the most holistic reads on a topic that matters greatly in all walks of life—resilience. I have a completely new appreciation for what resilience means and how to develop it more in myself and others. I will refer to this book often as it is a field guide for the journey all of us walk."

> —Teresa Roche, vice president and chief learning officer, Agilent Technologies

"Christian Moore's powerful book resonated strongly with me for many reasons. His story is more than just a raw, honest look at a difficult life; it is a living example of how he chose to live that life. Never giving in to the demons of despair and defeat, Christian inspirationally transforms his hardships into stepping stones toward higher ground. This is resilience! A timely, uplifting, and enlightening read."

> —Stephen M. R. Covey, author of the *New York Times* and #1 *Wall Street Journal* bestseller *The Speed of Trust*, and coauthor of *Smart Trust*

"The truth is simple: individuals work harder, better, and more passionately when they know how to approach challenges without fear. *The Resilience Breakthrough* is the perfect tool for any business interested in more confident workers, unstoppable teams, and bigger profits."

> —Liane Davey, *New York Times* bestselling author of *YOU FIRST: Inspire Your Team to Grow Up, Get Along, and Get Stuff Done*

"If you are at all interested in self-actualization, then Christian Moore's *The Resilience Breakthrough* is required reading. You'll learn that psychological resilience is the portal from which your true inner potential can be released. It's all about perspective! Perspective along with common sense, step-by-step applications. Fasten your seat belt and be prepared for your weaknesses to fuel your strengths, your negatives to be transformed into positives, and your hesitations to become actions."

> —Joseph J. Luciani, PhD, bestselling author of *Self-Coaching:*
> *The Powerful Program to Beat Anxiety & Depression*

"Do you sometimes find yourself paralyzed by the adversities of life—the challenges, troubles, and problems that consume and drain your vision of future success? If so, *The Resilience Breakthrough* was written for you. Christian Moore's authentic, refreshingly honest, and actionable guide to self-reliance will transform your life."

> —Scott Addis, president and CEO of The Addis Group; author of
> *Summit: Reach Your Peak and Elevate Your Customers' Experience*

"Helping students and clients overcome life's obstacles is the pivotal focus of each of the human service professions; e.g., education, social work, health sciences, and psychology. And there are few, if any, persons who are more qualified than Christian Moore to enunciate effective strategies for helping these individuals overcome barriers that confront them. He, himself, has overcome poverty, learning disabilities, living in the 'street,' and other serious challenges; earning a master's degree, working as social worker, becoming a prominent speaker, and developing and implementing the empirically founded Why Try? program that is widely used in building the resilience of youth. I highly recommend this book. It is an insightful, well-researched, and useful resource that has utility for persons challenged by life's burdens and in the work of human service professionals."

> —Dr. David E. Herr, professor, Educational Foundations and
> Exceptional Education, James Madison University

"As a national nonprofit focused on transforming communities and the lives of at-risk youth, the power of a resiliency is vital. The Cal Ripken, Sr. Foundation was founded by a family known for its perseverance and resilient nature—Christian's book brings these concepts to life."

> —Steve Salem, president of the Cal Ripken, Sr. Foundation

"Christian's own irrepressible life story and practical tools for succeeding in the face of hardship are a powerful combination."

> —Kim Capps, CEO of InsideOut Development

The RESILIENCE BREAK-THRUGH

{ 27 Tools for Turning Adversity into Action }

CHRISTIAN MOORE, LCSW

with Brad Anderson and Kristin McQuivey

GREENLEAF
BOOK GROUP PRESS

Published by Greenleaf Book Group Press
Austin, Texas
www.gbgpress.com

Distributed by Greenleaf Book Group LLC

For ordering information or special discounts for bulk purchases, please contact Greenleaf Book Group LLC at PO Box 91869, Austin, TX 78709, 512.891.6100.

Design and composition by Greenleaf Book Group LLC
Cover design by Greenleaf Book Group LLC
Cover image ©iStockphoto.com/hemul75

Publisher's Cataloging-In-Publication Data

Moore, Christian.
   The resilience breakthrough : 27 tools for turning adversity into action/Christian Moore, LCSW ; with Brad Anderson and Kristin McQuivey.—First edition.
      pages ; cm
   Includes bibliographical references.
   Issued also as an ebook.
   ISBN: 978-1-62634-093-0
   1. Moore, Christian. 2. Resilience (Personality trait) 3. Adjustment (Psychology) 4. Success—Psychological aspects. I. Anderson, Brad, 1952- II. McQuivey, Kristin. III. Title.
BF698.35.R47 M66 2014
155.2/4   2013954954

Part of the Tree Neutral® program, which offsets the number of trees consumed in the production and printing of this book by taking proactive steps, such as planting trees in direct proportion to the number of trees used: www.treeneutral.com

TreeNeutral®

Printed in the United States of America on acid-free paper

15 16 17 18 19   10 9 8 7 6 5 4 3 2

First Edition

Other Editions
eBook ISBN: 978-1-62634-094-7

To my wife, Wendy, the most resilient person I know.

To my two sons, Cooper and Carson: May you
always carry with you the knowledge that resilience is
the greatest truth your dad ever learned.

CONTENTS

FOREWORD

In my books, *The Speed of Trust* and *Smart Trust*, I make the case that trust is essential to prosperity, energy, and joy. After reading Christian Moore's new book, I feel I've been introduced to another essential: *resilience*.

When a friend of mine gave me a copy of *The Resilience Breakthrough*, I was instantly struck by the title. It espouses a timeless truth: When we find our inner resilience in the midst of a world of unrelenting change and uncertainty, it truly is a breakthrough. Indeed, I've become convinced that the key attribute that enables an individual, team, or organization to thrive in the midst of the turbulence we all encounter is resilience. Christian has written a book that not only shares a fascinating personal journey of resilience but also gives us a set of principles, tools, and skills that anyone at any stage or station in life can learn and apply, giving them a resilience breakthrough.

My father, Stephen R. Covey, grew up in a different time—an era in history when relationships with neighbors and colleagues were built on the solid foundation of trust; when people viewed challenges as a means to a better life; and when discipline, humility, and integrity were esteemed more highly than they seem to be today. The world looks somewhat different now than it did when my father was a young man. My book, *The Speed of Trust*, takes a good hard look at society's trust crisis, but Christian is the first author I've seen who directly addresses our "resilience crisis." As my father would often say, "It's not what happens to us, but our response to what happens to us that hurts us." Truly, too many of us are responding to challenges and adversity today in a way that's less than resilient, and, just like trust, resilience is an essential attribute that we can't afford to lose.

The reality is, we never know when we're going to experience professional or personal challenges. There is so much in life that lies outside of our control. A layoff, personal loss, economic challenge, or illness could be just around the corner. While that might seem like a grim outlook, Christian's book shows how life's inevitable misfortunes can actually serve as *fuel* to propel us into even better circumstances. Once we have a resilience breakthrough, we're prepared for whatever adversities may come our way, giving us the ability to bounce back from every challenge.

One of the things I like most about this book is that it gives us a common framework, language, and process for understanding how to develop resilience to handle life's challenges. Just imagine the power that would come to a business, family, or team if everyone inside it spoke the common language of resilience! This is the kind of empowerment that can literally transform individuals and organizations.

Christian's words resonate strongly with me, not just because of the raw, honest account he gives of the cruel realities he's faced in life but also because of the personal, engaging stories he shares of never giving in to the twin demons of despair and defeat. Christian's greatest gift is in his ability to translate his hard-won lessons of resilience into practical, accessible, and invaluable lessons for the reader. His book is, in part, a captivating memoir about living with learning disabilities, growing up in a blended home, and inspirationally transforming hardships into stepping-stones toward higher ground. More important, it also provides readers with real tools that, when applied, have the capacity to lift individuals, and ultimately society, out of their resilience crisis. These tools are delivered in a way that's accessible to everyone—the frontline worker, the stay-at-home mother, the successful CEO, the high school student. It's so full of aha moments that I personally had a hard time putting it down.

I write in *The Speed of Trust* that "contrary to what most people believe, trust is not some soft, illusive quality that you either have or you don't; rather, trust is a pragmatic, tangible, actionable asset that you can create—much faster than you probably think possible." I believe resilience to be similar—it's a skill that all of us are born with, but that most of us have forgotten. But, just as we can increase trust, we can restore our propensity to be resilient. Indeed, resilience is a skill that can be developed and increased. Christian references the groundbreaking research of Stanford professor Dr. Carol Dweck to support his premise that resilience is learnable.

I can promise you that, as Christian says, "if you're a human being breathing oxygen on planet Earth," *The Resilience Breakthrough* is for you. It will give you the courage to face whatever storm you're currently facing or might someday face. It will give you the skills you need to bounce back. I invite you to read it, apply it, and then share it with everyone you know who's faced adversity (that is, all of us). I think Christian is delivering something that people in our society are hungering for—skills of resilience that are not only helpful, but essential—and I'm convinced that the application of these skills will lift us out of our resilience crisis.

I hope you read this book with the expectation that it's going to change you for the better. It certainly did me.

Happy reading.

Stephen M. R. Covey
Cofounder and Global Practice Leader
FranklinCovey's Global Speed of Trust Practice

ACKNOWLEDGMENTS

I'd like to thank my wife, Wendy, who has been incredibly patient our whole marriage, but exceptionally so in the last three years. Without you, I would have never made it past page 1.

I thank my longtime friend and 15-year business partner Hans Magleby, who demonstrated his belief in me and in this book by putting so much on the line.

Thanks to my collaborator, Brad Anderson, without whose knowledge and expertise this book would still be a jumble of handwritten scribbles on a shelf in my office.

I thank the talented writer Kristin McQuivey, who was able to capture my voice on paper far better than I ever could have done myself.

I thank Valerie Bagley, WhyTry's director of communications, who contributed her valuable insights, guidance, and editing skills to the creation of this book.

My heartfelt thanks go to my mentor David Murray for his incredible support and wisdom.

I am grateful to Darrell Scott, a friend, a mentor, and a great example to me.

I extend my thanks to the WhyTry team for listening to my "book epiphanies" and for keeping us in business as I've thrown myself into this project.

Thanks to Bruce Bushnell for making me more resilient because of his constant sacrifice, love, and support. You're the best!

I am grateful to Dr. Shirley Cox for believing in me during my lowest times in life. Thanks for telling me to write this book.

Moses, Pat, and Shawn Jackson—thanks for showing me what love and kindness are early in life.

Nana and Papa Ash—thanks for your unconditional love and support.

My gratitude goes to the editor of this book, Aaron Hierholzer, and to other members of the Greenleaf Book Group, for capturing the vision of the book so quickly and being a pleasure to work with.

Finally, thanks to all the friends, mentors, advocates, clients, and family members whose examples have inspired me and helped me become a more resilient person.

THE RESILIENCE BREAKTHROUGH

I was curled up in the fetal position on my cold kitchen floor, sobbing like a child. Tears covered my red face and the linoleum beneath me. I was twenty-eight years old, far beyond the age this would be considered acceptable behavior, but I had never hurt so deeply in my life. My worst fear had just been realized—I had been found out as the academic fraud I always feared I was.

Yet slowly I wiped off my face, letting the anger surge through me as I thought about the last six years. *I'm not an academic fraud!* I insisted to myself. I wanted to prove it so badly that I began mentally preparing myself to go toe to toe with a man whose power, at least as far as my future was concerned, was beyond immense. I felt myself drawing upon all the anger and pain and frustration inside me, transforming it into fierce determination. I stood up.

I'll always remember that spring afternoon. It was a moment of truth; the day I learned one of my greatest lessons in the power of resilience and realized what it means to jump back up when life has literally brought you to your knees.

This happened on the last day of my senior year of college, but to help you understand where I'm coming from, I'll have to rewind a few years: back to me as a nineteen-year-old high school senior, struggling academically and ridden with anxiety, knowing that my severe learning disabilities would prevent me from ever making anything above minimum wage.

To say that school was difficult for me is a great understatement—it was my mortal enemy. I often acted inappropriately to cover up my inability to process anything the teacher was saying. As a special-ed student with severe learning differences, I struggled all through the public education system, ever since I'd been held back in the first grade. By the time I was nineteen, the high school counselor knew me by name, not because I was on the college track, but because college was the furthest thing from being part of my future. By some miracle, I managed to make it to high school graduation, but the question of what to do next scared me to death.

I still remember wandering the school commons on yearbook day at the end of my last high school year. College campus booths and recruitment reps lined every wall, but before I could go investigate, the counselor intercepted me. "Christian," he said, "if you want to take off after you're done signing yearbooks, you don't have to stick around." And I knew he was right. College was not an option for me. So I left.

After that, I went to live with my grandparents, an old-school, World War II–era couple who insisted I do something with my life. They even promised to pay the $700 tuition at the local community college. So I applied—and got in! I kept thinking to myself, *Why didn't my school counselor, why didn't my parents, why didn't someone tell me that the real requirement for going to college in America is a GED and all D minuses?*

I got a job as a telemarketer to pay for books and stepped warily into my first day of classes. But old habits, forged through years of neglecting serious study, die hard, and I soon found myself sitting in the back of the classroom, showing up late, or not showing up at all. I started failing my lower-level general-ed classes, and I got a sinking feeling in my stomach every time another test came back with an F. I felt beyond guilty that I was wasting my grandparents' money and destroying their trust, but I couldn't even do the bare minimum, let alone get an A. That's when a classmate gave me some incredible advice: "Just get a D minus. You get just as much credit with a D minus as an A." Shocked, I rushed to confirm this new piece of information with the school counselor, who matter-of-factly replied, "That's correct, Christian. You only need a D minus to pass. But you won't be able to get into graduate school with all D minuses." I chuckled at this, since graduate school was the furthest thing from my mind. All I cared about was that $700 I was wasting. I walked out of that office and scribbled down what I now call my "No F Game Plan":

- Go to every class.
- Sit in the front row.
- Connect with the teacher.
- Do all the homework.

I started following it right away, and it worked—in 70 percent of my classes. But in the other 30 percent of my classes, those that were completely dependent upon reading comprehension or taking a test, my No F Game Plan didn't work. Tests were my dead end. That's when I created the last point of the plan: the Extra Credit Hustle.

Here's how it worked: I'd walk into the professor's office and say, "Can I do some extra credit?" Ninety percent of the time, guess what the professor told me? "No. It's not in my syllabus. If I give you extra credit, it's not fair to the other students." In other words, "Kiss my left foot and get the hell out of my office."

Fortunately, as a kid who wandered the streets between DC and Baltimore at night with older kids and drug dealers, I'd picked up a few things about not taking no for an answer. When I was nine and there was no food in the fridge at home, I would walk up to shoppers in the local grocery-store parking lot and help them unload their carts, often walking away with small tips as a reward (which I usually would instantly spend on nutritious items like Jolly Ranchers).

These experiences gave me the boldness necessary to almost hold these professors hostage when my D minus was at risk. I'd look at them and say, "Listen, I'm not leaving your office until you tell me how I can get a D minus out of your class." I would watch them fidget in their seats from the other side of their desks, with nervous looks on their faces that said, *Is this kid for real?* Then I'd make them really nervous. "How much money do you make?" I would ask. Without fail they would tell me it was none of my business. I'd reply, "I've never made over six dollars an hour. My whole life I've been told that the more education you have, the more money you earn." And I'd insist again: "I'm not leaving. You have a future! You know how you're gonna buy groceries tonight. I don't know how I'm gonna buy groceries or put gas in my car." And that was the truth. I desperately needed that D minus.

I'd then pull a list out of my pocket, unfold it, and lay it on the desk in front of them. There were five to ten handwritten bullet points with extra-credit options I'd thought of beforehand. "Can you just pick one of these?" I'd beg. At this point—when I was placing real options before them—my professors usually conceded.

I had a lot of help pulling off the No F Game Plan after an incredible girl named Wendy came into my life. We started dating as I strained to juggle a minimum-wage job and a college education in the face of my learning differences. I fell in love with this amazing person, but I knew I couldn't marry her. I was petrified to commit, certain that I wouldn't be able to provide for her. I distinctly remember sitting her down and saying, "Wendy, you've got to marry somebody that can make over $40,000 a year." You might think that amount small, but $40,000 might as well have been a million for me. At the time, it was four times more than I'd ever made in a year. "You've got to marry one of those guys in the high-tech industry," I continued. "Someone more functional than I am. I might be fun to date, but your life will be hell if you marry me." I was devastated to let her go, but I was trying to set her free from what I feared was a lifetime of minimum-wage living.

Wendy asked me to meet her a few days later. She approached me with a shy smile and a speech prepared. "Christian, I know you love me deeply. And I know you have huge anxiety about earning a living." Nothing could have prepared me for what she said next. "I have so much love for you, I want to take this fear and anxiety off the table. If you marry me, Christian, you'll never have to get a job," she said. "I'll take care of that. That's how much I care about you." I held her close and thought, *I may be learning disabled, but I'm not stupid. This is the woman for me.*

As a matter of fact, Wendy did one better than keeping her promise to take care of me. She did everything in her power to make sure I made it through school and was my biggest ally in the No F Game Plan. Because I could only read at a seventh-grade level, we'd lie in bed late at night and she'd read textbooks out loud to me. I would handwrite all my papers and she would type them up. I still don't know how to properly type on a computer, and thanks to Wendy, I shaved off thousands of hours of pecking out every assignment.

One of our biggest tests came when I was failing my American Heritage class and went to see Professor McBride about some extra credit. Like all the others, he strictly refused to help me until I whipped out my handwritten list and unfolded it on his desk. At the top I had written, "I'll write a fifty-page paper on the Civil War in ten days." Professor McBride pointed to this first option and said, "Do that one." He had a sly look on his face, and as I turned to leave, he said, "Christian, you could have said a ten-page paper. And you gave yourself ten days to do it? How smart was that? You could have asked for fifteen." He shook his head as he said it. He was mocking me, but I wanted to prove to him that this is how hard I was willing to work.

The professor didn't realize my advantages: I can talk a mile a minute,

Wendy can type just as fast, and I grew up in Civil War country. I raced home that night, pulled out my half dozen books on the Civil War and an encyclopedia, and began talking while Wendy typed.

We hit page fifty at about one a.m., and Wendy was exhausted. "You have nine days to finish this, Christian," she pleaded. "Please, let me go to bed." I pleaded right back, "Wendy, I know this is going to sound crazy, and it's going to be difficult. Just stay up with me. Let's do a sixty-page paper. Let's show those academic elites." So my incredible wife stretched her fingers and started typing again. We didn't stop until sunrise, and when I dropped the paper on Professor McBride's desk that morning, he was shocked. Then he read it over and was even more shocked: no hot air, no shortcuts. A solid, sixty-page paper on the Civil War.

Professor McBride pulled me aside after class that day, and my life literally changed with that conversation. "I read your paper," he said, an incredulous expression on his face. "It was powerful. That was a real paper. I can tell you worked really hard on it. I find it interesting you did ten extra pages."

I replied, "Sir, I cannot even begin to pass your tests. I'm just trying to show you, that's how bad I want a D minus out of your class."

That's when Professor McBride told me about the Ambassador Scholarship, awarded to the hardest-working students by the school's scholarship committee, of which Dr. McBride was a member. He gave me the application for that scholarship, and it was awarded to me shortly thereafter.

I was twenty-two years old. Because of my learning differences I couldn't tell you what nine times six was. I couldn't use a computer. But suddenly I was at college *on a scholarship*. I don't know if I would have made it through college if it weren't for that scholarship. The financial benefit was great, but what it did for my confidence was ten times greater. What's more, that experience taught me something magical about the No F Game Plan: If I did more work than the person helping me, that person was much more likely to open another door for me.

I also learned that D minuses were nonexistent with my plan. Most of my grades rose to As, Bs, and Cs, and before I knew it, I was applying as a transfer student to a full-scale university.

My application was sparse. I wrote the university a passionate letter that detailed my goals and aspirations and how badly I wanted this opportunity. In my mind's eye I could see a room full of huge stacks of applications—all of them awesome and impressive—being read by a meticulous admissions committee. Mine was the thin one with frayed edges at the bottom of the pile. Because I couldn't pass a math or language class, had never taken the SAT, and had never gotten an associate's degree, I nearly fainted when I got the acceptance letter. It was a miracle: I would be a student on the campus of a highly selective, privately owned university. Every day I was there it was like I'd won the lottery, but some days I felt like an academic fraud for being there. I kept waiting for campus security to come and tap me on the shoulder and say, "Young man, we've looked over your records, and it's apparent you don't belong here," before dragging me kicking and screaming off campus. I kept thinking, *How long do I have before they figure out I can't even tell time on a hand clock?*

I decided early on in college that I wanted to become a social worker. My dream was to be able to help kids who struggle like I did growing up, and this goal helped me fight on as I realized that my university course load was far heavier than any I had struggled to manage at the community college. Every day was an exhausting battle to keep my head above water.

I woke up every morning at two a.m. to vacuum a college lecture hall the size of three movie theaters. I attended classes during the day, and in the afternoons I worked in a hot window-production warehouse as the cleaning guy. The glass would cut through my rubber gloves until my hands bled (I still have the scars from those days), and I'd return home in the evenings and study until I couldn't keep my head up. Wendy was working full-time and helping me with papers, and together we were constantly exhausted.

For every test I took, I would ask the other students, "How many hours did you study for this?" and they would usually respond, "Oh, three to five hours." For difficult tests I would often start studying weeks in advance, often twenty to thirty hours for one exam.

I stayed faithful to my plan all along, and I tried to look confident and composed as I purchased the textbook for Math 110, a class required for graduation that I'd been dreading since my first day on campus. Adding to my dread, this was the same class that had prevented me from getting an associate's degree at the community college. I feared it would also prevent me from getting my bachelor's. I carried my book into the library, determined to soak up everything I could about college algebra, but when I looked at that first page, my head began to swim. Numbers and letters blurred together in an incomprehensible mess. I looked down at my shaking hands and realized they were sweating profusely, completely soaking the numbers and letters on the page they were resting on. That's when I had my first full-blown panic attack. It was the end of my junior year, and I thought of all the money I'd spent, of all the time Wendy had sacrificed, of my dream of becoming a social worker and starting a family, and I began sobbing onto the pages as I realized it would all be for naught because of Math 110. I kept thinking, *What in the hell does math have to do with me being a good social worker? Or preventing suicide? Or saving someone's marriage?*

My school counselor had told me that the only way I could graduate was by passing this class, and I knew, plain and simple, that this was impossible. But I used every negotiation skill I'd ever learned on the streets, and after some time, I convinced them to find me a different class. It was finally decided that as a social work major, I could take a statistics class called Social Research Methods as a Math 110 replacement. It was such a relief that I did a jig on my way home that day, knowing that my future was bright once again. I realized that I might actually be able to make a livable wage one day, and it strengthened my resolve to do everything in my power to finish my education.

I was still religiously devoted to my No F Game Plan when I reached my senior year, and I was determined to make it to the end without missing a single day of class. I even ignored doctor's orders and went to class after I got a serious strain of the flu. I ended up in the back of the class, heaving into a trash can, with students yelling for me to leave. The professor took me outside but, seeing my determination, allowed me to take out the bag and sit through the rest of the class.

My proudest moment was approaching. I had survived years of cut-up hands, dusty early-morning vacuuming, anxiety attacks in the library, and thousands of study hours. They told me I could graduate, and after excitedly picking up my freshly pressed cap and gown, I opened my closet every time I was home to take another peek at it. I bragged to everybody, "The dumbest person in the world is about to get a college degree!" The kid who sat in the back of the class in school and didn't know how to read, the kid who was afraid to run a cash register at McDonald's, who was told to leave the high school job fair, who had never made more than minimum wage, who used to run the streets at night, was about to graduate from a major university. On top of that, I had been accepted into the masters of social work program. In those last weeks before graduation, I felt like I was walking on air.

Then I got the phone call that put my resilience to its ultimate test.

My wife was at work that afternoon. It was a few days before graduation, and I'd been home for only a few minutes when the phone rang. I picked it up and was greeted by an unfamiliar man's voice on the other end. "Hello, Christian, I'm the dean of the College of Home and Family Sciences."

Intense anxiety overcame me at hearing his authoritative voice and title. My throat went dry and my stomach began churning. I swallowed hard and asked hoarsely, "What can I do for you, sir?" There was a grim pause. "I have your academic history laid out in front of me. I understand you've been told that you're going to be able to graduate and that this

Social Research Methods class has replaced Math 110. I have to make the final decision. And I want you to know that, based on your academic history, I cannot allow you to graduate."

He was still talking, but those words, "I cannot allow you to graduate," rang loud and painful in my ears. I felt like someone had punched the wind out of me and my legs had stopped working. From somewhere far away, the voice was saying, "My decision is final," "You should not even be on this campus," and "I understand you've also been accepted in the master's program. That's not going to be possible . . ." I tried to catch my breath enough to respond, but between sobs all I could get out was, "Sir, can I come meet with you, talk to you?" I waited long enough to hear, "Okay, come right now," before hanging up and slamming the phone over and over into the linoleum floor as I curled into the fetal position and sobbed.

I called Wendy at work and told her it was over, that I had done everything I could but that I wouldn't be graduating after all. Years later, she told me that she locked herself in the bathroom after that call and sobbed for over an hour. She had never heard me sound so hopeless.

I mentioned at the beginning of this story that I was able to pick myself up off that kitchen floor because of the anger and determination that burned inside me during those painful moments. Just then, that dean had given me enough fuel to convince *anybody* that I not only had earned that degree, but that I was going to change the world once I had my master's degree in hand.

My wife had our only car, so I hopped on my ten-speed and began furiously pedaling to campus. As I approached the dean's office, I could hear him shouting on the phone at a professor from the social-work program, one of my greatest advocates and mentors. "He shouldn't even be here! If a kid like this can graduate with a college degree, then what does that say for our school's credibility?" I tried to take deep breaths. He was giving me more fuel.

Finally the door opened, and a burly man stepped out. His gruff, angry voice suited his build. "Christian, come in," he said sternly. I walked into his office and saw a desk covered with transcripts and other official documents. I saw my name and my Social Security number everywhere. My entire academic life stared up at both of us, and I knew what those papers had been telling him: that I was making a mockery out of the integrity of the academic system that he held dear.

I sat down across from him. He leaned over his desk and shouted, "How did you pull this off?" He then slammed his fist on the table; the condemning papers jumped with the force.

I took a deep breath. My Extra Credit Hustle, my childhood grocery-cart exploits, and my years of fighting for this degree had all prepared me for this moment of truth. I was not going back to the fetal position. I was not going to back down. I was going to be resilient.

I looked that dean in the eye and said, "When I asked other students how many hours a day they studied for a test, they said three to five. Sir, I studied twenty hours for the same test. I did ten times more work than any student in the history of this university. I am the hardest-working student who ever showed up on this college campus. I didn't miss one day of school. I worked as hard as I possibly could. I learned everything there was to learn about my profession. If you let me graduate, I'm going to impact millions of lives. I will make sure everybody has access to the kind of hope I discovered being here. Going to this school has been like winning the Super Bowl. I know I shouldn't have been accepted, but I was, and I deserve every credit. Sir, you can't stop me from getting this degree! I earned it." As I explained my dreams and goals to him, I began to see a visible change in the dean's demeanor.

He leaned back in his chair. His face was more relaxed now. "Wow, I wasn't expecting that," he said. "I can see that you're here under very unique circumstances." He looked up at the ceiling, then back at me. "Christian, you're going to graduate this week. Good luck in grad school, son."

I stood up and thanked him, barely able to maintain my composure. I turned at the door and said, "I will not let you down." And I'm proud to report that I never have. A few years after this experience I received the highly coveted Social Worker of Promise Award, an honor given by my peers in graduate school to the person most likely to have an impact for good on the world. I received awards from my university and internship offers as an undergraduate student from the US assistant secretary of education. A few years after that I started WhyTry, a resilience program that so far has reached over two million youth and adults in sixteen thousand schools and organizations.

That spring day with the dean was both the lowest and the highest point in my life. It was the first time I realized that my lowest point could actually be converted into my best friend. It gave me my greatest lesson in resilience and a resolve to make it available to the world.

YOU CAN TRANSFORM PAIN INTO POWER

Becoming resilient starts with the realization that the adversity you experience—*any* pain, discrimination, or challenge—can be converted into powerful fuel that can actually bring opportunity. According to the Christian Moore dictionary, there are two definitions of *adversity*:

1. A state or instance of distress, calamity, hardship, or affliction
2. Fuel; energy; your best friend

That second definition may seem odd, but this book is about to completely reframe the way you see your problems and, I hope, bring tremendous light into your life.

Resilience, this process of using that adversity as fuel, has fundamentally changed my life. I truly feel hope is always alive, because absolutely *everyone* can benefit from resilience. But before we get ahead of ourselves, let's also define *resilience*:

Resilience is the ability to bounce back when you have every reason to shut down—but you fight on! Resilient people have both tapped and untapped reserves, enabling them to overcome and thrive as they face the setbacks, challenges, and fears of daily life.™

Second only to love, resilience is life's most important principle. (Love and relationships are the most important things; they bring happiness and fulfillment and are an essential need for every human being.) Resilience enables you to deal with the day-to-day grind, the pain and challenges of life. It will give you the tools to cope and thrive.

Resilience showed me how my problems, even my very worst problems, could become my greatest resource. If we are able to reframe our challenges and recognize them as emotional fuel, we can operate like a refinery, channeling the emotion generated out of something negative, like pain—or even something positive, like love—and turning it into fuel that can be used to propel us forward.

Once you see how resilience works, your problems can become a never-ending source of fuel. Pain can equal power. Everyone has emotions, good and bad, that they carry around with them, like a big bucket of energy. As a therapist, my job is to show people how to channel that energy in positive ways. Positive emotions—feelings you get from being loved, being heard, feeling gratitude, experiencing two-way communication and connection—can generate fuel. Negative emotions are equally powerful, and potential fuel exists from the feelings that accompany depression, anxiety, disappointment, anger, being disrespected, and other painful emotions. When you have your *resilience breakthrough*, you realize that the fuel is there, know how to access the fuel, and are able to access it quickly. Once you can do that, you are on the road to long-term resilience.

In my life, the learning process of transforming pain into a powerful resilience source began when one of my greatest mentors recognized something in me that I couldn't see yet. Mama Jackson was an

African-American woman living in my neighborhood who watched me struggle and sensed my fears and anxieties. She saw me running the streets as a seven-year-old drug mule, and she reached out and became a second mother, planting a seed of confidence that eventually helped me build enough courage to attend college. That might not sound like a big deal, but you have to remember we're talking about me—severe learning differences, ADHD me. I wanted to live up to what Mama Jackson saw in me, and I wanted to save the world.

It was during my college years that I first began to realize that I was using the disrespect I had felt in my life from others as fuel to do better. I saw that I was using my disabilities as motivation to fight my way to that degree. I was using all the nos I had heard as a reason to fight for a yes. I began to recognize the resilience skills that were helping me bridge the gap between my challenges and my dreams. A professor in my master's program suggested that I take the time to write these skills down. So I made a list, and that list eventually became a resilience curriculum that has now reached millions of people and is now included in college textbooks.

Perhaps you're wondering, though, why in the world you should read a book written by this highly flawed, anxiety-ridden guy. Well, Christian Dan Moore is an internationally renowned author, speaker, and advocate, only because I am an expert in anxiety, fear, and failure. I have used this anxiety to create some success in my life, but I also know that it's the trigger for many of the failures that I have experienced. For most of my life, I've struggled with an internal conflict—a fight with myself that sometimes verges on an all-out battle. What helped me to finally start winning this conflict was realizing that I had *unlimited ammunition and fuel* that came from the very things I was trying to escape—that dreaded fear, anxiety, and failure. Will I ever totally overcome them? No! But today I know how to use the emotional fuel associated with that fear, anxiety, and failure to be a better father, husband, friend, colleague, and business executive.

The power to be resilient is already inside of you. Whatever battle you're fighting, this book will show you how to convert your challenges into fuel that can lead to the greatest fulfillment of your life. I'm writing this book so that it doesn't take you the forty years it took me to figure out how to tap into something you already have.

People ask me all the time, "Christian, if you could get rid of your learning differences, or change your background, or erase the hard parts of your personal history, would you?" But before I respond, I reply with my own questions: "Was it fun coping with learning differences, or being neglected and humiliated, yelled at and hurt? Was any of it easy? No. It wasn't fun. And it definitely wasn't painless. But if someone told me they could take all that away from me, I would beg them not to." Am I crazy?

All those experiences have given me the fuel I need to be resilient. When I speak to groups of people, I do it with great passion. This energy that audiences can see and hear coming out of me—this passion—is actually intense emotion. If I took this emotion and did bad works, they'd lock me up for the rest of my life. If I use this same energy, this same emotion, convert it to fuel, and use it to do good works, I get the chance to give my audiences a glimpse into their own resilience reserves. It has been my life's mission to figure out why some people take their challenges and use them as fuel to better their lives, while others' challenges are the excuse they use to hurt themselves and others. Now it's my life's mission to share everything I've learned about this important message with you.

VULNERABILITY: THE BIRTHPLACE OF RESILIENCE

For my entire professional career, I've always wanted to show people where resilience is born—where it begins—so you can always access more of it when adversity increases. In this book, I will share the four main sources of resilience—something that took me forty years to identify. But first, I want to give you a separate, universal tool and insight that will help you access resilience long term. I want you to look at the idea of vulnerability and how it ties to resilience.

The times when I'm least resilient are when I'm "frontin'"—putting on a facade—like everything's perfect. It takes vulnerability to open the door to resilience. I see vulnerability as a window into our humanity. When you show other humans that you're human, too, a bond is created that would be impossible if you only showed your roles, titles, and most appealing attributes. In my experience, the great majority of us spend a lot of our time frontin' and putting on pretenses. If you are part of the minority that choose to live authentically and allow yourself to be vulnerable, then you have a resilience advantage that the majority is missing out on.

It isn't easy to be vulnerable. Think about a time you've felt really, truly vulnerable. Did it create fear, anxiety, dread, or the desire to flee? Feeling vulnerable can be really uncomfortable. When I approached my professors and desperately begged them to let me do extra credit since I couldn't pass their tests, it was really hard to be that vulnerable. I had to open up and expose all my weaknesses to them—my learning differences that I wanted to keep hidden under the rug. In our society we are often judged so harshly that many of us keep our defenses up at all times—an unyielding, titanium wall that shields others from our authentic selves. These facades that we work so hard to create hold us back and make us less resilient. And I get that being 100 percent vulnerable 100 percent of the time isn't the wisest approach either—you have to use common sense and be aware of your surroundings. But our unwillingness to be vulnerable is such a common problem that it's important to cover it before we move on. Keeping up those thick walls requires a lot of energy, and I don't want to waste any energy on hiding from my pain, because I need every ounce of energy I can muster to keep me resilient. This allows me to turn pain into emotional fuel more effectively.

Brené Brown, a professor at the University of Houston Graduate College of Social Work, has studied vulnerability for over a decade.

"Vulnerability is our most accurate measurement of courage—to be vulnerable, to let ourselves be seen, to be honest," she explains. "Vulnerability is not weakness." After delivering an extremely popular speech on the subject, she received offers to speak all over America. What amused and surprised her were the requests, particularly from Fortune 500 companies, to please not mention the words *vulnerability* or *shame*. When she asked them what they'd like her to speak on, the business sector requested topics like innovation, creativity, and change. But, Brown says, "Vulnerability is the birthplace of innovation, creativity, and change. To create is to make something that has never existed before. There's nothing more vulnerable than that."[1]

Think of a time you've been resilient. Was vulnerability a component of that? I'm betting it was. I can't be resilient in my business—create new products, remain competitive, and figure out how to adapt to change—if I'm unwilling to be vulnerable. If you're not willing to be wrong and sometimes fail—to be vulnerable and take a risk—you'll never come up with something original. It's equally true in regard to my personal life. True connection requires honesty and vulnerability. Relationships with mutual authenticity are stronger and last longer, and since relationships are the lifeblood of resilience, being vulnerable, in my opinion, is a prerequisite for resilience. I challenge you to allow yourself to be part of that authentic minority and read this book with vulnerability.

BUT CAN RESILIENCE BE LEARNED?

I once had a conversation with an expert on resilience who had just heard me speak. We were talking about what we would do for someone who feels like giving up. I argued that I would increase their ability to be resilient. This expert was taken aback. "Resilience would be a very difficult thing to teach," she said. "If you had a resilience pill, you'd be worth a lot of money. Resilience is something you have to be born with. People are either resilient or they're not." In other words, she was adamantly telling me that resilience can't be taught.

I didn't disagree with her completely. Just as with other capabilities and talents, some people are born with more innate ability than others. But completely deprived of the capacity to be resilient at birth? No way! I've seen it over and over: people at their lowest point—even rock bottom—who eventually bounce back, even when everyone else had completely given up on them. I remain convinced there's a way to help anyone, no matter their natural abilities or where they fall on the resilience spectrum, to become more resilient. Based on years of experience, I believe it is an attribute that can be developed in anyone's life. Like any other skill, the more you focus on it, the more you improve.

But here's what gets me really excited. In her groundbreaking book, *Mindset: The New Psychology of Success*, Dr. Carol Dweck, a professor of psychology at Stanford University, backs me up with science! With twenty years of research she makes it absolutely clear that resilience *can* be learned.

"What are the consequences of thinking that your intelligence or personality is something you can develop, as opposed to something that is a fixed, deep-seated trait?" Dweck asks. She then makes the distinction between a *fixed mindset*—which is when you believe you're stuck with what you're born with; that you have only a certain amount of intelligence and character—and the *growth mindset*, "the belief that your basic qualities are things you can cultivate through your efforts." A fixed mindset means you think your qualities are carved in stone. You're smart or you aren't. You're talented or you're not. You believe you were born with personality traits and characteristics that are only available in finite amounts. This kind of thinking creates a constant need to prove yourself. It keeps you from exploring and risk-taking and believing in the possibility of growth. Instead, you focus on protecting yourself, lamenting, blaming, and validating. Instead of admitting and correcting deficiencies, your energy is spent trying to hide them. She explains, "It's startling to see the degree to which people with the fixed mindset do not believe in effort. When we temporarily put people in a fixed mindset, they quickly fear challenge and devalue effort."

Conversely, you have a growth mindset when you have "passion for stretching yourself and sticking to it, even (or especially) when it's not going well." Cultivating a growth mindset means you like a challenge, enjoy effort, and learn from mistakes. In other words, a growth mindset is a resilient mindset! People with this mindset believe even geniuses have to work hard. Dweck cites as examples Leo Tolstoy and Charles Darwin, both of whom were considered to be very ordinary as children. The growth mindset is to "believe that a person's true potential is unknown (and unknowable)." People with a fixed mindset only want to attempt things they know they'll be good at, and give up quickly when something gets hard. But the growth mindset appreciates effort. Most important, those with a growth mindset believe that human qualities can be enhanced, changed, and improved through that effort. "People may start with different temperaments and different aptitudes," she says, "but it is clear that experience, training, and personal effort take them the rest of the way.... Although people may differ in every which way—in their initial talents and aptitude, interests, or temperaments—everyone can change and grow through application and experience."

If you have a fixed mindset and experience something traumatic, you aren't equipped with ways to overcome it. A failure means you *are* a failure. But here's the good news: According to Dweck, people who are willing to adopt a growth mindset "seem to have a special talent for converting life's setbacks into future successes. This is the mindset that allows people to thrive during some of the most challenging times in their lives."[2]

Because *resilience can be taught*, there is hope no matter your circumstances. This is why I truly believe hope is never dead despite any conditions. Just ask anyone who has overcome seemingly insurmountable odds. Being able to access resilience is like pouring gas on the fire of hope.

THE PROMISE OF THIS BOOK

I am going to be pretty darn bold and make you, the reader, a promise. I promise that this book contains clear and specific instructions on becoming more resilient. I'm not just going to describe what it means to be resilient. That's been done before. What makes this book unique is that I will show you exactly how to tap into your emotional fuel and turn it into resilience. In fact, I'll make you an even more specific promise:

> If you are a human being breathing in oxygen on planet Earth
> with a desire to increase your ability to withstand and even thrive
> in the face of life's challenges, *reading this book will be like going to
> your pharmacist and getting a prescription for developing resilience.*

Other books simply tell you the traits of resilient people. This book makes it accessible, and, based on the principles and skills you'll read about, gives you real hope and the tools that will enable you to become resilient.

It doesn't matter what neighborhood you were born into, or who your parents are. It doesn't matter if you've lost a loved one, lost a job, or been to prison. Regardless of your race, education level, or socioeconomic status—wherever you're standing, whatever the daily battles are that you're fighting, or if you're simply a human being trying to be a better human being—if you understand the principles we're going to show you in this book, you can transcend all these issues to have a better ability to cope with the reality of your life, and you will learn how your worst pain and problems can be converted into emotional fuel. This can propel you toward a life of hope and an ability to thrive.

This book is not about success. It's about *resilience*, which means it will help you to thrive regardless of your circumstances. Resilience is the ability to endure pain, to press on, even if you're not winning. The ability to show up, to keep going, or even to just continue to go through the motions while you're dealing with failure, depression, anxiety, hopelessness, addiction, legal problems, an abusive spouse, unemployment, a terminal illness—the list of struggles that are part of the human condition is endless—creates dignity. It creates self-respect. There is an honor in pressing through even the worst of circumstances.

Success, especially worldly success, has nothing to do with being resilient. Now, let me be clear: Achieving greater levels of resilience *is* success, but not necessarily success as the world defines it. Success in becoming resilient isn't measured by the outcome, by your outward achievements or the number of problems you overcome. When you're successfully resilient, your problems are still there—but you're forging ahead in the middle of the mess. We must remain relentless despite the world's constant negativity. *That's* real success.

I'm living proof of the hope that comes from resilience. Just consider the odds: Forty-eight percent of individuals with learning differences like mine are unemployed. Forty-three percent live below the poverty level. Only 13 percent ever make it to college, and even fewer graduate or go on to graduate school. As I look to my future, and to my children's future, it's clear that resilience is *the* vital skill we need to thrive. I became the exception to the norm when I discovered that resilience is something I can access, not just *despite* my disabilities and challenges, but *because* of them. Resilience is the X factor that's helped me transcend my biggest challenges, and I know it can change your life, too.

There is an honor in pressing through even the worst of circumstances, and this is because of one of life's most important truths:

Pain channeled in a positive direction is the greatest thing that can happen to you.

{ PART I }

CORE PRINCIPLES OF RESILIENCE

FLIPPING THE SWITCH

RESILIENCE IS INSIDE YOU—SO LET IT OUT!

As someone who has experienced plenty of life's hardships and has worked with others who are dealing with intense challenges, I understand that most of us are experiencing pain from something in life. It's unavoidable. How we handle our pain is what makes the difference. The following examples show pairs of people facing comparable circumstances who handle their pain in different ways. As you read each example, think about how you would respond if placed in a similar situation:

- Two frontline workers in a retail store have to deal with a difficult manager who seems bent on breaking their spirits. One goes on to thrive and advances in the organization, while the other does the bare minimum required each day, going through the motions while hating his job.

- Two people are in a difficult marriage that requires a lot of work and attention. A combination of financial problems and the stress of raising children has taken a toll on their relationship. One wishes to seek solutions through marriage counseling, while the other is ready to give up and thinks divorce is the easy way out.

- Two managers in the same corporation are told they have to do more with less: fewer employees, less budget, all while increasing productivity. One finds ways to cut costs, acquire new customers, and increase quality, while the other manager fails to adjust and is fired.

- Two individuals struggle with addiction, and despite numerous attempts to turn from this lifestyle, each has failed many times to attain long-term sobriety. In spite of seemingly overwhelming compulsions, one individual continues her efforts to overcome her daily desire to use, while the other decides recovery isn't possible and continues to spiral.

- Two kids grow up in the same neighborhood with poverty, abuse, and discrimination. One child works hard to overcome his circumstances and eventually makes it out to live a productive life. The other succumbs to a difficult existence and continues the same cycle of violence he has always known.

- Two college graduates attempt to enter the workforce in a time of diminished opportunity. One seeks to find problems and solve them, looking for ways to add value when given the chance; the other possesses an attitude of entitlement, believing that employment should be guaranteed to a college graduate. As a result, the latter goes jobless.

What made the difference for those who overcame their circumstances in all of these examples? Answering this question became my life's work, and I believe I've done it: The answer is resilience, the ability to use adversity as fuel.

Because of the vastness of the human experience, we all process pain differently and with varying levels of ability, and we must have great compassion for others and not judge someone who appears less resilient. However, resilience is what makes the difference between those who succumb to problems and those who fight through them. In each of those scenarios, one person got caught in self-pity and blaming, becoming a victim and shutting down. The other person, however, was resilient. They were able to say to themselves, *I'm going to use this difficult situation as fuel to try harder.*

I call this "Flipping the Switch." When you Flip the Switch, you stop for a moment, realize that you can turn your pain into power, and move forward, committed to being resilient. Let's look closer at the powerful edge that Flipping the Switch can give you.

HOW AN INMATE CAN HAVE AN ADVANTAGE OVER A HARVARD GRAD

I've taught the concept of Flipping the Switch in some interesting places. After speaking to a group of students in an inner-city school, I was approached by an administrator immediately after my speech and asked if I had time to speak to a group of juvenile offenders in a local detention center that very afternoon. I had time before my flight, so I agreed, and they rushed me over to a lockdown facility full of boys ages twelve to eighteen who had committed terrible crimes, including rape and murder. This was definitely a rough crowd.

Since the decision to have me speak was made last minute, the director of the facility didn't have much warning that I was coming. She didn't know anything about me, or what I was going to be speaking about. These juvenile offenders are on a highly regimented schedule, and usually I need twenty or thirty minutes to set up my equipment. The director was obviously agitated, and as I started to get ready she angrily said, "They're coming in right now! You don't have time to get set up. Do you know who these kids are? What are *you* going to say to these boys?" In her defense, she was caught off guard, but it wasn't hard to hear what she was really saying. I imagined her looking at me, a short, fat, white guy from upper-middle-class suburbia, and thinking I was way out of my league. What could I possibly have to say of value to these young men?

The offenders—mostly African-Americans and a few Latinos—started slouching into the room. "Put your computer away," she said. "Go." I walked to the front of the room, and she left the room as I began to speak.

The boys leaned back in their chairs, not making eye contact with me. Their body language said, *What you got?* and there was a ton of attitude in the room. They weren't into it at all. I walked over to the wall and started flipping the light switch on and off. The room—with only one small window by the door—went very dark each time I turned off the light. And every time light once again flooded the room, I saw the boys looking at me like, *Are you crazy?*

With my finger still on the switch, I said, "I'm about to teach you something, and if you are able to really understand it, every one of you in this room could have an advantage over a student at Harvard." That got the room quiet; the scraping of chair legs and shuffling of feet stopped. Now I had their attention.

I explained to them what it means to Flip the Switch—that they had the power to see their challenges differently and convert their anger into the fuel to be better. "The only thing that really gives someone in jail an advantage over someone at Harvard," I said, "is how *quickly* they realize that the switch is there. That Harvard guy, he might not realize it's there until he is sixty years old. Or never. You guys right now are fifteen, sixteen, seventeen years old. Can you imagine the power of knowing that switch is there when you're fifteen or sixteen? The switch equals the awareness that you can use pain, disappointment, and tragedy as fuel to overcome life's challenges. That you can see your problems as your best friend. I'm telling you, there are a lot of adults who never knew they had this capacity. I have family members who have lived on this Earth eighty years and they never knew they could Flip the Switch. They only saw their problems as a reason to be angry, upset, feel disrespected, and turn to depression, anxiety, or hopelessness. These are educated people! And they only saw their pain as a reason to give up.

"Anybody here ever messed up?" I asked them, scanning the room. "Anybody here have any great pain in your life?" All of those boys raised their hands, and most were now making full eye contact with me. "You've got the fuel! You've got the fuel already in you! You've got to use that fuel to become greater. I don't care where the fuel came from, whether it's poverty, abuse, you hurting someone else, your dad dying, or your mom in prison. . . . I don't know where your fuel comes from. But you got the fuel. Anybody here frustrated?" Again all hands went up. "Use the fuel, I'm telling you! If you use the fuel you have an advantage over somebody at Harvard who doesn't know how to use the fuel. There are people who run multimillion-dollar corporations or have PhDs that don't get this. If you understand how to Flip the Switch, you *will* have the advantage."

I paced the room and tried to look into each of the boys' faces. They were looking up now, leaning forward eagerly. I shouted out a challenge: "Every night I want you to ask yourself, 'Am I Flipping the Switch?' When you mess up, are you giving up or trying to become greater? Because the reality is, everyone messes up. The most resilient people use the mess as the reason to become greater. Everyone has nights when they go to bed with fear, frustration, anxiety, and anger. You've got to Flip the Switch, and consciously decide to wake up tomorrow and work as hard as you can to do the best that you can. You consciously decide to not get hung up in all the crap. That's what resilient people do. When you walk out of here, you can use your pain as fuel to be a better employee, a better son, a better father. Because of this difficult situation, you're going to become greater."

I explained to them that the reality is, they're in jail. They're going to sit there for five, ten years—however long their sentence is. Time is constantly moving, no matter where they are, and they could spend their time there being angry and rebellious, or they could work on Flipping the Switch. I told them that the minute they Flip the Switch, their emotions flip as well, and that if they do this, previously unforeseen options will eventually open up to them. Things they might never have dreamed of will come together. Once they were committed to this course of action, I said, doors would open for them, doors they didn't even know existed.

By the end of my speech, those young men were fully engaged. You could've heard a pin drop in that room. Afterward, they stood in line to talk to me. They were emotional and sincerely thanked me, saying things like "I see the world different" and asking me questions, hungry for more. They were extremely respectful, former attitudes and wariness forgotten. It was an intense and amazing experience for me as I felt their emotional eagerness. They'd come in rolling their eyes, and they left shaking my hand.

When the director returned, two supervisors who had remained in the back of the room pulled her over and talked to her. She then came to me, thanked me for coming, and apologized for being upset earlier. "I misjudged you," she said. "My staff told me this was one of the best speeches they've ever heard."

(As a side note, it's interesting that I had to Flip the Switch during my interactions with this director. I agreed to volunteer my time and speak to this group last minute. When she was condescending and rude to me, not allowing me to set up, my initial reaction was to get angry and defend myself. However, I knew that the most important thing was for me to have the chance to help these kids, not to get even with her. With that thought in mind, I was able to Flip the Switch—to draw upon my anger and convert it into energy for my talk.)

THE PROOF

I really do believe that Flipping the Switch can give a convicted murderer an advantage over a Harvard student. I've seen firsthand that academic and business success don't equate to an ability to thrive, but author Shawn Achor *proved* it—from the heart of Harvard itself.

I stumbled upon Achor's ideas just over a year after speaking in the detention center. Achor was a Harvard student himself, and describes in his book, *The Happiness Advantage*, how excited and honored he felt to be at such a prestigious university as an incoming freshman. He quickly fell in love with Harvard—so much, in fact, that he stayed on as a lecturer and proctor following graduation. After twelve years of observing thousands of Harvard students, Achor discovered something fascinating: Despite the obvious advantage many of the students had—parents' money, perfect SAT scores—they were supremely unhappy, they did not feel the privilege of their position in life, and they were certainly not resilient. "They fretted incessantly about their future, despite the fact that they were earning a degree that would open so many doors," Achor writes. "They felt overwhelmed by every small setback instead of energized by the possibilities in front of them. And after watching enough of those students struggle to make their way through, something dawned on me. Not only were these students the ones who seemed most susceptible to stress and depression, they were the ones whose grades and academic performance were suffering the most." Based on the opportunities surrounding them, these students should have been thriving. Instead, they were unhappy and tense. They were brilliant students, but they had never been taught resilience: the second-greatest principle in the world.

Achor explains, "It's the lens through which your brain views the world that shapes your reality. And if we change the lens, not only can we change your happiness, we can change every single educational and business outcome at the same time."[3] In other words, your ability to thrive and be happy has little to do with IQ, employment status, or anything external whatsoever. It has a lot more to do with your ability to "change the lens."

When I heard this idea, I was awed by its similarity to Flipping the Switch. I realized that I was hearing from an actual Harvard graduate the very thing I had explained to that roomful of youth: If you wake up every morning with a willingness to change the way you look at your problems, it makes little difference whether you attended a prestigious university or were serving time for a serious mistake—you could make your situation better.

"WHAT IF THE SECRET TO SUCCESS IS FAILURE?"

When I came across a *New York Times* article titled "What If the Secret to Success Is Failure?" I was further pleased to see that research backs up the concept of Flipping the Switch. In the piece, Paul Tough shows that drawing on failure and pain can indeed give less privileged kids an edge against their more elite peers.

Tough describes two New York City school principals, Dominic Randolph and David Levin. Randolph works at a prestigious private school, and Levin in a low-income-area charter school. They both had been thinking that traditional education was missing a critical piece; Randolph thought that his students had lost the idea that started long ago in America: "That if you worked hard and showed real grit, you could be successful," he said. "Strangely, we've now forgotten that. People who have an easy time of things, who get eight hundreds on their SATs, I worry that those people get feedback that everything they're doing is great. And I think as a result, we are actually setting them up for long-term failure. When that person suddenly has to face up to a difficult moment, then I think they're screwed, to be honest. I don't think they've grown the capacities to be able to handle that."

Levin, principal of the less-advantaged school, kept tabs on his graduated students, and he noticed something interesting: "The students who persisted in college were not necessarily the ones who had excelled academically at the charter school; they were the ones with exceptional character strengths," he said. He goes on to describe these "character strengths" as things like optimism, persistence, ability to recover from a bad grade and resolve to do better, and to persuade a teacher to give them extra help after class. All these things—Randolph's "grit" and Levin's "character strengths"—sound a whole lot like resilience to me.

"The idea of building grit and building self-control is that you get that through failure," Randolph explains. "And in most highly academic environments in the United States, no one fails anything."[4] Because of the ease of life—be it overprotective parents, true ability, or a high IQ— these kids are actually at a disadvantage to others who have experienced setbacks and failure. This is precisely why I can confidently tell a kid who is pretty darn familiar with failure and who is stuck in detention that he can indeed have an advantage over an Ivy Leaguer.

But remember: Despite this proof that your background doesn't predict your ability to be happy and resilient, you can *only* have an advantage over the less-than-resilient Harvard student if you start using the pain of your mistakes to be a greater human being. I've had the opportunity to be around leading experts who went to some of the best schools in this country, but I've seen these people struggle with the tremendous challenges in their lives. The person at Harvard might well be educated in math, science, and history, but one of the most important things to be educated in is human capacity, to know what your ability is as a human being to use pain.

THE FIRST STEP: KNOWING YOU HAVE A SWITCH

Everybody has a switch that can be flipped to make a difference in their life. Wherever you're sitting—in a cubicle, in first class, in a jail cell— you've just got to know the switch is there. You Flip the Switch when you say to yourself, *Okay, I have a crisis, a real difficulty in my life, but I'm going to use this crisis to become greater.* Flipping the Switch is second nature for some people. To others, it is a completely new idea. But the good news is, we can all learn how to do it.

The first step is just becoming aware that the switch is already inside of you, waiting to be flipped. This awareness leads to believing that something positive can happen, and that's when options start to become possible. And here's the thing—that energy is there whether you Flip the Switch or not. But you have to know the switch is there and that you can flip it before you access the energy.

Not convinced that it's already inside you? Well, look back at what you've previously been through and overcome. Think of both the big and small things. The reality is that you are already practicing resilience. Take today, for example. Did you get out of bed today? Did you take a shower? Did you show up to work? Was it one of those days where you continued to go through the motions even though you wanted to shut down? The fact that you're whatever age you are right now and that you picked up this book is strong proof that you are resilient. You might not realize how resilient you have been. Greater awareness can equal greater resilience.

Every day adults and children alike go to bed at night with no concept of their ability to Flip the Switch. Children aren't learning this skill because adults aren't teaching them. How can they, when they don't know how to do it themselves? Most adults don't see their problems as their best friends.

The person who realizes that the switch is there, and knows how to flip it, has a major advantage over someone lacking that knowledge and ability. It's also important to realize that the faster you can Flip the Switch, the more likely you are to stem the damage, recover quickly, and bounce back.

ONE MORE REHAB—WITHOUT THE SWITCH

A week after I spoke to the boys in that detention center, I had a vastly different experience with someone on the opposite end of the socio-economic spectrum. As I returned from giving a speech in the South, I found myself sitting on an airplane next to a woman in her midfifties who was dressed to the nines and very put together. She was highly educated and worked for a nonprofit foundation that raised money for charitable causes. She was obviously affluent. She drank the entire flight. We started talking after the third time she ordered alcohol, when she turned to me and said, "I'm going to rehab. And I'm going to drink all the way there!" I knew I had to hear her story.

She told me she had always been very professional and coped well until her life started falling apart. Her first marriage failed when her teenage daughter died of cancer. By the time her second marriage failed, she'd turned to alcohol to try to get by. This was her third time going to rehab.

I listened as she shared her story with me. Then I told her, "Look, I teach people how to take their challenges and struggles and use them as reasons to be better. You have to use your daughter's death as a reason not to drink." I explained the idea of Flipping the Switch to her. I think it was the first time anyone had explained to her that her daughter's death could be her fuel to try to achieve sobriety. I told her that she couldn't go back and undo her daughter's death. She couldn't get rid of her past failures in treatment programs. But she could use these failures and setbacks as the fuel to make a comeback.

She kept talking about her age, as if it were too late for her. I told her that life is going to keep going. It won't stop. The good news is that she could spend the next three months in that place, working on learning to Flip the Switch, and she could come out ahead. Time will pass anyway, and she may as well use that time in rehab, as painful as it might be now, to put herself in a better position.

At the end of our talk, she hugged me three times and followed me to my departure gate, almost missing her connecting flight. I hope she realized after our conversation that she had the ability to change her life by Flipping the Switch.

LEARNING HOW TO FLIP THE SWITCH

Once you are aware that the switch exists, you will need the ability to flip it. Follow these steps to do so:

1. **Combat denial and acknowledge that there is a problem.** Realize the reality of your pain from where you're standing. Pain can occur anywhere across a wide spectrum—it could stem from a true crisis or simply the day-to-day hardships that mow you over. Whether you're overwhelmed by laundry or losing your home, accept that the situation is your reality. However, a word of caution here—it's also important to keep things in perspective. Don't overdo it and get bogged down in negativity; acknowledge that you can still get up and do something no matter what your reality is, and that while everything may seem hopeless, life evolves quickly.

2. **Ask yourself the Flip the Switch question:** How can I use this emotional pain, challenge, or situation to better my circumstances and make me more resilient—today, this hour, this minute, this second?

3. **Do the opposite of what people would normally do in a similar situation.** Even if a certain response is understandable, valid even, do the opposite. When you Flip the Switch, you're turning your situation on its head—you're turning bad into good, pain into power.

4. **Pay attention to how you feel inside when you decide to Flip the Switch.** You're likely to feel more energized, hopeful, and motivated. This will inspire you to continue to Flip the Switch in the long term. This will increase your awareness and allow you to feel more in control. Hope and optimism grow. The other benefits are powerful, and include the following:

- You give hope to others as they watch you handle your situation with strength.
- Your dignity, self-respect, and confidence increase.
- You get your power back because you're making a decision that puts you in control.
- Inner healing occurs more quickly.
- It gives you something to do with the pain.
- Your anger is put in check, because now you have a new perspective and you see anger as fuel.
- You perform real service to others because your focus is turned outward.
- You have increased compassion for others because of increased empathy for anyone dealing with pain.
- You think more clearly because you have insight that pain can be converted into positive fuel.

These benefits are so tangible that you will want to Flip the Switch again and again. This creates a cycle that becomes self-perpetuating.

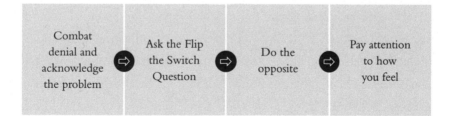

WENDY FLIPS THE SWITCH

My wife, Wendy, and I had an experience that demonstrates this process. Years ago, due to my learning differences, I was holding down a number of minimum-wage jobs while working on my degree. This put Wendy under a lot of pressure to provide for our family. Times were rough, and there were very few jobs to be had. She had applied at dozens of places and spent each day searching for employment and sending out resumes. After weeks of disappointment, we were starting to lose hope.

One day I drove her to an interview, and on the ride we discussed her frustration at the rejections. We came to the conclusion that we wouldn't give up, but that we had to do something different. Before she got out of the car, I said to her, "You've got to go in there, hand them your resume, and tell them you are going to work the first two weeks for free. Let them know you want this opportunity bad enough, and are certain enough of your abilities to do the job well, that you'll do it for free."

She took a deep breath and went inside. When she came back out, her huge smile told me how it had gone. They'd said she stood out from all the other applicants. She knew they were really interested in her, and she was fairly certain she had the job. And she did—in a few days they called and offered her the position, with pay.

This story was an instance of Wendy and me Flipping the Switch together. Let's take a look at how the steps worked in this case. Step 1 is combating denial and acknowledging the problem. In the beginning, we were both in denial. We assumed that sheer perseverance would pay off. If Wendy kept sending out resumes and applications, eventually she'd find a job. However, the reality was that she was sending out applications all day long but not getting hired. We finally realized that unless we did something differently she was probably not going to find work. We came to accept this reality. But we also knew there were jobs out there and we needed to keep trying.

Next, Wendy and I moved on to step 2: We asked ourselves the Flip the Switch question. What could we could do, right then, that day in the car, to channel our frustration into something positive? Fortunately, Wendy was open to marshaling her feelings of rejection and letting them fuel a new approach to the very interview we were driving toward.

Step 3, doing the opposite of what someone else might do, took place next. Certainly, no one expected Wendy to walk in, present herself with confidence, and offer to work for free in order to prove her desire and abilities. It definitely caught the attention of the employer and worked to her benefit. Her ability to pull it off was a testament to her resilience.

Step 4 is to pay attention to how you feel after you Flip the Switch. How did Wendy and I feel after the first three steps? Well, she was smiling from ear to ear when she came back to the car. She felt very confident, and she should have—she did the hard part! But I felt great, too. We both sat in the car celebrating. We were lucky because it worked the first time, but we both realized that won't always happen. The thing is, even if she hadn't got that job, she would have felt better. She would have still felt more in control and empowered because she had done something proactive, aggressive, and positive. Even with no job, she'd been bold and advocated for herself. She had additional dignity and self-respect. So even if she hadn't been hired, she'd have tried again, because she was stronger.

I've had countless experiences like this. Flipping the Switch makes all the difference! Channeling the pain you are experiencing is incredibly empowering. Flipping the Switch also helps you be "more human"— kinder, more authentic, more willing to reach out to others—and gives you the ability to connect with people in a very authentic way. The only time that life is at its peak is when two human beings are communicating with each other without strategizing or angling for success or glory. Being "more human" draws people to you and leads to better relationships, which increases your resilience and gives you more options.

YOU HAVE TO CONSTANTLY FLIP THE SWITCH

Flipping the Switch isn't a one-time event; you can't do it once and hope it stays on for your entire life. You have to be constantly Flipping the Switch. You might have to Flip the Switch ten times in one day. You might have days where you have to Flip the Switch every hour, or every ten seconds. Sometimes I only have to Flip the Switch once a week. But I have to constantly say to myself, *Okay, this is the problem I have to deal with, and I'm going to channel the pain and make the conscientious choice to maximize the situation and become greater.*

For example, say I've been on the road for three days. I'll be home two days, and then I leave again for four days. I'm already prepping myself, because I know I'm going to have to Flip the Switch. Do I want to go on the road for the next four days? Absolutely not. I'd rather do anything else. But the reality is, my body is going to have to get on that airplane and go somewhere. So I'm going to Flip the Switch. I'm going to do the best that I can, wherever my body has to go. I'm going to make the best decisions I can. I don't want to do it, but since I have to, I'm going to be as nice to the TSA folks and flight attendants and people sitting around me as I can. I'm going to Flip the Switch and be as loving, kind, motivational, and patient as I can be.

FLIPPING THE SWITCH IS FOR EVERYONE

Anyone can Flip the Switch—the wealthy, the imprisoned, the highly educated, the blue-collar worker, the white-collar worker. When I was first developing these ideas, I was focused on special-education and high-risk kids, but I have since seen that they apply to absolutely anyone. A few years ago a school superintendent told me they were going to put all seventy thousand of their students through my WhyTry resilience program. When I told him it was intended specifically for high-risk kids, he explained that he had a son who could've gone to Harvard, but he lost him to suicide. His son succumbed to the pressure that so many high-achieving kids face. This superintendent was certain the outcome would have been different had his son been familiar with these principles. From that moment on I became an advocate for all kids and adults. This isn't just for at-risk people. Everyone needs to understand the principles of resilience. Resilience is for the world.

A MIDFLIGHT FLIP OF THE SWITCH

I hurried onto my flight after giving a speech to three hundred people in Philadelphia, shoving my two bulky bags into the overhead bin before squeezing into my aisle seat. The woman next to me was wearing a flight-attendant uniform from another airline, and the older, overweight woman next to her was fidgeting nervously, eyes darting back and forth. I had an immediate hunch that the woman by the window had some mental-health issues—a hunch that would be confirmed before we landed in Denver a few hours later.

I struck up a conversation with my flight-attendant neighbor, who introduced herself as Julie. I was on what I call a "speaker's high"—full of adrenaline from my speech combined with excitement that I was finally on my way home. Despite the fact that she was probably exhausted from a long week of work with her airline, I began chatting with Julie at a million miles an hour, explaining how many days I fly each year and joking that I'm probably in the air more than she is. My broad shoulders invaded her small seat space as I talked, and the woman next to her continued to fidget and glance around, wide eyed. Imagine this poor flight attendant: sandwiched between a woman with mental-health issues and a euphoric overweight business traveler. And we hadn't even taken off yet.

The voice on the intercom announced that it was time for takeoff and asked passengers to please buckle their seatbelts. Just then the woman next to Julie darted out of her seat, looking panicked and trapped, her back against the window. Julie turned to her and said politely, "Will you please sit down?" She then turned back to me and muttered under her breath, "I'm off the clock and this isn't my airline. I hope the flight attendants will come do their jobs." The lady slowly sat back down, and the plane took off.

I found out the lady's name was Sarah. When they started passing out drinks, she loudly ordered a twelve-dollar bottle of wine. They opened a bottle, handed her a glass, and she poured a drink. But you have to use a credit card to purchase these beverages, and she didn't have one. She sat there awkwardly while the server waited for a solution, unsure of what to do now that the bottle had already been opened. I took out my credit card and paid for her. Next to me, Julie rolled her eyes and whispered, "Are you kidding me? You have to pay for her alcohol?" I smiled and assured her it was all right.

Sarah sat there, shifting nervously for a few minutes. All of a sudden, the bottle slid to the back of her tray and spilled everywhere, covering Julie's legs and bag. She was livid. "What's the matter with you!" she exclaimed before rushing to the restroom at the back of the plane. She returned a moment later with a handful of paper towels, which she threw down before ordering, "Clean this mess up!"

At this point, I was annoyed at how this flight attendant was treating her seat neighbor. Sarah tried to clean up the spilled wine around her, but she couldn't bend over very well and did a pretty bad job. She began muttering senselessly about unconnected aspects of her life, and about how rude the people were who brought her wine. Julie gestured toward me and said, "Well, not everybody's rude. He bought the wine for you." Sarah didn't seem to be listening. Her trail of muttering continued into all the things that were hard about life and how crazy the world is.

By now it was dawning on me that Sarah likely had no friends and lived a very isolated life. She was obviously a lonely woman in a tough situation. She didn't fit in with society.

Julie was now beyond ticked. The two women began insulting each other, and it was getting ugly. And this was only the beginning of a long flight! So I said to Julie, "I thought when you were in that uniform you had to be nice all the time." She retorted, "I don't work for this airline, and I don't have to be nice."

Soon the food cart came by. Sarah turned to me and asked, "Could I borrow that credit card again? I'm hungry."

In exasperation, Julie cried, "Are you kidding me? He already bought you a twelve-dollar bottle of wine, and now you're going to have him buy you dinner?"

I laughed and replied, "I would be more than happy to buy you that food, ma'am." And I bought her a full meal. Now Julie was completely beside herself and watched in disgust as Sarah quickly and untidily ate her meal. When she finished, she was covered in crumbs and had sauce on her mouth. Julie continued to stare at her, and Sarah became so uncomfortable that her legs began nervously tapping, and I saw all the social cues saying that she was scared to death of the flight attendant next to her. Sarah finally stood up abruptly and said she had to go to the bathroom.

When she had gone, Julie looked straight ahead and sighed, "I'm tired of these types of people."

In the flight attendant's defense, she works with difficult people a lot, and she was tired. She just wanted to have an uneventful flight home after a long week of work. Now obviously, I'm much more naturally aligned with the cute but annoyed flight attendant. But the social worker in me knows I'm being a bystander bully if I don't speak up, and this is where the magic happens. So I said to her, "I see you're very frustrated with that woman. On the surface, you have every reason to be upset. Now, you don't have to listen to me, but I'm going to share something with you. Do you want to see the world completely different for the rest of your life? You don't have to listen to me, but if you do, I want to share something with you."

Julie sighed and said, "Well, it obviously can't hurt."

I introduced myself, telling her that I'm actually a licensed clinical social worker and experienced therapist. "If you want to tune me out you can, but I'm going to be this lady's voice for a minute and tell you who she really is," I said. Then I tried to take Julie directly into the world of this person that she had just treated horribly. "Imagine this: I wake up in the morning. I don't have any friends. I don't have anyone to call. I might watch daytime TV or read the newspaper. If I can get myself up, I might go on a walk. I'm going to think about relationships in my life that I've lost. I'm unemployable. My day is long and lonely, and much like every other day. That's probably her normal day. In this airplane, she is pinned against the wall and she doesn't know how to cope with the anxiety of all that's going on. To top it off, she's probably going home to an empty apartment."

I could tell the lightbulb was starting to come on for Julie. I continued, "If I get diagnosed with cancer, my wife and kids would rally around me. But if my ADHD gets crazy and out of control, my family will run from me. We're accepting of people with physical problems, but not of people with mental-health issues. If I have cancer, they rally. But if you have mental-health issues, it's seen as a character flaw. We say these people are rude, stupid, or take advantage of us. They're sloppy or erratic or lazy. We use all the labels. If she had a physical problem, you and I would be treating her like gold right now."

Julie's face had softened and there were tears streaming down her cheeks. "I get it," she said softly. "I think they taught us some of this in our training. I'm exhausted, but you're right, it's no excuse. It's horrible how I've treated her."

Now, Julie had already taken a poor approach to handling the situation with Sarah, but was it too late for her to Flip the Switch and convert her annoyance, disgust, and possibly even rage into respect for her fellow passenger? No! That's the beauty of this technique: It works even late in the game, after you've messed up. It's never too late to Flip the Switch.

When Sarah returned from the restroom, Julie was ready. She smiled at her and gently apologized for her earlier behavior. The rest of the flight was like heaven on Earth. Why? Because Julie made the decision that she was going to see her fellow passenger for what's right with her, not what's wrong. She Flipped the Switch and decided to treat her with respect.

◆ ◆ ◆

Whenever I speak to any group—whether it is the hardened youth offenders in an inner-city detention center or highly educated professionals—my goal is that they walk out of that room believing in resilience. I want them to understand that human beings, no matter their plight, have a switch that they can flip. They can flip it every day, every hour, every moment. It might not get rid of the problem or the pain, but it will help them manage their current plight and better their situation. Flipping the Switch will allow you to access previously unforeseen options and the Four Sources of Resilience, which we'll discuss next.

ASK

What adverse issues or challenges you currently face have come to mind as you've read this chapter? In what situations can you begin Flipping the Switch in your own life?

Have you ever Flipped the Switch during a crisis or challenge? What were you thinking and feeling that enabled you to access resilience rather than shutting down or reacting poorly?

TASK

Practice the "Do the Opposite" principle. Instead of responding without the awareness that you can Flip the Switch, do what no one, including yourself, would have thought you'd do—do the opposite.

If you know someone who's dealing with serious adversity and your relationship is solid with this person, consider sharing this information with them, perhaps explaining its value to you.

FINALLY! WHERE RESILIENCE COMES FROM!

HOW I DISCOVERED THE FOUR SOURCES

In my early years of teaching resilience, I was often confronted with the question, "What about someone who doesn't have any motivation to be resilient?" I used to look at the people who asked this like they were requesting a miracle. Were they crazy, thinking I could tell them where resilient people drew their power from? I could teach strategies on how to increase resilience, and talk for days about how important this concept was, but I couldn't exactly say where, fundamentally, resilience came from.

But one day a tiny Polynesian woman approached me after one of my speeches. Although she was petite, I could tell she was a force to be reckoned with. She reminded me of Mother Teresa, a powerful little woman with an intense desire to help others. This lady looked up at me and said, "Christian, I'm working with so many children who have no idea why they shouldn't give up. Please, please reflect on your experiences and see if you can explain what would motivate someone to be resilient." She said she'd been trying to figure this out her whole life. I could tell that my speech on resilience had brought her closer to this knowledge than ever before, but she wasn't quite there.

From that day on I was obsessed. The question "What is motivating this person to be resilient?" became my filter for everything. I wore my

"Where does resilience come from?" glasses every day for about seven years as I tried to solve this problem.

MY TRIGGER EVENT

Finally, something happened that changed everything. I call it my "trigger event." I had been working nonstop and was traveling over twenty days a month. I started having panic attacks on planes and severe anxiety in hotel rooms. I was emotionally crashing. I was facing multiple personal crises in my life, and it was a very low point for me. Both my business partner and my wife confronted me and told me I had to cut back on my travel and slow way down. So, for the first time ever, I had time to just be in the office. This downtime was very new and difficult for me, but now I had time to really focus on my quest for the answer to that question—where does resilience come from?

One day I was sitting in my office, feeling like giving up and shutting down. I asked myself, *What is it that has enabled me to overcome the obstacles in my life? I have had so many barriers to face. Now my barrier is this anxiety. What's going to get me through it?* A word popped into my head, and I wrote STREET on my whiteboard. To me, it referred to the way I had used challenges, like disrespect I had felt or mistakes I had made, as fuel. I used my weaknesses in life, whether they were learning differences or delinquent behaviors as a child, to my advantage. I had learned how to channel these challenges and find ways to turn them into assets. Dealing with them had given me an edge.

I thought, *Christian, this is how you overcame your childhood. This is how you made it through college. It's Street Resilience.* I started to feel excited. I knew everybody in the world had felt disrespect or made mistakes in their life; it was universal. I realized that if I could teach this to someone in great pain, or someone who felt like giving up, or even someone who is already highly functional, they'd be more motivated to be resilient. They'd have an edge. They'd have Street Resilience. Street Resilience enabled me to get through elementary school, to survive my neighborhood, to graduate high school, to stay in a marriage, to have the desire to be a social worker.

My brain started racing as the ideas came quickly. I decided I needed a heading for all of this, and I wrote "Resilience Motivation" on the board. I thought of my business partner Hans. He is brilliant and very resilient, but he doesn't have an ounce of "street" in him. Where did his resilience come from? With Hans in mind, I wrote RESOURCE on the board. Hans has access to many resources, he is extremely good at utilizing his gifts and abilities, and he came from a place completely different than I did. Resource Resilience—a second source.

Next, I thought more about what had kept me going. What was it that had helped me to get out of bed each morning, even when I was crashing? It was my two kids. They were completely dependent on me. I absolutely had to make good decisions for them. I wrote RELATIONAL on the board. My social-work background taught me that relationships are the backbone of resilience. Support systems are key to mental health. When other people really need you, you are much more motivated to increase your resilience. I refused to give up because I knew my family needed me. I had identified a third source.

I then reflected on the times when I'd been at my very lowest. I wrote ROCK BOTTOM on the board. I knew instantly that it qualified as a fourth source. These lowest moments in life helped me dig deep and find resilience, and I knew it wasn't just me. As a therapist in a homeless program, I observed people with no family or any visible reason to keep going. Yet they did. This sheer will to live has always been an inspiration to me. I'd spent my whole life being fascinated by people who have every reason to give up but don't.

As I looked at these four categories that I'd written on my board—STREET, RESOURCE, RELATIONAL, ROCK BOTTOM—it felt like the moment from years before when I'd finished developing my WhyTry curriculum, which had since helped thousands of kids. That day I did a little jig in my office. Now, with these four sources identified, I knew I had something that explained where resilience is born, something I'd been trying to solve for years. And I did a little celebratory jig again.

MY SIXTY RESILIENT HEROES—
AND WHAT I LEARNED FROM THEM

Next, I wrote sixty names on the board, those of people like Gandhi, Oprah, Richard Branson, Nelson Mandela, and Christopher Reeve. I spent the rest of the afternoon alone in my office identifying which types of resilience each of them had. The sources held up—I could identify at least two of them for every person I considered.

Since that day, I've found that most people have at least two of the four sources. I'm not saying that people are born with them. A person may have an innate propensity for one of the sources, but usually it has to be developed. Sometimes life circumstances force them to be developed. The great thing is that all four sources can be acquired. And the more sources of resilience you can access, the more resilient you are.

For twelve years I'd been teaching resilience, and I knew it could be learned, but that day I gained more insight than I'd ever had before about where resilience comes from. My breakthrough had come from reflecting on my own life, just as the little Polynesian woman had begged me to do. I realized that I was really strong in Street and Rock Bottom Resilience, and weakest in Relational and Resource. I also realized that if I could strengthen these other two sources in my life, I'd be much more likely to be consistently resilient. I knew, and it was very emotional for me, that if I could develop the sources where I was currently weak, it could change my life. I also knew I needed all four sources if I was going to make it through the second half of my life. And if I could teach others to do the same, it had the potential to impact individuals, families, and organizations.

◆ ◆ ◆

Relational, Street, Resource, and Rock Bottom Resilience comprise the foundation of resilience. Without these four sources, you might have all kinds of hope and optimism, but you won't know where your motivation to act on them will come from. Hope without strategy is a failed effort. Here at our office we call it "hopium." It's a short-lived and false high. But if you combine that positive energy with the sources of resilience, you'll find your drive to actually *do* something rather than just relying on hope and a good attitude.

My goal is to help everyone have access to at least two of these resilience sources and to share strategies to help you develop all four. As we explore the Four Sources of Resilience in the next four parts of this book, you'll naturally reflect on how well you're using each of them. Where are your strengths? Where can you improve? What inspires you to be more resilient? It is my hope that as you draw on these sources, you will find increased motivation, and increased ability, to be resilient in every aspect of your life.

ASK

Which of the Four Sources of Resilience do you connect with the most? Which do you think would be most difficult for you to tap into?

TASK

Make your own list of "resilience heroes" in your life and try to put your finger on their strongest source. Pick a person from the list who is strong in the source you think you're weak in, and then talk to this person about how they developed their strengths. Decide to remind yourself of this person's resilient actions the next time you're facing adversity.

> **BEFORE YOU KEEP READING:** If you'd like to find out which source of resilience you're strongest in, I encourage you to take the optional resilience self-assessment at the back of this book.

{ **PART II** }

RELATIONAL RESILIENCE

The power of human connection

WHAT IS RELATIONAL RESILIENCE?

The first time I realized the power of Relational Resilience, my face was covered in spit.

Several years ago, I was working as a counselor in a group home with some pretty rough kids. One night I was taking them bowling, a rare privilege that had them pretty excited. It was up to me to make sure they all cleaned and vacuumed their rooms before we could go, and everyone had finished and was ready. Everyone except a young man named Sam. He flat out refused to clean his room, swearing at me and insulting me the more I tried to negotiate with him.

I pulled the van around to the front of the house, knowing the others were counting on me to get Sam to move so they could enjoy a night out. I was starting to get desperate, so I loaded the kids into the van and pointed out to Sam that he was making them wait. As I climbed in behind them, listening to them telling Sam to hurry up, their expressions turned panicked and they started pointing to something right behind my head. "Mr. Moore! Mr. Moore!" they cried. "Turn around! Turn around!"

In my mind's eye I saw a baseball bat or golf club waiting to clock me in the back of my head. But it was way worse than that. When I cautiously climbed out of the van and turned around, Sam's scowling face was inches away from mine. He made that disgusting noise—the one that comes when you're pulling up snot from the back of your throat—and spit in my face. Huge, warm, dripping spit. It oozed down my forehead, my hair, on my eyebrow. It covered my face. But when I felt the warm, disgusting snot sitting on my lip, I lost it. Being OCD about germs was bad enough, but I'd been conditioned by the environment I grew up in that spitting in someone's face was the ultimate disrespect. It could literally get you killed.

I distinctly remember feeling my body tingle with rage. I felt it from my toes clear up my spine. My hands made a fist purely as a reflex. There was a stucco wall about twenty feet away, and in that moment all I could visualize was dragging Sam's face across it. This all happened within half a second, and I knew I had to get control fast. So I went from straight rage to saying to myself, *Christian, Christian, Christian. Calm down.*

The week before, I had seen this child's psychosocial history, and it flashed through my mind as I tried to get myself under control. He'd come from a horrible situation and had been through a tremendous amount of pain. As I looked at this young man, I Flipped the Switch. In a single moment, I went from almost uncontrolled rage to careful calm, instituting damage control that would not only affect me but also all those kids that night that depended on me. If I had retaliated, I could have lost my ability to be a social worker, but more important, I would have taught the kids in the van to strike back. I would have hurt Sam and reinforced to him what the world had taught him to do his whole life—to hurt those who hurt you—which only leads to more pain.

So instead of retaliating, I wiped Sam's spit off my face with my hand, took a deep breath, and said, "Look, I understand why you just spit in my face. If I had a life like yours, I would be spitting in someone's face, too." Sam started shaking like a leaf, and I asked, "Every time you spit in someone's face, your whole life, what's happened?"

"We'd start fighting," Sam retorted.

When Sam spit in my face, he was 100 percent sure that we were going to fight. He looked at me and shouted, "Mr. Moore, you're weak! You're a sissy. I disrespected you, and you didn't do anything!"

The other kids were still sitting behind us in the van, expressions of shock on their faces. To be honest, I was just as shocked, because I didn't know I could control my anger like that. I realized that this was an important moment for us, especially me. I had to stay in control of my emotions if I was going to spend my career helping others. I looked Sam in the eye and declared, "Listen. If you lined up a hundred people and you punched or spit at all of them, ninety-nine would probably punch or spit back. But the one person that doesn't? He's ten times stronger than the other ninety-nine! If you always hit back, you have no future. It takes no strength, no backbone to fight back. Hitting back is simply human nature. 'You hurt me, I'm gonna hurt you.' It takes all the strength I have not to fight back."

I took Sam in the house that evening and counseled him for about twenty minutes before loading the van and heading to the bowling alley. He calmed down, apologized to me, and had tremendous respect for me after that. For the rest of his time in the group home, he tried to show empathy and self-control and reminded others to do so as well.

What stopped me from reacting that day and helped me stay in control of my emotions? It was the knowledge that those kids—including Sam—depended on me. Imagine the cost if I hadn't used the kids' dependence on me as a reason to be resilient in that moment. What if I'd forgotten in my rage how much this child needed me?

When others are depending on you, you do what it takes and find strength you didn't even know you had. Even when you really, really want to, you simply don't give in, or give up. This is one important aspect of Relational Resilience.

BOOSTING RESILIENCE THROUGH THE HUMAN CONNECTION

When you have **Relational Resilience**, your greatest motivation to make good decisions, put more effort into life, and not give up is the knowledge that others depend on you. You also draw strength from the emotional support of friends, family members, deceased loved ones, a pet, or even a stranger who smiles your way. These support systems can come from simple or in-depth interactions. You recognize that influence is reciprocal and that you can both give and receive resilience in the ways you approach your interactions with others throughout your life, even those that seem trivial and mundane.

As human beings, our connection to other human beings is essential. No matter our circumstances, we need each other. We need to know that we are influencing others, and we need to feel the influence of others in our lives as well. It doesn't matter if you are married or single, come from a huge family or are an only child whose parents have passed away. Connection to other human beings is vital to our ability to be resilient and thrive. I'm always amazed at how quickly I can feel lonely and disconnected. I've learned that I need frequent, consistent connection, and I believe this to be true for all human beings. Extroverts and introverts alike need to influence and be influenced by others.

Loneliness is a powerful enemy of resilience, and loneliness is something that many people struggle with. You can have lots of people in your life and still have bouts of loneliness. It's even possible to be lonely in a crowd. The need for inclusion varies greatly from person to person; the important thing is that you are aware of your needs so that you do what you can to fill your life with the amount of human connection you need to be resilient.

THE POWER OF BEING COUNTED ON

They say that everyone needs to be needed. Dr. Mark Katz, an expert on resilience and a longtime mentor of mine, would agree. In his book *On Playing a Poor Hand Well*, Katz describes a study conducted by Hanita Zimrin in 1986, which followed abused children into adulthood. Although the majority of these children had struggles throughout their adult lives, a few of them were seen as "survivors" based on differences like scholastic achievement, absence of severe emotional problems, and constructive future plans. Zimrin determined there were a number of variables that distinguished those who were able to adapt. As summarized by Katz, "Members of the survivor group also took on the responsibility for helping someone else; for example, protecting and nurturing a sibling in some specific way. Some survivors mentioned the importance of caring for a pet that depended upon them. The nonsurvivors did not mention a similar type of responsibility."[5]

Katz often tells schools and people in the mental-health arena that if they want to see change in a child who is struggling, they should create a meaningful role for the child. Give him a job or an important responsibility, something that he can do well, and see what can happen. "A teacher once told me that she gave one of her toughest students the assignment to water the plants in the school," Katz shares. "Other teachers and the principal began acknowledging how great the plants were looking. This kid started showing up twenty minutes early to school to make sure he took care of those plants. His teacher said it was so eye-opening for her—he was literally a different student, just because he had a task and was needed."

Whether it's a member of your family, someone completely unrelated to you, or a pet, everyone needs to be needed by someone. These relationships matter. They are meaningful. It's really a matter of awareness. I think to myself, *Is what I'm doing impacting those who depend on me?* This is a great source of untapped fuel in our lives. A relationship might be the main fuel to get you to stay in college. It might be the fuel to get you to stay off drugs. Or the reason you get up day after day, go to work, and face that condescending boss who never listens to your ideas. It might be the only reason you got out of bed today. It's a big gas tank of resilience fuel! And it's just waiting to be used. You simply have to be aware that it's there.

STAYING SOBER THROUGH
RELATIONAL RESILIENCE

Bill Clegg was a high-profile literary agent for several well-known authors and co-owner of his own agency in New York City when he descended into a life of drug addiction. After experiencing relapse after relapse he finally became sober and was able to relaunch a successful career. In his book *Ninety Days* he tells the powerful story about how Relational Resilience was a major motivating force in helping him through his arduous and long battle with drugs.[6] Clegg had lost everything—his business, his relationships, his money—and was trying to stay clean after his latest six-week stint in rehab. Ninety days is the goal, a seemingly impossible goal, as over and over he relapses, succumbing in his fight with the overpowering demons that have taken over his life. He says, "As any recovering addict knows, hitting rock bottom is just the beginning."

It's a pretty raw story, and your heart can't help but go out to Clegg as he repeatedly fails to stay sober and have a semblance of a functional life. He spends his days and evenings attending recovery meetings, where he meets a few indispensable allies. Polly, also a recovering addict, becomes essential to his journey. They see each other every day at twelve-step recovery meetings and at the park. Polly struggles every day to stay sober, especially since her twin sister and roommate is a user with no intention to get clean. Bill and Polly support each other through good days and bad days, until Polly's sister almost dies from an overdose, and Clegg pulls some strings and gets Polly into a two-week rehab program.

For about a month after rehab Polly does great. But then she falls, and falls hard, telling Clegg that she is done—done trying, done going to meetings, done. A huge part of Clegg wants to be done, too, and the next day he almost decides not to go to the recovery meeting, until he has the thought that maybe Polly will be there. What if she goes, and he's not there? This thought keeps him going to meetings for days, and then weeks, but still there is no Polly.

On a particularly bad day, the cravings attack again, and he finds himself walking toward his dealer's house. Normally, if he even crosses into this section of the city, it's over. Addiction and desire consume him, and all his sober days dissolve into days and nights of a drug-hazed binge. He stands in front of his dealer's door, ready to ring the bell. But this time (although he doesn't call it this), Relational Resilience is what stops him. "But before I press the buzzer," Clegg explains, "I think of Polly. What if she calls me when I'm in there? What if she hears I've relapsed again? What if I don't make it to the meeting tomorrow, stay up for a few days, and miss her when she comes back in? What if my picking up gives her another excuse to keep using? It's narcissistic, I realize as I'm thinking it, but I can't help but ask myself: What if my picking up results in Polly dying? The logic is suddenly so plausible, so powerful, and so likely that it stops me in my tracks. It stops me less than ten feet from the buzzer I've pressed countless times over too many years and with the same grim results. I've never been this close and not gone in."

This moment for Bill Clegg becomes a turning point in his recovery. Over the next weeks there are dozens of times he goes to call his dealer, or thinks of showing up at the house, just like he always has. But this time, when he feels the claws of craving start to get him, he thinks of Polly. Or of someone else he's given his number to and told to call when they need him. And each time he stops long enough to call someone that's told him the same thing, and eventually the urge passes.

I found this brutally honest account to be a fantastic example of how, when it truly is all you can do to hang on, when life seems harder than you can possibly stand, Relational Resilience can give you strength. Bill Clegg realized that other people were counting on him—and that realization motivated him to be resilient, even in the face of crippling addiction. That's Relational Resilience at its finest.

ASK

Who in your personal life depends on you? What support do you provide for this particular person? What would happen if this person could have full confidence in your ability and desire to be dependable and supportive? How would it change the relationship?

Who depends on you at work? What service or product do you provide for them? What would happen if this person couldn't count on you? Does the knowledge of their dependence on you matter? How so? Is there anything you could do that would make you a more reliable, dependable coworker?

TASK

In spite of any obstacles that may arise, or that may have arisen in the past, follow through on the commitments you've made to anyone depending on you. This could include performing tasks or acts of kindness completely unexpected by the other person.

RELATIONAL RESILIENCE BOOSTERS

There are many ways to cultivate Relational Resilience. I've thought long and hard on some of my favorite tools for strengthening the ability to create and access this resilience source, and the material in this part of the book contains those techniques and skills—I call them "boosters." They are designed to fortify your relationships with other people, and to help you remember that your decisions affect everyone in your life. With healthy, vital relationships in place, and with the constant awareness that other people are depending on you, you'll be better able to find relational motivation to be resilient, even through the hard times.

Relationships have been the source of my greatest pain and greatest joy. Relationships amplify life's experiences. I've eaten a piece of pie alone, and I've eaten it with someone I love. It tastes so much better when I share it with someone I care about. It's this amplification of the highs and the lows that gives me the determination to fight on. It gives me the motivation to be a good friend. It gives me a reason to keep reaching out. It amplifies my resilience. There is no maximum capacity for love, no saturation. At the end of the day, the reason why relationships are so important is that they give me a feeling of being significant. As my sense of significance increases through my connections to other people, I become more resilient.

I have flown over two million miles around the world. I have eaten in the nicest restaurants. I've seen the best entertainment. I've had standing ovations. I've experienced all these amazing things. These all provide a temporary high and mimic lasting happiness. But the most amazing thing I've ever experienced, by far, hands down, is sitting on my couch, watching a basketball game on TV with my son Cooper. Or having Carson run to meet me at the door after a trip, a huge smile on his face. Nothing compares with being wanted and wanting connection from someone else. Nothing compares to meeting others' emotional needs and having your own emotional needs met. It's the greatest rush you'll have in life.

When it's all said and done, the only things that really matter are relationships. Just like you, I have heard this speech a thousand times. And honestly, it's taken me forty-three years to get it. Even three years ago I didn't completely comprehend it. But I finally understand: When someone needs me and I need them, this is real wealth. This is the highest level of fulfillment—and the only way to long-lasting resilience.

SURRENDER THE ONE-UP RELATIONSHIP

RELATIONAL RESILIENCE BOOSTER #1

Early in my career I started to recognize an interesting phenomenon. I noticed that in almost all social situations, I felt that I was either in a position of superiority or power or in a position of inferiority or "less than." In simpler terms, I was either "up" or "down" in relation to the other person. Think of the most recent interaction you've had today. Were you up or down in relation to the other person? We have been socialized to measure ourselves against others, and even though we don't do so purposely, we judge others' influence and power and how they can impact us positively and negatively. For a lot of my life I have felt "one-down." Because of my learning differences I often felt like the dumbest person in the room, and whether that was true or not, it affected how I felt about myself and my relationships with others.

Many relationships have a natural hierarchy—boss and employee, parent and child, teacher and student. But even when the ranking isn't so obvious, we tend to rank ourselves in relation to the other person. Think about it—who is the "one-up" in these examples: popular versus shy, thin versus fat, or wealthy versus poor? It's not hard to figure out who would have the natural advantage.

The most powerful interpersonal tool I know is something I term "surrendering the one-up relationship." This means that when I have power or influence over another person, I use that advantage in their best interest. That person goes from feeling inferior, or "one-down" to feeling equal, or even "one-up." This is the opposite of what we are socialized to do. We're taught to be competitive and win everything we can. Today, however, I know that when I practice surrendering the one-up, I help create an environment where everyone can thrive.

My first memory of this concept was taught to me as a child when I learned the biblical story of Jesus washing his disciples' feet. Even then I knew this was a powerful principle. I was further reminded of its importance a few years ago as I was walking on a college campus late one evening and noticed someone coming toward me on the sidewalk. It only took me a second to realize it was one of my childhood heroes: San Francisco 49ers Hall of Fame quarterback Steve Young. I stopped him to ask for his autograph and began telling him how great he was. Instead of letting me go on with my praise he asked me all about what I was studying and what I wanted to do with my degree. He ended up interviewing *me* for about twenty minutes! I was shocked when he told me how much he admired me after learning about my passions and interests. There I was, talking with a football legend, a two-time NFL MVP, yet after he walked away I felt like *I* was the celebrity! It would have been so easy for him to sign the autograph and walk away, but he gave me real time, focus, and interest. He surrendered the one-up, and that exchange had a lasting impact on my life.

YOU TAKE THE NICE CHAIR

As a therapist I constantly had kids sent to me who had failed—in their home life, in school, in the juvenile justice system. All of these failures put these kids one-down in all their relationships. One way I was able to surrender the one-up with them was as simple as where my client and I sat in my office. I had a nice leather chair and a metal folding chair that was beat up and in bad condition. When a child would come in, they would always go right to the beat-up chair. Just before they would sit down I would ask them to sit in the nice leather chair. The child would smile, lean back, and enjoy the comfy chair for a few minutes. Then they would say, "Here Mr. Moore, you can have your nice chair back." The child instinctively understood the boundaries. I was the "expert" and should have the nicer chair.

But I would say to them, "No, you are the expert on your own life. You have lived your life for the past ten [or twelve, or sixteen] years. You stay in the nice chair." The look on the child's face every time I did this taught me that everyone needs a person—especially one with a natural advantage over them—to serve and respect them. Surrendering the one-up creates an unlimited amount of motivation and real mutual love and respect. It also resulted in far fewer dropouts in my program. When I treated those kids like they were just as important as myself, they felt like they were winning—and they were hungry to be in an environment where they felt like they were winning.

Ask yourself: What relationships do you have in your life where you need to, metaphorically speaking, give up the leather chair? Any time you do this—any time you motivate, inspire, encourage, and build up another person with no thought of anything in return except a more meaningful relationship with them—you are surrendering the one-up. This changes any relationship for the positive faster than anything else I know.

SURRENDERING THE ONE-UP, THE HP WAY

Surrendering the one-up helps boost your Relational Resilience in your personal life, but it can also help build resilience in the business world. Hewlett-Packard is a great example. HP was the original garage start-up, founded on a couple hundred borrowed dollars in 1939 by Bill Hewlett and David Packard. For years it was the goal of many a talented engineer to work at this cutting-edge, multibillion-dollar company, which was perennially ranked at the top of the most admired companies to work for. Because of various marketing realities and leadership changes, it is no longer what it once was, but for decades it was a world-class company built on "the HP Way"—Bill and Dave's egalitarian approach to running their company.

In the 1950s, '60s, and '70s, HP fostered a corporate culture that was ahead of its time. The founders insisted on being called "Bill" and "Dave" and made themselves accessible to all employees. In stark contrast with much of the rest of corporate America, at HP nobody had an office; rather, employees worked together in open spaces, and executives mingled with employees.

In 1958, David Packard presented what he called his "11 Simple Rules" at an internal meeting in Sonoma, California. As I read them, I realized that each of these principles rests on the idea of surrendering the one-up:

- Think first of the other person.
- Build up the other person's sense of importance.
- Respect the other person's personality rights. (My personal favorite.)
- Give sincere appreciation.
- Eliminate the negative.
- Avoid openly trying to reform people.
- Try to understand the other person.
- Check first impressions.
- Take care with the little details.
- Develop genuine interest in people.
- Keep it up.[7]

One story in HP's history became part of the folklore around its strong corporate culture. Chuck House, a longtime HP employee, was working at an HP laboratory in Colorado Springs and knew both Bill Hewlett and David Packard well. Packard reviewed a large-screen oscilloscope that House was developing and ordered, "The next time I come here I don't want to see that product in the lab."[8] Instead of abandoning the project, however, House took vacation time and went to California, stopping along the way to show potential customers a prototype. He took out the front seat of his Volkswagen Bug, put the monitor in its place, and visited forty customers in three weeks. The positive feedback and orders he received inspired him to complete the project, even though it had officially been discontinued, and he rushed it into production. The next time Packard visited the lab, he thundered, "I thought I told you to kill that product!" to which House replied, "No, you said you didn't want to see it in the lab. It's not in the lab anymore."[9] House's invention was a huge success. It was used in the first manned moon landing, and HP ended up selling seventeen thousand of them, making $35 million for the company—quite a chunk of change back then. Some years later, Dave Packard himself proudly presented House with an award for "Extraordinary Contempt and Defiance Beyond the Normal Call of Engineering Duty."[10]

Of course, I'm not advocating that employees ignore or defy their bosses—there are many instances when that would not be beneficial for anyone and might not end happily. But House said it never occurred to him that it might cost him his job. Because of Packard's accessibility and habit of focusing on the other person's importance, House knew that his boss's inherent nature was to surrender the one-up. And because Packard built that habit, his resilience—and that of his company—increased.

ASK

Think about a time you were "one-down" in an interaction. What emotions did you experience during this interaction? Who may feel one-down in their interactions with you?

TASK

Tomorrow, approach *every* interaction—with colleagues, family members, friends, and service workers—with an attitude of "surrendering the one-up." Make sure those people walk away from you feeling better about themselves.

ENGAGE EMOTIONALLY
RELATIONAL RESILIENCE BOOSTER #2

One day I was lying in bed next to my wife after a long trip. I had been traveling over two hundred days a year for several years, and I noticed that I felt extreme loneliness even though she was right there next to me. Looking back, I now realize this was because being on the road so much takes a toll, and I wasn't doing what I needed to have the amount of emotional intimacy with my family that I required to be able to thrive. My wife hadn't done anything wrong. I had emotionally disengaged in countless little ways and was using my work travel as an excuse. It was easy to blame it on the demands of my job, but I wasn't doing what I needed to do to stay connected.

A strong marriage, a healthy family life, and ongoing relationships with friends all require work. I hesitate to even say something that seems so obvious. But maybe it's not as obvious as I assume—marriage authority Aaron Beck says that one of the most destructive beliefs is "If we need to work at it, there's something seriously wrong with our relationship."

The truth is that all relationships—even the healthiest—are subject to entropy, the tendency of everything in life to deteriorate into chaos. Yet somehow many people assume that their friends and family don't require constant attention. It's especially true with family: Although most people claim the family is the most important concern in their lives, very few behave this way. They mistakenly believe that if they are providing for their material needs, that is all that is necessary. Dr. Mihaly

Csikszentmihalyi, former head of the University of Chicago Psychology Department and author of bestsellers *Flow* and *Finding Flow*, says, "The most widespread attitude seems to be that as long as material needs are provided for, a family will take care of itself; it will be a warm, harmonious, permanent refuge in a cold and dangerous world. It is very common to meet successful men in their late forties and fifties who are stunned when their wives suddenly leave or their children get into serious trouble. True, they never had more than a few minutes each day to talk, but how could they have done otherwise, with all the demands from the job."[11] It's a powerful point. All significant relationships dissolve into entropy without attention, effort, and care. This is what had happened in my situation when I was pouring all my energies into my business.

> **All significant relationships dissolve without attention, effort, and care.**

Emotional intimacy—which applies to all relationships, not just that of husband and wife—is a mutual understanding of each other's life experiences, strengths, weaknesses, mistakes, fears, hopes, and vulnerabilities. This means there has been adequate time invested, a shared understanding and real connection, caring, safety, and trust. It's a mutual desire to renew and build the relationship, and there is safety to express how you *really* feel. Emotional intimacy requires effort and is vital to our ability to access Relational Resilience.

EMOTIONAL ENGAGEMENT AROUND THE TABLE

Restaurants are one of the greatest places to observe the Relational Resilience that comes from emotional engagement. Due to my travel schedule, I have eaten thousands of meals in restaurants by myself. This has given me plenty of time to people-watch and learn a few things. One thing I've observed is that meals with other people fill our emotional needs much more than our stomachs. The social dynamics at each table fascinate me. In one corner of the restaurant I might see six women in their forties. I can tell by how comfortable they are with each other, the high energy level, and big smiles and hugs that they have been close friends for years. At another table I will see a family laughing and teasing each other. I will see tables with businessmen and women strategizing their next moves. I will observe lovers building on their relationships, or just starting relationships, and I have even observed several people ending relationships. (I eat out way too much!) I will also see other business travelers like myself, staring at their smartphones, desperate for some type of entertainment or connection. Anything to push off boredom and loneliness.

At first glance you would think the loneliest people in the room are the travelers like me. After twenty years of observing people, however, I've learned that sometimes the loneliest person in the room isn't me, although I certainly have been lonely in many a restaurant. Sometimes, the loneliest person is sitting at a table with two, or sometimes even ten, people.

After many years of scientific observational study (the layman's term would be "people-watching") and my own battle with loneliness, I can spot these fellow lonely diners in seconds. They are usually casually listening to the person in front of them. In some instances they are not listening at all to the people around them. They often have a very good fake smile and a rehearsed nod that well-practiced people-watchers like myself might notice. They are often looking past the person in front of them. Their emotional investment in that moment with those people in that restaurant is very small. They are experiencing emotional disengagement—the ability to be with people and still feel very alone.

Emotional disengagement is the opposite of a resilience booster. I am most concerned when I see this happening in close relationships, such as with a spouse, children, or good friends. Emotional disengagement—which may eventually lead to emotional numbness—is one of the greatest resilience killers. Relationships and emotional engagement are some of the most important components that help us weather the storms of life, and emotional disengagement does the opposite.

There have been so many times in my life where I have hurt or weakened my emotional connections and friendships. One of my first defenses, when I feel threatened at all, is to emotionally disengage. I pull back and the walls go up. But when I do this, I am not only hurting those around me who care about me; I am hurting myself.

TURN TOWARD THE OTHER

The absence of emotional engagement can wreak havoc in a marriage, but in the presence of it, the relationship blossoms. In the book *The Seven Principles for Making Marriage Work*, marriage expert Dr. John M. Gottman describes the importance of "love maps"—his name for the part of your brain where you store all the relevant information about your partner's life. Emotionally intelligent couples are intimately familiar with each other's world and have richly detailed love maps. They have made plenty of cognitive room for their marriage. These connections can be small but they are deceptively important, happening during "the grind of everyday life," says Gottman. "Comical as it may sound, romance actually grows when a couple are in the supermarket and the wife says, 'Are we out of bleach?' and the husband says, 'I don't know. Let me go get some just in case,' instead of shrugging apathetically. When couples engage in lots of chitchat like this, I can be pretty sure that they will stay happily married. What's really happening in these brief exchanges is that the husband and wife are connecting—they are turning toward each other."[12]

When we're constantly turning toward the others in our lives—wife or husband, brother or sister, friend or colleague—we build rich relationships that keep us strong and resilient. Engage emotionally at every chance you get, and you'll see your resilience soar.

ASK

What is your most significant relationship? What are some ways you may be emotionally disengaging yourself from this relationship? For example, do you find yourself tuning out everyday conversations with this person? Do you ever feel lonely in this person's company? Are there any areas that may be lacking your complete attention, effort, and care?

TASK

Identify one weak point in the significant relationship you've identified and commit to make a conscious effort in the next week to improve in this area. Pay attention to him or her. Don't go overboard and hyperfocus; simply ask yourself how you might make a slight change from prior emotionally disengaging actions. Try doing something you both enjoy, or say or write something that's truly heartfelt about their admirable qualities. Don't be afraid to be vulnerable—ask this person what areas you could improve in, or share your new goal with them.

Here are some other ways to increase your emotional engagement:

- Forgive a past grievance, whether real or imagined.
- Don't complain—about *anything*.
- Don't criticize.
- Find a simple way to serve this person that requires you to exert effort, not just spend money. Do something for him or her that inconveniences you.
- Don't isolate—stay available physically and emotionally.
- Look past an annoying behavior and remind yourself that you have your own that surely make you less than ideal company at all times.
- Monitor your use of the pronoun *I* and reduce it as much as you can. Start using *we* more often.

FRIENDSHIP—DON'T
TAKE IT FOR GRANTED
RELATIONAL RESILIENCE BOOSTER #3

The following fact blew my mind. A study in the *American Sociological Review* reported that in June 2006 American adults said they had only two close friends. When I read this I thought, *Really? Only two? What happens if one moves away?* This number was down from only three close friends in 1985, which shocked pollsters at the time. Even more troubling is the finding that men and women of every race, age, and education level reported fewer intimate friends than the previous study, and one of every four said they have no one to discuss important matters with.[13]

My eyes were really opened by another study conducted by researchers at the Minnesota Department of Corrections. This study, one of the largest of its kind, tracking sixteen thousand prisoners over nearly five years, discovered that inmates who received even just *one* personal visit from a family member or friend while incarcerated were 13 percent less likely to commit another felony when released, and 25 percent less likely to end up back in prison on a parole violation.[14] If you do the math, that 13 percent equals 2,080 people who won't commit another felony, and four thousand who don't return to prison—and that's just in Minnesota. Which means that 2,080 people won't burglarize, do drugs, commit rape, or even murder. That's astounding. The savings to society from the four thousand who don't return to prison is immense. That's the difference one personal visit can make! That's the power of a friend.

MY DEFINITION OF A TRUE FRIEND

Now there are friends, and there are true friends. Everybody wants to be your friend when you're on top and times are good. The real test of friendship comes during times of crisis. I've thought about this long and hard, and I've come to the conclusion that there is one key thing that determines real friendship: *A true friend is someone who shows an increase of love when you're at your lowest.* At your lowest, ugliest point, there will be very few people who are willing to increase their love for you. Especially when you are in a place where you are not meeting their needs.

Maybe you feel that plenty of people like you, but remember that popularity is fickle and fleeting. It is easy to forge bonds quickly but not deeply. For example, even when I get a standing ovation from thousands of people, afterward I can still find myself eating dinner in a restaurant by myself, depressed. The applause I receive is a counterfeit for true friendship. There is no true and lasting connection there. They loved my message, not me. It's a delusion. Have a big, life-upending crash, and you will see who your true friends are.

True friendship is unconditional. True friendship is absolute loyalty. Youth fades, looks fade, wealth and popularity fade, but true friendship never fades. True friends stand by you through the highest highs and the lowest lows. They are genuinely happy for your successes. They can be more therapeutic than any therapist (although I'm certainly not suggesting that a skilled therapist isn't extremely valuable and at times completely necessary). True friends speed up healing faster than anything in the world. True friends are those you can set your watch by. That's real friendship, even if it doesn't seem very exciting. I would rather have three true friends than a busload of people who are my friends only as long as I can do something for them. The more of this rich, unconditional love you have in your life, the more resilient you are.

A few years ago, I was crashing, hard. On the surface I had all these supports: my community, neighborhood, business partner and team, in-laws and extended family, friends, wife, kids. I reached out for help to everyone. But I found that not many people were willing to reach out to me. I quickly realized that my true friends, those who had the ability to show an increase of love when I was too low to have anything to offer them in return, were very few. But I found them. And they were my lifeline. They pulled me back from the edge when I needed them. They helped motivate me to stay resilient. In a strange way I'm grateful for this experience—it encouraged me to cultivate more friendships like these to boost my Relational Resilience, and it has made me try very hard to be this kind of friend to others.

ASK

Do you have more or fewer true friendships today than you did five years ago? What do you think has made the difference between now and then? In what ways can you become a better friend?

TASK

Make a list of ten individuals who once played an important part of your life but with whom you've not had contact for some time. For the next month and a half, reach out to at least one of them a week in some meaningful way.

TURN OUTWARD

RELATIONAL RESILIENCE BOOSTER #4

When you're disconnected from others, you'll likely turn inward. One of the best ways to feel connected with other human beings is to turn outward and serve in the moment. I'm not talking about going to Tibet on a service mission (although I think that's an awesome thing to do). I'm talking about "in the moment" service—little ways to look out for someone else on the spot. It's a small thing, really, but man it makes all the difference!

I know you're probably tired of hearing me whine about all the traveling I do, but here's a good example of how turning outward and seeking to serve others has made a huge difference for me. I had just gotten back from a trip and I was tired. The last thing I wanted to do was leave again, but the next day I had a business trip. I really didn't want to go, but I knew I had to. So I accepted that, and then I thought to myself, *I'm going to make the best of this.* And here's what I did. I decided to turn my focus from inward to outward, and to really see people. Sometimes when I travel I don't even see all the people who are serving me. I'm tired and ornery and I don't see the person behind the counter at the airport. I don't see the person driving the shuttle. I don't see the person who cleans my hotel room. But on that trip (and I've made a conscious effort to do it on every trip since) I tried to really *see* people.

This has made travel come alive for me. I feel lonely and isolated when I travel. This is going to be a reality for me with the career that I've chosen, a reality that has required some serious radical acceptance and overcoming denial. But if I can really see all the other lonely people out there, the difference is huge. When the shuttle doors open up, instead of going straight to the back of the bus, I sit up front and say to the driver, "Hey, how are you doing today?" We make some small talk. I thank him for picking me up at six thirty in the morning. And I can tell if he's bored or frustrated or a little depressed, and I maybe have the ability to make this guy's day just a little bit better. Then, instead of just tossing my bags on the platform, I make eye contact with the Delta agent and say, "Good to see you again! How's your day going?" I look forward to my interactions with the TSA folks the most—they're the best. Most people don't even want to look at them. But if I say, "How're you doing? Busy day for you, huh?" they look up, startled, and the cold-as-ice veneer starts to melt a bit. They're not used to it. But when I do this, it's like the energy of the day changes.

It makes a huge difference for me when someone sees me, too. They have these delicious green olives at an airport deli that I frequent. There's a lady who works there who, every time she sees me, puts a couple olives on my plate. She recognizes me and knows I like them. What that does for me is huge—that I walk up and this lady acknowledges me. The payoff isn't the olives, even though I like them. The payoff is the connection. The payoff is that she saw me and made me feel significant. It might be the highlight of my day. It's a powerful service she's doing for me.

Stanford psychologist Kelly McGonigal explained in a recent speech how the stress of everyday life can actually be healthy—especially if we're spending some of our time reaching out to others. According to McGonigal, the relaxation hormone oxytocin is released when we're under stress, and if we put ourselves in the right mindset, the hormone can help our heart regenerate. The cool thing, she says, is that these benefits increase with social contact and support, "so when you reach out to others under stress, either to seek support or to help someone else, you release more of this hormone, your stress response becomes healthier, and you actually recover faster from stress. I find this amazing, that your stress response has a built-in mechanism for stress resilience, and that mechanism is human connection."[15]

Any time you're in the presence of another human being, you have the opportunity to focus on them and serve them. And the payoff for you is huge. You feel much more human. You feel connected. Your body literally undergoes a healing process. It's so easy to let exhaustion, stress, or other emotions get in the way of reaching out. But if you can Flip the Switch and serve in the moment, I guarantee you'll feel better—and more resilient—right then.

> The roots of interpersonal conflict are often an excessive concern for oneself, and an inability to pay attention to the needs of others.
> —Mihaly Csikszentmihalyi

REMEMBER—IT'S NOT ALL ABOUT YOU

Selfishness is a powerful destroyer of relationships. In all my years of counseling people, if I could, as Dr. Gottman says, get two people to "turn toward" each other, it was a win. When counseling couples, if I could get both of them to grow toward each other, I could almost guarantee a happy marriage. There's no such thing as a stagnant relationship. You're either growing closer together or further apart. Selfishness equals growing apart. Dr. Csikszentmihalyi says it well: "The roots of interpersonal conflict are often an excessive concern for oneself, and an inability to pay attention to the needs of others. It is sad to see how often people ruin a relationship because they refuse to recognize that they could serve their own interests best by helping others achieve theirs."[16]

I have a friend who has been married a long time. He and his wife are empty nesters. Most evenings after work, my friend can easily spend all his time surfing the Internet, unwinding with a book, or simply letting the time get away from him. His wife also enjoys reading in the evening and has a couple of television shows she likes to watch. They could spend most nights in separate rooms, doing what they both prefer to do, but they realize this is not good for their relationship. His wife often makes an effort to find small ways to spend time together. She'll call down to him on the intercom that a show is on and invite him to watch with her. It might even be a show he has no interest in. But he is interested in her and appreciates that she wants to watch it with him. They have found that doing things together, even if it is just sitting next to each other watching a show, makes a difference. They choose unselfishness with small but meaningful ways to connect with each other.

Another good friend has a professor who spent one summer taking his son to see a baseball game in every major-league park in the country. Somebody once said to him, "I didn't know you liked baseball that much." His response? "I don't. I like my son that much." The time spent with his son traveling to all those ballparks was a priceless investment in his relationship with his son, and an unselfish way to show his love for him.

ASK

When was the last time you went out of your way to acknowledge the people in your path who help your day go smoothly? This includes janitors, bus drivers, security workers, store clerks, postal workers, and any other service-work position. How do you feel when you make this small effort?

TASK

Cheerfully acknowledge everyone you encounter in a service position today by expressing gratitude or paying sincere compliments. While you're at it, find simple ways to serve others around you "in the moment." Make small talk while standing in line. Hold the door for someone else. Try to really *see* the people around you.

PUT DOWN THAT DEVICE!
RELATIONAL RESILIENCE BOOSTER #5

You'd have to be living under a seriously large rock to not be aware of the electronic revolution surrounding us. There is no escape! We are plugged in every minute of every day, everywhere we go. Although these technologies mean that our loved ones, colleagues, friends, and bosses can easily reach us, I also believe they distract us from cultivating meaningful relationships and diminish our Relational Resilience.

In late 2011, essayist and novelist Pico Iyer wrote a column for the *New York Times* that resonated with the world. In it, he talks about the Internet rescue camps in South Korea and China designed to save kids who are addicted to the screen, and about expensive "black-hole resorts," where guests pay high prices for rooms without TVs or Internet. "The more ways we have to connect," Iyer says, "the more many of us seem desperate to unplug."[17]

I'll admit it—I'm just as addicted as the next person, and I couldn't run my business without these devices. But there are many startling facts about our technological addictions. The average office worker can spend, at the most, three minutes at a time at his or her desk without an interruption. The average American spends at a minimum eight and a half hours a day in front of a screen, and sometimes more than one screen at a time, as we are often on our computers while we watch television. Most web pages are visited for ten seconds or less. And here's a frightening thought: A journal about cardio-pulmonary bypass surgery found that 55 percent of technicians who monitor bypass machines admitted that they had talked on cell phones during heart surgery—personal calls involving vacations and family plans. Half confessed to texting while in surgery.[18] It's such a problem that it actually has a name—"distracted doctoring." Yikes. Iyer says, "The information revolution came without an instruction manual," and I believe our resilience suffers for it.

Our brain development suffers for it as well. According to scientists, children's developing minds are not only adversely affected by bad stimulation but also by a lack of good stimulation. Studies that have followed children for nearly four decades show that those who are raised with a lack of emotional attunement—who aren't "in tune" with someone else emotionally—experience brain-development differences that deeply affect a child's ability to regulate stress. These physiological changes increase that child's risk for addictive behaviors as the child tries to self-soothe through extra TV watching and overeating. These children have actual differences in brain anatomy that make it difficult for them to thrive at school or be successful in the workplace. Being raised by a parent who is emotionally distracted—stressed out, depressed, constantly working, or always focused on an electronic device—produces what has been called "proximate separation."[19] This means that even when the parent is present and the child knows he is loved, if attunement isn't a regular parenting practice, the stress level for the child is heightened and long-term side effects follow.

As a parent, this information scares me! But it matters even if you don't have kids. Other studies suggest that lack of attunement due to constant electronic connection is taking a measurable toll on our biological capacity to connect with people. Just as the muscles in our body follow the "use it or lose it" law, the more we spend time disconnected socially, the more our ability to positively connect with others atrophies.

I'll be honest: I've frequently caught myself not being attuned while in a conversation with another person, and I know this hurts the relationship, whether they call me on it or not. I've also been on the receiving end, with the other person's device commanding far more of their attention than they're giving me. That never feels good. Obviously, being 100 percent attuned to another's emotional state all the time isn't possible or even desirable. But if I'm in any kind of meaningful dialogue, I expect myself and the other person to give each other appropriate mental attention, which just can't happen when the device is the center of either of our focus.

Recently when I was with my nine-year-old son at a basketball game, I had an important call. He said, "No phone, Dad. This is *my* time." And he was right. I needed to focus on my son. I turned my phone to silent and decided to worry about important calls later. I've also realized that leaving my phone at home when I go on a date with my wife makes a significant difference in the quality of the date. This actually started by accident, when I left my phone at home one evening. Feeling anxious without it, I started to head back home when my wife convinced me I'd survive phoneless for a few hours. We had such a nice evening without the usual distractions that I committed to always leaving it behind on date night. I find I'm much more attuned to my wife when she isn't competing with my phone for my attention! And of course, when our relationship is strong, we're both more motivated to be resilient.

TAPPING INTO THE POWER OF MINDFULNESS

While most MBA students start class by opening their laptops, those in the Executive Mind class at the Drucker School of Management at Claremont Graduate University begin every class by putting away their smartphones and computers, closing their eyes, and focusing on the meditation session directed by their professor. In a *Los Angeles Times* article on the subject, journalist Robin Rauzi explains, "This might seem like an awfully touchy-feely way to train future corporate executives. But all manner of research supports the idea. . . . Companies including Google Inc. and General Mills Inc. are embracing mindfulness training with the aim of making their workforces less reactive, more resilient—even more creative."[20]

These companies really understand the value of being more present and less distracted, even by the very technology that is essential to running a successful business. Google has offered mindfulness training to its employees for over four years, with a waiting list of over five hundred, and its campus has multiple meditation spots for employee use. If you are feeling frustrated by the nonstop distractions at work (remember how the average office worker gets to spend a whole three minutes, at most, without an interruption?), perhaps a little mindfulness could help.

WHAT'S YOUR ELECTRONIC-DEVICE DISORDER (EDD) SCORE?

I've put together a short self-assessment to help determine whether your own use of electronic devices (or, as I like to call them, EDs) is having a negative impact on your emotional intimacy—in other words, whether you have electronic-device disorder (EDD). To get a better sense of how important your EDs are to you, give yourself one point for each statement that describes you and then read the recommendations for your score. (Remember: The assessment is only valuable as long as you are willing to be honest and do your best to avoid self-deception. You might want to consider asking someone who knows you well to answer on your behalf to give you a more complete and accurate perspective.) If you find that even just one or two of these questions describes your use of EDs, you may need to make a conscious effort to connect more with actual people and limit the amount of time you spend electronically connected. I know this is easier said than done, but it is absolutely vital to a healthy relationship.

❏ When spending time with other people, I can't help occasionally pulling out my ED and checking it for updates.

❏ The information I obtain on my ED is more relevant to me than the information I am receiving from people in front of me.

❏ I can't sit through an entire movie, game, or other event without checking my ED.

❏ The first thing I do in the morning or the last thing I do at night is look at my ED.

❏ When driving, I have a strong desire to reach for my ED.

❏ I can't attend a family event without using my ED.

❏ I can closely predict the remaining battery life on my portable ED.

❏ The frequency with which I check email is much greater than the actual number of emails received.

❏ When I don't access social media, I feel disconnected or frustrated.

❏ I communicate with more people through my ED than I do in person.

❏ People close to me have complained about the amount of time I spend on my ED.

❏ I feel anxious if I leave my ED at home or am ever away from it.

❏ I always know where my ED is.

❏ I feel a surge of excitement when I receive notifications on my ED.

How to Interpret Your Score

You should have one point for each of the statements in the list that describes you.

1–2 points: You've got it under control. You are in the safe zone. If you can maintain the balance you currently have between the real world and technology, you'll never be at risk of electronic-device disorder.

3–4 points: You have symptoms. You like your ED, but you're not nearly as hooked as the majority of the population, and use your ED primarily for communication and a little bit for entertainment. Be careful not to get hooked on too many ED features that can slowly detach you from the people around you.

5–6 points: You're mildly disordered. In my observation, most people fit in this category. You *love* your ED, and without realizing it, you may be disengaging from others. Your family and close friends are probably the most aware of your EDD when they're trying to make conversation or get your attention. Try putting your ED in another room for a few hours a day and really focusing in on your loved ones, other significant relationships, or a worthwhile hobby.

7–8 points: Electronic-device disorder has fully kicked in. If you scored this high, you're in the danger zone! Pick one night a week to turn off your ED and focus instead on your family, friends, or a worthwhile interest. Gradually increase the number of nights a week you do this until your EDD score is between 1 and 3.

9 or more: EDD rehab is in your future. This is a severe case! Your life would literally cease to function if you were deprived of your ED, and that means you're shutting yourself out of the relationships and endeavors that matter most. Turn off your phone when you are driving, in a meeting, or eating a meal with someone you care about. Once you're able to do this without experiencing anxiety, start turning it off one night a week, gradually increasing the number of nights a week you do this until your EDD score is between 1 and 3.

Note: You may be tempted to give this assessment to someone you think needs it. Be careful, as this could make someone defensive without more context.

WHAT MESSAGE ARE YOU SENDING?

If you are a parent and this is something you struggle with, you might want to give your kids permission to ask you, "Mom/Dad, is what you're doing on your phone right now more important than paying attention to me?" when they feel ignored or frustrated by your EDD. It's also good to be aware that our kids themselves are growing up addicted to and overstimulated by these devices. We may one day feel rejected as our kids choose electronic devices over us, and at the same time we may be contributing to their addiction if we don't give them guidelines and rules about their usage. Remember that song from the '70s, "Cat's in the Cradle"? It was a popular song about a dad who didn't have time for his son, and then the son grows up and doesn't have time for his old and lonely dad. That may be us one day, recognizing the sad irony as the next generation grows up to be just like us—too plugged in to connect.

I saw a Christmas card this year that pictured a family where every family member had their head down, texting or using their cell phones. It was funny, but it's also sad—because it happens all the time! As Thoreau pointed out many years ago, we have more and more ways to communicate, but less and less to say. In his popular article, Iyer refers to a series of tests that have shown that subjects who spend time in quiet rural settings "exhibit greater attentiveness, stronger memory, and generally improved cognition. Their brains become both calmer and sharper. More than that, empathy, as well as deep thought, depends on neural processes that are 'inherently slow.'" That last part—that really important part about one's ability to develop empathy—has been validated by neuroscientists. I'm not planning on moving to a farm, but I definitely intend to make an effort to disconnect from my EDs more often and focus more on the person actually in front of me.

I feel especially strong about this resilience booster because of my own struggles in this area. When I got my first smartphone, I found that social media was dominating me. I'm highly social to begin with, and I had a grand time entertaining everyone with funny stories or sending out an inspirational thought and getting thousands of validating responses. It was like heroin to me. I began to realize it was a severe problem. I was interacting with my phone more than actual people, and it was affecting my relationships. For my business, the instant access to information was great. But for someone like me with ADHD, a smartphone is like a slot machine. So for a time I had to cut off all ties with social media. I was 100 percent abstinent. I had to get it under control.

Of course, if used with balance and self-control these devices can strengthen our relationships. An experience that really drove this point home to me happened—you guessed it—on a plane. I was sitting next to a Catholic priest, and we'd had a nice discussion during the flight. As the plane landed, I immediately started making a phone call. This wise priest said to me, "You know, the first person you call when an airplane lands reflects your deepest priorities." His words stabbed me in the heart. I had dialed my business partner. I immediately hung up and called my wife. Now, I can't say that I have always followed his advice, but ever since that experience, I think about it each time my plane lands, and I try to always call my wife first.

ASK

Have you ever felt disrespected due to another's use of electronic devices? Do you feel others could feel the same way about your own use of electronic devices?

TASK

Set aside time this week to spend at least one hour in solitude—completely free of interruptions and devices. Go for a walk, spend time in nature, or find a quiet place to read a book. If at all possible, plan another day that you will spend completely electronic-device free, focusing instead on nurturing the important relationships in your life. If you observe others who are spending too much time in front of a screen, invite them to join you.

DROP THE FACADE

RELATIONAL RESILIENCE BOOSTER #6

As a public speaker, I always try to cultivate a good relationship with my audience. Sometimes, however, there are blunders—major blunders. Years ago, I was addressing a group of mental-health professionals, and during a break I went to the restroom. I am proud to say that I am a multitasker who always uses his time as productively as possible, so while there I also called my wife. She asked me how my presentation was going. I vented to her, "This audience is dead! They seriously have no energy in there today!" She offered me some words of encouragement, and I told her how much I loved her and missed her and couldn't wait to get off the road to see her. When I came out of the bathroom, a friend of mine was there yelling at me, "Christian! Turn off your microphone! Everyone can hear everything you're saying in there!"

I was mortified. Not only did the whole audience get a soundtrack of my bathroom experience, they heard me disrespecting them! Not to mention my personal exchanges with my wife! It was seriously the most embarrassing moment of my life. I had to go back on stage and finish speaking, which was incredibly nerve-wracking. But it all worked out. Luckily, the audience was highly forgiving. They had a great laugh at my expense, and, actually, the energy was better for that half of the conference.

Now whenever I am speaking and have mic problems, I share this story. And every time I start by admitting to one of my worst moments of idiocy, I'm instantly bonded with the audience. They love the vulnerability I share when I tell this experience. Suddenly they can relate to me as they think of their own embarrassing moments, and we're all equals in the human condition.

In the introduction, we learned that vulnerability is the birthplace of resilience. Vulnerability means you admit your weaknesses and your need for help. You aren't afraid to look foolish. You're proud to say, "I need you and you need me!" As you reveal your fears, mistakes, and weaknesses, people will feel closer to you. Intimacy is increased, along with our motivation to be resilient.

It's taken me over forty years to learn that real expression of real emotions takes real courage and real strength. Denying emotions is easy and much more cowardly. But a word of warning: This requires balance. You don't want to emotionally "throw up" on people. If I entered a room full of people who didn't know me and introduced myself with, "Hi! I'm Christian, and I suffer from anxiety," it would drive people away. I'd scare away any chance for regular social interaction with them. But authentic expression of your vulnerabilities has the potential to increase intimacy. This applies to both people in the relationship. If either person decides not to be vulnerable, that relationship will most likely not last.

Remember frontin'? It kills vulnerability. As the owner of a company, sometimes I'll front—acting like everything is great when I'm really stressed out. Once I was talking to a friend of mine who owns a company that we often partner with. Things had been really tight for my company economically and we'd taken a couple of recent hits. I was worried. But his company was doing great, and my ego didn't want to admit our struggles to him. I told him everything was fine. He called me back two days later, asking, "Christian, what's really going on?" and explained that he'd picked up on the anxiety in my voice during our previous discussion. I dropped the act and opened up to him about the rough start we'd had that year. Because I was honest with him, he was able to help me problem-solve. We were able to partner with him, and he opened up some doors for my company that were really beneficial. Showing vulnerability in business is hard, but had I not told him the truth, my company would have missed out on some great opportunities.

I have used this strategy of acting like everything is fine as a defense mechanism to keep people at a distance from me. There are times when I don't let people get close or help me because of my pride. This kills opportunities to create real connection or help people grow closer to me. When life is at its most difficult is when relationships show what they're made of, and they will usually either become stronger or they break. Being honest about your real challenges can create lasting connections. Plus, I want people around me who still love me when I am at my lowest, or when I just experienced my biggest failures. It's when things aren't perfect that you find out who you are really emotionally connected with.

ASK

Is there anyone you are around on a somewhat regular basis with whom you feel a sense of discomfort or unease and with whom you rarely, if ever, share your vulnerable self?

TASK

Take a risk and share something you normally wouldn't say that's appropriate to the situation and the relationship, and that puts you outside your comfort zone. Share something about yourself that shows the other person more of "the real you" and less of your superficial exterior. Do you feel this interaction improved your relationship? If so, try to find appropriate ways to "drop the facade" in other relationships as well.

CONNECT WITH SOMETHING BIGGER THAN YOU

RELATIONAL RESILIENCE BOOSTER #7

Don't worry: Everyone—from self-proclaimed atheists to Christmas-and-Easter churchgoers to the devoutly religious—can benefit from this next booster. Regardless of your spiritual or religious practices, connecting with a higher power is a vital facet of Relational Resilience. In the early twentieth century, lecturer and writer William James used the term *higher power* in a broader way, describing it as that which takes a person outside or beyond themselves and connects them to others, an idea that was later used as a founding principle of Alcoholics Anonymous. Your relationship with a higher power is one you develop, either within you or outside of you, that lifts you up, gives you motivation to thrive, and provides refuge during difficult times. This higher power can be almost anything, as long as it is meaningful and powerful to you. It could be nature, love, God, internal drive, the universe, moral principles, Buddha, self-respect, a dead ancestor, patriotism, hope, a sense of dignity, service—whatever you believe in and that moves you. It's your relationship with something bigger than you, whatever that is. This is one of your very most important relationships.

If such a connection does not exist in your life, then I urge you to at least be open to the possibility of connecting with something bigger than you. For some people, belief in a higher power comes naturally and easily. It's not even a question. For others, it doesn't resonate at all. However, almost everyone would agree there is something bigger than themselves. If you don't believe in anything else, believe in these four things:

- Connection
- Options
- Hope
- Resilience

I have found that if you can believe in connection, options, hope, and resilience, it will help lead you to something bigger than you. These beliefs will guide you to enough love and connections that you will want to go on, even when life is dark and difficult. When you truly believe in something bigger than you, options present themselves that you never saw coming. You feel hope for something better, or even just the hope for eventual relief from current pain.

A UNIQUE AND PERSONAL RELATIONSHIP

Your relationship with your higher power is completely unique to you. It can be formal, or it can be very relaxed. My relationship with my higher power is ever present. It's a very personal relationship for me, and my higher power plays various roles in my life. One minute he is like my brother. The next minute I'm in a comedy routine, and I verbally spar with him. Next I'm pleading with him for help. I simply talk with my higher power. I do it all the time. It's a support system for me. I've been doing it my whole life. I even remember doing it while walking to elementary school. Sometimes I'm almost in a meditative state when I do it. Sometimes I'm multitasking. I communicate with my higher power about all the small things. As soon as my eyes are open in the morning, I'm in conversation. I know I'm manic about it, and I'm somewhat self-conscious about it because people assume you're crazy. I walk about mumbling in conversation, and people ask me all the time, "Who are you talking to?" They must think I am mentally ill. But I believe completely in the connection, and it is a true source of resilience for me.

My connection and belief in my higher power is on a continuum. There are times it is stronger than others. Sometimes my faith falters. Sometimes I question. I can intellectualize too much and have moments of internal battle. I'm a flawed person who is trying to figure out what role believing in something bigger than me has in my daily living. Sometimes I feel like I'm walking every step with my higher power. Some days I feel like we're not even in the same universe. I just never close the door completely.

A relationship with a higher power transcends the limitations and weaknesses of the human condition—anxiety, fear, pain, addiction. Connection with a higher power helps put mistakes, disappointments, and failures in perspective. A belief in a higher power helps us better understand who we are and who we want to become. Believing in a higher power, whatever that may be for you, allows you to feel more unconditional love toward others. However you are connected to your personal higher power will make you more resilient. As long as whatever you believe in doesn't make you hurt yourself or others, go for it. Knowing I always have a relationship with something bigger than me leaves the door open for a comeback, no matter how much I've messed up. Healing can happen and relationships can be renewed. Life requires multiple comebacks. That's what resilience is.

ASK

Who or what would you identify as your "higher power," your "something bigger"? Is there anything you can be doing to strengthen this connection in your life? Is there a limitation or weakness you are currently facing that your higher power can help you confront more easily?

TASK

Connect with your higher power by doing one or both of the following:

- Start your day reading something that motivates you and inspires you.
- Write down all of your life's most amazing experiences. What was the best day of your life and why? Ask yourself, *How can I have more days like this?*

RELATIONAL RESILIENCE FUEL

Part of accessing each of the four sources is accessing the energy that comes from the specific *emotions* and *mindsets* that fall under that source. That's why, at the end of each part, I've put together a list of several emotions and mindsets that relate to that source. Chances are you're experiencing at least a few of them, whether positive or negative, and I'd like you to circle all the ones that apply to you. The more emotions and mindsets you circle, the greater your capacity to access that source. Just harness the energy from those emotions into resilience.

- Love
- Ostracism
- Needed
- In conflict
- Caring
- Neglected
- Responsible
- Invisible
- Fulfilled
- Let down

- Secure
- Vulnerable
- Emotionally intimate
- Lonely
- Accepting
- Cared for
- Rejected
- Significant
- Heartbroken

- Included
- Hate
- Inspired
- Respected
- Excluded
- Supported
- Love lost
- Valued
- Connected

PART III

STREET RESILIENCE

Drawing strength from mistakes, disrespect, and discrimination

WHAT IS STREET RESILIENCE?

There are two simple words that most people with learning differences hate to hear: *Just think*.

The first time I remember hearing those two dreaded words was in the first grade, while learning addition. Even now, decades later, I vividly remember the teacher leaning over my shoulder, saying, "Just *think*! Two plus two equals what? It's right in front of you. If one plus one equals two, then what would two plus two equal?"

Then she said those words again. "Just think! If two plus one equals three, then what would two plus two equal? Think about it!"

As I sat there looking at the paper, I thought to myself, *What in the heck do two twos have to do with a four, and when is this teacher going to walk away from my desk, and when is she going to stop tapping her long red fingernails on the number four? I'm starting to wonder if the answer is in her fingernails, because "just thinking" is not helping me get the answer. Maybe when she walks away everyone will stop smiling at me and looking at me like I am an alien because I don't see how a two and another two magically create a four.*

Later, I found myself in a special spelling class; I'd been informed I was special because I was the only kid in the third grade who couldn't spell his name. Instead of the teacher standing over my shoulder for a few minutes with thirty other kids in the class, it was just me and another teacher in the room, and she would stand over my shoulder for a whole hour. In our first session, the two dreaded words jumped up and bit me: "Just think! Sound it out. Write a *C* ten times, then an *H* ten times, then an *R* ten times, then an *I* ten times. . . . Just think! You can do it."

What do ten Cs have to do with my name? I asked myself. *And what in the world does the C sound \"kä"\ have to do with my name being Christian?*

In third grade, I was placed with other kids like me for the first time. There were about five of us who were constantly told to "just think," and we sat at a table in the back of the room. All the other kids in the class—the ones who could think, apparently—had individual desks, and I also noticed that we had dumbbell math and reading books, different from everyone else's.

My next recollection of the magic words was in the seventh grade. One of my biggest fears at that time was the simple question, "What time is it?" The teacher would tell me to "just think" as she tried to explain to me that a quarter to five means fifteen minutes to five, when to me and my nonthinking self, a quarter equaled twenty-five. All I could do was come up with excuses to get out of the pressure of telling time: "What time do *you* think it is?" or "It's time for *you* to get a watch," or "You can see the clock just as good as I can."

When you are in your teenage years and you are struggling with telling time, you soon start to have a lot of self-doubt about your future and how you will be successful and make a living, when doing something as simple as running a cash register at McDonald's seems impossible and terrifying. Chances are the McDonald's manager won't tell you to "just think," but will tell you to come back when you have some basic math skills.

The feelings of fear and frustration in school make school as fun as going to the dentist every day—only there is nothing to numb the pain except acting out enough to divert the attention away from the real issue. The real issue is the inability to process information in a way that will bring you positive feedback, respect, and a passing grade.

This is the best way I can explain the feeling in my gut during eight hours of classes every day. Imagine that you're with a group of people and someone tells a joke. Everyone is laughing, except you. You don't get it. The person who told the joke realizes you don't get it, and says to you, "Just think!" They tell the joke again, slower this time, and say, "Don't you get it!?"

It was this sense of inferiority that planted the first seeds of Street Resilience in me. That experience of feeling left out is with me often, even now, but today I use it as fuel for **Street Resilience**—for taking the pain of disrespect, discrimination, and regret and using it as fuel to propel me forward.

I call it "Street" Resilience because life on the streets is raw. On the streets, people will put you down and disrespect you and take advantage of you. On the streets, you're alone. You lack resources and support, and you have to fight for your basic needs. You have to use your mistakes as a reason to rise above. Of course, you don't have to literally be on the streets to have Street Resilience. As we'll see shortly, even people whom others might see as privileged can draw on the disrespect and discrimination and regret they experience. Anyone can learn to be a fighter, a survivor, to do what it takes to make it.

I also want to be clear that Street Resilience isn't the same as street smarts—being aware of the world around you, having common sense, or excelling at smooth talk. Being street smart can work to your advantage, but it doesn't necessarily mean you're Street Resilient. Street Resilience is much more. Someone with Street Resilience is a fighter. They know it's up to them to channel their pain and use it as positive energy.

Street Resilience is channeling your emotions—guiding them, directing them, and using them for a productive purpose, instead of letting your emotions use you. Let's look at some short examples of this in action:

- Sara is a forty-two-year-old advertising executive who has excelled during her fifteen-year career. She has consistently received the highest performance reviews, but each time she has applied for a senior management position, she's been turned down. Things became very difficult for her at work when she announced that she was expecting a baby, and projects she would usually manage were given to a male coworker with less seniority and expertise than she had. After returning from maternity leave, Sara found herself out of the loop and ostracized. She has decided to use these rejections as the fuel to take a risk and start her own advertising agency.

- Tim is a heavyset man who hates to fly because the seats are too small and uncomfortable for someone his size. A death in his family necessitates him flying cross-country, a trip he dreads taking. After boarding the plane, he finds that the seat belt doesn't fit and asks for an extension. When he makes this request of the flight attendant, she rolls her eyes and looks annoyed. Tim quickly decides that despite the rudeness he's experienced, he is going to Flip the Switch: He uses the disrespect as fuel to be extra kind to the attendant during the flight, and to treat those around him with the same increased kindness, refusing to allow himself to treat others as he's been treated.

- Bill is a recovering meth addict who has been sober for six months. After hanging out for years with a really rough crowd and spending a lot of time on the street, he found out he had a two-year-old daughter. He has been trying to get his act together in order to be a better father to her than his own alcoholic father was to him. After leaving rehab he tries to find a job, but given his sketchy history, no one wants to hire him. Almost desperate, he uses the pain of all the rejections, and his regret at the choices he made earlier in his life, as a reason to volunteer at the local food bank. After seeing his hard work, the manager offers him an entry-level job as a driver.

Each of these examples demonstrates the power of Street Resilience. Each person experienced some form of disrespect or regret, but instead of shutting down, they chose to channel their challenges.

My own history is rampant with examples of Street Resilience as a source of fuel. I am definitely a survivor. I will do almost anything to make it, which is probably why this source strikes such a chord with me. After all those years I spent struggling in school I had a decision to make—I could use those feelings to tell myself, *I'm done. I'm stupid. I'm a loser.* Or I could use those feelings as a catalyst to try to prove them all wrong, to do things that would enable me to progress. I may be lacking in some of the other sources, but I have unlimited Street Resilience because of my challenges early on in life, and especially because of the disrespect I experienced from my learning disabilities. It's my personal X factor. The pain you hear when I talk about my own experiences is the fuel I've used to impact kids around the world.

Street Resilience is really all about channeling your rage. The rage that could have put me on death row if I used it to hurt someone is the same energy that I use to do good works. If you use your anger to do bad works, they lock you up. If you use it to do better, you get a standing ovation, or more important, self-respect.

> **Street Resilience is channeling your emotions—guiding them, directing them, and using them for a productive purpose, instead of letting your emotions use you.**

We're all born with resilience inside of us, though life has a way of crushing it out. When we're in the midst of disrespect, discrimination, or mistakes, we tend to forget it's there. But you've got to use adversity, or adversity will use you. Street Resilience will help you use disrespect and discrimination and regret for good, no matter the circumstances.

WE'RE ALL "THOSE PEOPLE"

You might be thinking to yourself, *But I've never really experienced intense disrespect or discrimination. I haven't made any massive mistakes. That only happens to "those people," not to me*. But you must remember that life does not stay the same. It's always evolving, and it's likely that some form of disrespect, discrimination, or regret is on its way. One day, chances are you will be one of "those people."

Just ask anyone over sixty-five if they've ever felt discriminated against. Ask if they've noticed that younger people seem to get more attention in a store or restaurant from younger workers. Ask someone who's overweight if they've ever felt disrespect or discrimination. Ask someone who has lost a job or can't get a job if they've ever felt disrespected or discriminated against. We all will be one of those people, because of age, unemployment, economic challenges, disability, health problems, depression, anxiety, or fear. The ups and downs of life are sure to happen—all you have to do is let time pass—and one day you will need Street Resilience, whether you're a PhD or a prisoner.

Consider the story of Michael Gates Gill, an executive at one of the top ad agencies in the country. He had no criminal record and enjoyed a generous $160,000 annual compensation package. He'd dedicated his life to working there for over twenty-five years when he was blindsided by a layoff. A much younger woman whom he had personally hired and mentored for years broke the news to him. Suddenly, Michael's life was falling apart. The economy had crashed, and his chances of finding a $160,000 job were slim. The discrimination he faced as an older person in the job market was different than that faced by a felon, but it was there—and very real to him.

After months of searching, Michael was offered a job as a janitor and gopher at Starbucks. His lifestyle changed drastically; he'd gone from power suits and personal drivers to an apron and a toilet brush.[21] This humility and willingness to adapt to current realities is a great example of Street Resilience, and in the end, it ended up being the best job Michael had ever had. It opened great doors for him, including a bestselling book and national speaking opportunities. I get that this is highly unusual, but options you can't foresee open up when you show up, even when what you have is less than ideal. Street Resilience enabled Michael to apply for and excel at a job most would have considered beneath him, in just the same way that Street Resilience can help a reformed criminal do what's necessary to get back on his feet.

DON'T LET DISCRIMINATION TURN YOU INTO A JERK (LIKE I DID!)

Though Street Resilience is one of my strongest sources, I have *plenty* of moments where I mess up, where I forget all about Street Resilience and channeling my anger for good. As an example, let me share one of my not-so-fine moments.

Years ago I took a red-eye flight from Seattle to New York, where I was the keynote speaker at a very large administrator's conference. I had spoken in two or three cities already, had been living out of a suitcase, and I had probably only had about eight hours of sleep in four days. When we arrived in the airport, I was a mess. I was wearing a T-shirt and jeans (my travel clothes that had already been worn on this trip), my hair was a mop, I was unshaven, and I probably had bad breath. It wasn't pretty. There was a very professional-looking lady—perfect hair, manicured nails, high-end jewelry, dressed in a business suit—holding a sign that said "Christian Moore" in front of baggage claim, waiting to welcome me and get me to my accommodations for my stay. The driver of her Lincoln Town Car limo was with her. I approached her and said, "I'm Christian Moore."

She looked at me. "You mean you work for Mr. Moore?"

"No, I promise you, I'm Christian Moore. I'm sorry; I've been on an all-night flight."

She was still very unconvinced. "You *do* know you're speaking to three hundred school administrators tomorrow morning?" I kept trying to assure her that I really was Christian Moore. I could tell she was very concerned about the way I looked. In her defense, she was sticking her neck out, bringing me in as the keynote address to this event, and I looked like a homeless person. She was experiencing high anxiety, judging me on my appearance. Once she was finally convinced I really was who I claimed to be, we got in the limo.

Now, I'm not proud of what happened next. I'm really not. On that limo ride, I just couldn't resist. I threw Street Resilience right out the window. I was exhausted and feeling incredibly disrespected, so I started talking to her like I was an uneducated, inner-city thug, just like I used to as a kid on the street. I was definitely disrespectful to her, and I knew I was pushing her buttons. In the moment, I was thinking, *If you're going to treat me like this, then I'm going to act like this.* I totally regressed into that world and was the perfect example of what Street Resilience is *not.* I pestered her in a silly, uneducated tone, asking question after question about the hotel and where I could get food. "This homeboy needs some grub!" I exclaimed at one point. It was a twenty-five-minute ride, and it must have been pure misery for her. To say she was nervous is a huge understatement, and the more I talked, the more nervous she got. I was setting her up. I knew that when I got to the hotel, I was going to shave and shower, put on a nice suit that I'd ironed, slick my hair back, and give my speech. The next day I'd be the total opposite of what she saw in the car. But I'd bet she had a hard time sleeping that night; she was probably pretty worried about how I'd do the next day in front of her three hundred administrators.

Luckily, before it was too late I remembered my resilience skills. Because of the disrespect I felt, I decided to give the best speech of my life. I accessed Street Resilience and used the discrimination I had felt as fuel. I also drew on Relational Resilience—I knew I cared about the students in that area too much to blow an opportunity to help them. Because of that, I put my whole heart into that speech and received a fantastic response from the audience.

The conference host watched their reaction and approached me. Now, of course she knew at this point that she'd been played. Although I am sure she was relieved that the speech went well, there had to be a part of her that was hurt. But she said to me, "Christian, I am so sorry how I treated you. I can see why you were upset." I apologized to her for my immaturity. I had focused on the person and not on her behavior. I also realized that although I had eventually utilized resilience, my lack of it in the limo with her could have been incredibly costly. She could have fired me on the spot. Or, no matter how good the speech, she could've remained angry about my behavior and broken all ties with my company. I had put the chance to help thousands of students on the line because I focused my anger on her. Initially, instead of using the discrimination I felt as fuel, I discriminated back, which only made the problem worse. I should have used Street Resilience from the beginning, focusing on her behavior as motivation to give a powerful speech without demeaning her and risking future opportunities to help kids in that area. To this day, I'm grateful that she allowed me to recover from my mistake.

STREET RESILIENCE WORKS FOR ORGANIZATIONS, TOO

Part of Street Resilience is thriving on mistakes. Harnessing the regret and disrespect that often accompanies your errors can be incredibly effective—and that's as true in our personal lives as it is in business.

Given the percentage of time we typically spend working and the kinds of stresses we are often exposed to on the job, it is inevitable that we will make plenty such mistakes. A lot depends on whether we use them as a fuel source or let them take us down.

Failure, mistakes, and dysfunction exist at some level in every organization (if you know of a perfect workplace, let me know—I'll send in my resume!), and anytime we're truly trying to accomplish something it involves taking risks. But when we botch something at work, we're often really hard on ourselves. We think, *Man, I really messed up, and now I'm going to beat myself up for it.* Choosing to take that frustration and instead resolving to do something good with it is evidence of our resilience.

Most people in business would argue that innovation is key to success. But innovation can only exist through creative thinking and the freedom to explore new ideas, which can only happen in a workplace where you can respectfully voice your opinion (even when it's different from the boss's), submit ideas, and even—gasp!—make mistakes. As Gandhi said, "Freedom is not worth having if it does not include the freedom to make mistakes."

Our society has programmed us to be frightened of doing anything wrong. We learn this early on in a school system that sometimes tends to educate the creativity out of us. Ken Robinson, an international adviser in education and a creativity expert, says, "If you're not prepared to be wrong, you'll never come up with anything original. And we run our companies like this, by the way. We stigmatize mistakes . . . and the result is that we are educating people out of their creative capacities."[22]

The Failure Wall

Jeff Stibel has founded numerous highly successful technology and marketing companies and is currently chairman and CEO of Dun & Bradstreet. He describes one way to create a safe environment and encourage creative thinking that I think is brilliant. One night he and his assistant designated a large white wall in the company break room as the "failure wall." After stenciling on a dozen quotes about the importance of failure, they attached a dozen markers and some simple instructions: (1) Describe a time you failed, (2) state what you learned, and (3) sign your name. "The failure wall," Stibel explains, "was part of our efforts to create a company culture where employees can take risks without fear of reprisal."

He kicked things off by writing down some of his own most humbling mistakes and then watched as the wall became filled with failures. "Success by failure is not an oxymoron," he says. "When you make a mistake, you're forced to look back and find out exactly where you went wrong, and formulate a new plan for your next attempt. By contrast, when you succeed, you don't always know exactly what you did right that made you successful. (Often, it's luck.)"[23]

Forgive and Remember

Another way to create a safe work environment is to adopt a philosophy of "forgive and remember." Bob Sutton, a well-known business professor and writer at Stanford University, has said that the five books he has written specifically for managers can essentially be summed up in one sentence, and it backs up the idea behind Stibel's failure wall: "Failure is inevitable, so the key to success is to be good at learning from it."[24]

The old adage "forgive and forget" doesn't really work. Instead, it is important that we "forgive and remember," meaning that a willingness to forgive is essential, but forgetting means we repeat the same mistakes over and over. According to Sutton, "You forgive because it is impossible to run an organization without making mistakes, and pointing fingers and holding grudges creates a climate of fear. You remember—and talk about the mistakes openly—so people and the system can learn."[25]

Failure Is an Option

IDEO, an international design firm in the heart of Silicon Valley, has developed hundreds of products we take for granted—everything from the first Apple computer mouse to Nike sunglasses. It's been called the most influential product-development firm in the world. Sutton writes about the amazingly creative toy-development group at IDEO who, in a typical year, come up with about four thousand ideas of new toys to invent. Sutton references Dennis Boyle, an IDEO partner and key client manager, and explains in his book *Weird Ideas That Work*:

> Of these 4,000 ideas, 230 were thought to be promising enough to develop into a nice drawing or working prototype. Of these 230, 12 were ultimately sold. This "yield" rate is only about one-third of 1 percent of total ideas and 5 percent of ideas that were thought to have potential.... As Boyle says, "You can't get any good new ideas without having a lot of dumb, lousy, and crazy ones."[26]

> You can't get any good new ideas without having a lot of dumb, lousy, and crazy ones. —Dennis Boyle

IDEO has come up with a great formula for creating a safe work environment—a place where each employee feels safe enough to fail enough to eventually be brilliant. And it's paid off—rated as one of the most innovative companies in the world, this is a resilient corporation. So, instead of saying, "Failure is not an option," if we allow each other the room to take risks and make mistakes, learning as we go, our organizations will be much more resilient. Not only can mistakes eventually lead to great innovation, invention, and success, mistakes can be an immense source of resilience fuel. Rather than encouraging others to cover up their mistakes in an environment where mistakes are taboo, creating a safe environment where we can use them as fuel is much healthier, not to mention productive.

Good things can come out of mistakes. Things like learning, insight, maturity, new inventions, and increased compassion. Charles Goodyear accidently spilled rubber sulfur and lead together on a hot stove. This mistake led to vulcanized rubber and the creation of rubber-soled shoes, tires, and hockey pucks. It's just one such example among many!

Mistakes are often blown out of proportion. We live in a world where people are trying to be perfect. That's not reality. As George Bernard Shaw said, "A life spent making mistakes is not only more honorable but more useful than a life spent doing nothing." I believe this is one of life's great truths. I want my children to understand they don't have to be perfect all the time. They will learn much more from their mistakes than from a life cushioned by a parent with a parachute. My life is full of mistakes. They are the stepping-stones that have led me to where I am today. Overcoming mistakes has refined me and forced me to acquire resilience attributes such as patience, focus, hard work, and humility.

ASK

What types of organizations do you belong to? A family? A business? A school? Do you have a leadership role in any of these organizations? What happens when mistakes occur? Do you have a tendency to punish the mistake maker? Or do you have an attitude of "forgive and remember"? Do you forgive the person who made the mistake so they feel safe taking risks, while remembering the mistake so that learning occurs?

How did you respond the last time you felt disrespected, discriminated against, or regretful about a mistake? Are there ways you could have channeled the negative feelings into more productive responses? How can you remind yourself to harness the pain of similar situations in the future and use it as fuel?

Have you recently been the cause of someone feeling the pain of discrimination, disrespect, or punishment for a mistake? What actions on your part would be required to right this wrong? What could you do to make amends to this individual?

TASK

Disrespect, discrimination, and mistakes are all fuel sources; they can be used to redirect the pain they cause into positive, productive action. Identify an area where one or more of these have occurred. Approach your next project at work with the philosophy that failure *is* an option and with a determination to learn from it. See if you sense a difference in creativity and productivity as opposed to a time when you perhaps feared the prospect of failing.

STREET RESILIENCE BOOSTERS

Street Resilience is an extremely powerful resilience source that can be utilized throughout your life. It can give you the motivation to fight on and get back up. Remember, whatever mistake you've made or discrimination you've felt, others have been there before. When they see you fight on, it inspires and helps them. Street Resilience is a momentum that can't be stopped once it starts.

Unfortunately, all of us—young or old, rich or poor—will experience some form of disrespect, discrimination, and regret throughout our lives. It's therefore extremely important that you have Street Resilience in your toolbox at all times. Street Resilience needs to be always on your hip, ready to be pulled out at a moment's notice.

> **Street Resilience needs to be always on your hip, ready to be pulled out at a moment's notice.**

Discrimination and disrespect and regret can come from many sources, and we often don't see them coming. It can be done very passive-aggressively, or very subtly, behind closed doors, or under the table. It can come from otherwise benign sources, too: For example, who could have predicted the unique opportunities that social networking has created for discriminating, showing disrespect, and making irrevocable mistakes?

So how do we access Street Resilience when we inevitably run up against this kind of adversity? How exactly can we channel our mistakes and pain into fuel, transforming wrongs—both real and perceived—into motivation to be resilient? The following boosters can help you to access additional "power from the street."

GET THE WHOLE PICTURE
STREET RESILIENCE BOOSTER #1

One day, during my undergraduate years, I was sitting in a large, theater-style classroom with about 250 other people. The majority of students on this campus came from highly educated, upper-middle-class families, a far cry from my experience. We were listening to a lecture on welfare reform by a visiting professor from Cornell. He asked us, "Has anybody been exposed to people on welfare?" Several students raised their hands and talked about working in fast-food restaurants or grocery stores and the interactions they'd had with people on welfare there. They gave example after example of people using food stamps to buy nonessential items, most with an attitude suggesting these shoppers were lazy no-good bums taking advantage of the system. After about seven of these speeches, a girl in the back raised her hand and said, "I was working at a grocery store checkout, and this person comes through with Orange Crush, lobster, and ice cream. And they pay with food stamps! They should've been buying staples—milk, bread, diapers. They weren't buying items to meet their basic needs!"

Sitting on the fourth row of the large auditorium, looking up at this girl at the top of the room, I suddenly realized I couldn't take it anymore. I raised my hand, turned back toward her, and asked, "What's your favorite kind of ice cream?" In a mocking voice, she said she liked mint chocolate chip. Then I asked, "Why do you like it?" She scoffed and said it tasted good. "When do you eat it?" She said she liked it best at the end of the day, before she went to bed. I made her tell me all of the emotional perks of eating this ice cream, and she did, acting like I was an idiot the whole time. It was uncomfortable for everyone in the room, especially the visibly uneasy professor. But I kept going: She tells me she feels good when she eats it and that she likes to eat it with her favorite show. I ask her all about her emotional connection to ice cream. She says she likes to eat it with her girlfriends, and that sometimes, after a bad day, she'll eat a whole half gallon. "Is ice cream a bonding experience for you?" I ask. Luckily, the professor is being patient. I look over at him, and now he has a slight grin. He's figured out where I'm going with this.

After a good six or eight minutes of her in-depth ice cream descriptions, I hesitate, pause for a moment, and then say, "With all due respect, the reason that you like ice cream, believe it or not, is the exact same reason that a poor person likes ice cream." By now I am addressing the entire class. "They want and like the same things you do. And they may want it even more than you, 'cause they're hurting! It could be they're depressed. Maybe their lives are falling apart. That ice cream may be even more valuable to them than to you. There's no difference between rich people and poor people. They have the same needs, the same wants. They're no different than you, but the emotional urge for it might be even more intense. I get that the reality of economics is that someone on welfare might not be able to have access to ice cream. Growing up, a lot of my friends had food stamps. And they were great people. They often shared that food with me, and sometimes it was the only food around. I agree; they should be buying staples. But when you're hurting, when you're rock bottom, when you don't have access to basic things . . . little things are big things."

The professor invited me down to finish the lecture and handed me the chalk. That poor class—there was no stopping me now! "Most of us in this room, we could eat ice cream seven days a week if we wanted to. It's no big deal. To the poor person, that gallon of ice cream might be the highlight of their day. Even if they only have forty dollars on their welfare card, the four-and-a-half-dollar ice cream might be worth much more to them." I wanted her to understand that these people weren't bad because they were buying ice cream; in fact, it might be much more logical for them to buy ice cream than for her to buy it. That might be their one splurge for two weeks. We just don't know. We have a limited view of their situation. We cannot fairly judge them.

On the way out of class that day, there were definitely students who tried to avoid me. But there were also quite a few who stopped and said things to me like, "You literally changed the way I see the world," and "You're one of the bravest people—to take on that many who saw it so differently than you did." I wasn't trying to be brave. But because of my own experience, I have always been passionate about getting the whole picture.

When we feel like we're being judged or discriminated against, it's easy to lose sight of the big picture and do the same back to others. But this Street Resilience booster is about Flipping the Switch and using those feelings of judgment as fuel to get a better view of that whole picture, a sense of what's really going on. We have to realize that it's the human condition to just see part of the picture, like this girl who condemned less-fortunate people for buying ice cream. Had she gone home with that family and watched them eat the ice cream, her view would've flipped—and I'd bet you she would've been buying *them* ice cream. In the same way, when we commit to getting the whole picture rather than letting feelings of disrespect get the best of us, we open the door to a new frame of mind and become increasingly resilient.

THE DANGERS OF A HALF-PICTURE VIEW

When someone discriminates, it's usually because they only have a half-picture view of the situation—and they often don't even realize they have this giant blind spot. I really believe that most people aren't malicious or mean, and that most discrimination occurs due to a simple lack of exposure. With a half-picture view, you regard others as less than you, a view that breeds contempt. But when you boost your resilience by taking a whole-picture view, you determine not to disrespect others but to strive for understanding and respect on every level.

Think of how much harm comes from people lacking the whole picture. Bullying. Racism. Genocide. If you have conflict with someone, it's usually because one of you is not willing to look at the other half of the picture; you both see a polarized world. This applies to couples, to whole organizations, and to nations at war.

But a world that attempts to see the whole picture is a world of opportunity. It is a safer world, where people ask, "How can we all win? What is the mutual benefit for everybody? How can I join others? How am I part of all humanity? How do I create opportunity for others to win as well?" Compare this to the half-picture view: "What's in it for me if I reject others? How can I separate myself from others? How can I show I am superior or better? How do I keep my power, my dominance?"

Of course, it's impossible to ever see the whole picture in its entirety. All truth is not available to us. But, we can strive to see it and in doing so gain a more complete view. Conversely, a half-picture view doesn't literally mean we understand half of a situation. It means we have a limited view and understanding. One of the biggest problems comes from people having a half-picture view but thinking they have the whole-picture view, a very common situation. Ask yourself, *Is it possible that I don't have all the information about this? Is there a chance that I am not understanding the other point of view?* Because, chances are, you don't. We rarely have the whole-picture view and the ability to understand and empathize with all involved, which is good reason for giving others the benefit of the doubt and cutting everyone a little bit of slack. When we foster this kind of mutual understanding, we increase everyone's ability to persevere through hard times of discrimination and judgment—to access, in other words, the power of Street Resilience.

HOW THE WHOLE-PICTURE VIEW COMES INTO FOCUS

So how do we get the whole picture? Some have it due to experience. Others have to proactively seek it. Look for other points of view that are different from your own, and seek to increase your exposure to other opinions and ways of living.

A few years ago a colleague of mine was able to take his family on a trip to China. They had a tour guide who took them to all the touristy places, which were beautiful and impressive. My friend then asked the guide if he could take them to see a typical Chinese village, so that they could see how a group of Chinese people in an impoverished community really lived. The guide reluctantly did as he requested. What they saw was shocking and life changing: row upon row of cinderblock and rubble houses, with no semblance of any organization or community. Scrawny dogs and hungry people were everywhere, forlorn and hopeless looking. My friend's family hadn't realized that people actually lived in such extreme poverty. Their itinerary as listed would not have given them a whole-picture view; they had to seek it out. And it was worth it—before this part of their travels, they had an incomplete view of this part of the world. The increased exposure was incredibly valuable. When we have an expanded perspective like this, it's so much easier to Flip the Switch when we, ourselves, feel those creeping feelings of disrespect, discrimination, and regret.

I'm not saying you have to travel the world to see the whole picture, although that is certainly something that can happen if you're fortunate enough to be able to do so and you have the right mindset. There are many low- or no-cost ways to get the whole-picture view. For example, your library can be your best friend. Reading can open your mind in invaluable ways. President Abraham Lincoln lived in poverty and was denied formal education because he needed to work on the family's hardscrabble farm. His father was forced to loan him out to work on other farms to pay off debt. Lincoln went to school a week here, a week there, and calculated that in total he had one year of formal education. "Books became his academy," writes Doris Kearns Goodwin. "Relatives and neighbors recalled that he scoured the countryside for books and read every volume he got his hands on."[27] It was said that he couldn't contain his excitement whenever he got a new book—couldn't eat, couldn't sleep, but stayed up all night reading. Lincoln was confined to an extremely small world in terms of geography and diversity, yet took tremendous advantage of the one resource he did have—books about the world. Literature allowed him to transcend his surroundings.

If you only expose yourself to what you know and are comfortable with, growth and insight into other options are stagnant. Try to increase your exposure to occupations and cultures that are different from your own. Watch or listen to media that carry political views that vary from those you hold, for example. Research, ask someone for help, and experience something new. The opportunity I had to spend time living with my grandparents (the World War II generation), as well as spending time with Mama Jackson—my African-American "second mom" and mentor—and her family exposed me to different ideas and views. Living on both the East Coast and in the western United States has expanded my mind. I have learned that no one group of people has all the knowledge and insight. I can't settle for one perspective on an issue or situation if I'm going to continue to grow, discover my true purpose, and access my inner resilience.

It's important to note that exposure alone does not necessarily equal enlightenment and make you more resilient. It does not guarantee understanding. Rather, *exposure while seeking to get the whole-picture view* is what leads to insight and expanded perception. Getting the whole-picture view means you take the time to understand both that which you easily agree with and that which you don't. Instead of focusing on what is wrong, it's much more productive to focus on what's right with a community, culture, people, or organization.

> *Exposure while seeking to get the whole-picture view* is what leads to insight and expanded perception.

No one sums up the whole-picture view quite as powerfully as someone who has literally had the whole *world* view. Edgar Mitchell, of the Apollo 14 mission, said, "You develop an instant global consciousness, a people orientation, an intense dissatisfaction with the state of the world, and a compulsion to do something about it. From out there on the moon, international politics look so petty. You want to grab a politician by the scruff of the neck and drag him a quarter of a million miles out and say, 'Look at that, you son of a bitch.'"[28]

Michael Collins, an astronaut on Gemini 10 and Apollo 11, echoed that sentiment: "I really believe that if the political leaders of the world could see their planet from a distance of 100,000 miles their outlook could be fundamentally changed. That all-important border would be invisible, that noisy argument silenced. The tiny globe would continue to turn, serenely ignoring its subdivisions, presenting a unified facade that would cry out for unified understanding, for homogeneous treatment. The earth must become as it appears: blue and white, not capitalist or Communist; blue and white, not rich or poor; blue and white, not envious or envied."[29]

ASK

When was the last time you had a disagreement with someone that went unresolved? What was your opinion, and what was the other person's opinion? What could you have done differently to gain a better understanding of their point of view?

TASK

The next time you interact with someone whose opinion is different than your own, make a conscious effort not to argue, and instead seek a more complete understanding of that person's point of view.

CHANNEL PAIN INTO A CAUSE

STREET RESILIENCE BOOSTER #2

When we feel the pain of discrimination, disrespect, and regret, we can either give in, or we can seek to find a positive, proactive outlet that enables us to transform hurt into action. This Street Resilience booster is all about latching on to a cause—something that excites or moves you—and using it to transform pain into productivity. This cause acts like a fuel distributor, channeling adversity straight into your resilience engine.

The cause you identify could be either inward or outward. Inward, or personal, causes include things like staying sober, being more honest, forgiving someone, or losing weight. Outward, or societal, causes include things like the civil rights movement, equal pay for women, or organ donation.

In order to combat discrimination or overcome a mistake—to be Street Resilient—you have to increase your energy, passion, focus, determination, forgiveness, and love, and that's exactly why it's so crucial to pick a cause that really gets you fired up. Think of anyone who is passionate about a cause—they're overflowing with energy! It's that passion that opens the door to Street Resilience. Street Resilience doesn't look like someone lounging on a couch. It looks more like a mother who is channeling the pain and anger of losing a child in a drunk-driving accident and now volunteers her time with Mothers Against Drunk Driving, passionately working to raise awareness and prevent driving under the influence. It's devotion and commitment. It is the complete opposite of being low-key or passive. It's someone boldly saying, "I'm going to use the pain I feel from someone hurting me as fuel and have increased energy to make a difference in this world." It's an action.

Eleanor Roosevelt is a great example of turning pain into a cause. In 1918, future US president Franklin Delano Roosevelt returned from visiting the front lines of World War I in Europe. A packet of love letters fell out of his suitcase, and Eleanor discovered he had been having an affair with her social secretary, Lucy Mercer. Eleanor stayed with him for the sake of his political career, but for all intents and purposes the marriage was over. She lived like this for decades, and the American public never knew it was all a facade.

Years later, after FDR was elected president in 1932, Eleanor found herself hating the traditional role of first lady. Using the pain from the affair and her failed marriage as fuel, she channeled her energy into becoming the eyes and ears for FDR in her extensive travels throughout the country. Her husband was completely crippled from polio, and they worked hard to hide this from the American people. Eleanor traveled extensively throughout the country to find out how average people were living and coping with the Great Depression, which was devastating the lives of millions of Americans. She had boundless energy and wrote FDR so many memos about her findings that he eventually limited her to three memos per day.

The first lady came under attack for her tireless advocacy of New Deal reforms, and especially for her sympathies with the struggles of minorities. Dorothy Height, from the National Council of Negro Women, said, "Here was a woman coming from the top class in our country and here she was moving into poor neighborhoods. Here she was sitting in groups of people of all races and all backgrounds. She didn't have a program, but a lot that she did helped to lay the groundwork that we could build upon in later years in civil rights."[30]

You may not think of Eleanor Roosevelt as very "street," but she had Street Resilience in spades. She channeled her personal pain from the disrespect she'd experienced into a worthwhile cause and made a big difference in history as a result.

ASK

In what areas of your life do you currently feel the most pain? What is one personal struggle you can start channeling in a positive direction?

TASK

Now, identify a cause that you can begin channeling this pain into. It can be an inward cause (like reducing procrastination), or it could be an outward cause—something that benefits the wider community. Think of what you can do to begin converting pain into a cause today.

REFRAME YOUR LIMITATIONS
AS POTENTIAL STRENGTHS
STREET RESILIENCE BOOSTER #3

Gillian Lynne was born in 1926 in Kent, England. As a young girl she constantly underperformed in school—she couldn't focus, frequently disrupted others, and couldn't stay in her chair. At Gillian's teachers' request, her mother took her to see a specialist for help. For twenty minutes the eight-year-old sat on her hands in his oak-paneled room, trying her best to hold still, as her mother discussed all her shortcomings with the doctor. After listening to her list of problems, the doctor asked Gillian's mother to step out of the room with him so they could speak privately for a moment.

On their way out, he turned on the radio. "Just stand and watch her," he whispered to her. The minute they were out of the room, Gillian was on her feet. She was completely in her element, happily moving to the music. "Mrs. Lynne," the doctor said, "Gillian isn't sick; she's a dancer. Take her to dance school."

That decision changed the young girl's life. "I can't tell you how wonderful it was," says Gillian as she recounts her first day at the new school. "We walked in this room and it was full of people like me. People who couldn't sit still. People who had to move to think."[31]

Now, you might not know who Gillian Lynne is. But chances are you've seen her award-winning choreography: After a wonderful career at the Royal Ballet in London as well as founding her own dance company, she choreographed some of the most beloved productions ever performed on live stage, shows like *Cats* and *Phantom of the Opera*, sharing her creativity with millions of people.

Most likely, Gillian Lynne has what we now call ADHD. However, in the 1930s, ADHD wasn't yet recognized as a condition. Luckily, a wise doctor helped Gillian's mother see that a perceived limitation could actually be a strength, setting young Gillian on a path to success.

When we find ourselves feeling disrespected, discriminated against, or suffering from regret—in other words, when we need Street Resilience— our weaknesses often weigh heavily on us. This booster is about boosting your Street Resilience by looking at your weak points as strong points in disguise. When we pull this off, it further enables us to transform pain into positive action.

GOT ADHD? LET'S PARTY!

One of my limitations is similar to Gillian's: ADHD. But I've truly come to believe that attention-deficit hyperactivity disorder can be one of the greatest diagnoses in the world. Difficult as ADHD can be, it can also be an amazing source of fuel, and I want people to be able to see it this way. In therapy I used to bring a cake into my office and light candles to celebrate when a child got this diagnosis. "Great! You got ADHD!" I'd say to the parents and child. "We live in a very fast-paced society, and people would love to have your kind of energy! We're literally going to have a party. I'm going to show you how to use this as a way to get all your homework done. We're gonna use ADHD as the greatest fuel in your life." For the first time, they'd see the ADHD as a resource. Parents who had come in at their wits' end would leave my office with their heads up and full of hope. They'd started to reframe their child's diagnosis as a potential strength.

I don't mean to make light of ADHD—it is a serious condition that presents serious challenges. As someone who struggles with a severe case of ADHD, I know firsthand how difficult it is. (Also, please know I am not saying that this condition should never be medicated. This is an individual choice that should be made after careful consideration of what is most helpful to the child. I do believe, however, that medication should not be the only treatment a child with ADHD receives, as is unfortunately often the case.)

Some of the most brilliant and creative people in the world have (or had) ADHD, including Albert Einstein, Richard Branson (CEO of Virgin Airlines), Pablo Picasso, Justin Timberlake, Ingvar Kamprad (founder and chairman of IKEA), Whoopi Goldberg, the Wright brothers, Anderson Cooper, and Elvis Presley. And don't forget, me! I'm in pretty good company. In today's world, strong work ethic and rapid pace really can be a great advantage, and I've learned to use my condition as an advantage. I have ADHD, and I would attribute much of my success to it.

CAN PTSD BE A PLUS?

Reframing your limitations is applicable in so many situations. Once I was working with a soldier who had returned from fighting in Iraq and who suffered with a severe case of PTSD (post-traumatic stress disorder). He was in a state of constant hypervigilance, something that was useful and necessary for survival during wartime but that created anxiety and trauma in his postwar life. As a soldier he was always on defense, scanning windows, looking for the reflection of a gun barrel, and extremely focused on sounds and the threat of IEDs (improvised explosive devices). Now that he was home, his relationship with his wife was falling apart. Scared of his intense reactions, he had a hard time getting out of bed and was withdrawing from the family. When he was with his kids, he was tense and angry. When he was first referred to me, his wife told me, "I've lost my husband." She didn't believe there was anything I could do to help him.

Instead of simply giving him antianxiety medication, as often happens in severe PTSD cases, we worked on using his hypervigilance in helpful ways. All of those skills he learned in Iraq could be used in his relationship with his wife. When she got home from work, he needed to ask her about her day and "hyperfocus" on listening to her. When he gave her a hug, he needed to be completely present. When his kids got home from school, he could really listen to how their day was, paying attention to their body language when he communicated with them. I asked him to do this in his career as well, to pay attention to the details, to do everything thoroughly and with more intensity than he was currently doing it. In every aspect of his life, he could take the intensity he brought home with him and do good works with it.

Being constantly hypervigilant about a gun pointed at you during wartime may be necessary for survival, but it is a hard way to live. Being hypervigilant about your relationship with your wife can be healing. As he learned to focus this vigilance in healthy ways, his anxiety was calmed. Two months later, his wife told me her husband was back. It wasn't an overnight process, but he eventually became successful at reframing a huge challenge and using it as a strength.

THE DANDELION MODEL

Thorkil Sonne of Denmark quit his job and founded a company based on the idea of converting a limitation into an advantage. When he realized his autistic son had some unusual skills, such as incredible memory and precise execution, he conceived a business plan. Many companies have a hard time finding workers who can perform specific, repetitive tasks, tasks that some autistic people could be exceptionally good at. His company, Specialisterne (Danish for "the specialists"), provides jobs for previously unemployable people, jobs in increasing demand in a more and more specialized job market. The company's website describes Sonne's "dandelion model," which is a great description of reframing a limitation. "Most of us don't want [a dandelion] in our gardens—it doesn't fit in. But if you place the dandelion seeds in your kitchen garden and cultivate it, it can also turn out to be one of your most valuable plants, used in beer and wine making, salads, and as a natural medicine . . . Weed or herb? You decide."[32]

Even though I don't eat a lot of dandelion salad, it's a great metaphor. Instead of categorically condemning ourselves for our weaknesses, and letting the disrespect and discrimination of others get to us, is it possible to see a bit of brilliance there? If we are able to reframe the way we look at our limitations, we might be surprised at the strength and resilience we are able to find.

ASK

What's one of your weaknesses or limitations in your professional or personal life? It can be anything, large or small.

TASK

Now, think of a situation in which this perceived limitation could be used in a positive way. You may want to ask friends or family members for help. In the next week, try to put yourself in a situation where you can put this new strength to use.

FOCUS ON WHAT YOU
DID RIGHT TODAY
STREET RESILIENCE BOOSTER #4

I am trained in solution-focused brief therapy, a popular form of therapy attributed to Steve de Shazer and his wife Insoo Kim Berg. Shazer and Berg describe it this way: "Solution focused brief therapy focuses on the solution the client wants, not the problem. Solution focused brief therapy focuses on what can be done, not what cannot be done . . . not what cannot be changed. Solution focused brief therapy is about here and now, not what happened in the past."[33]

Each night, ask yourself these questions: *What did I do right today? How can I do more of that tomorrow?* One way to combat the judgment of others, because there will never be a shortage of critics, is to focus on what is right with yourself, and how you can do more of that. Then ask yourself what solution-focused brief therapy practitioners call the "Miracle Question": *Imagine that while you sleep tonight, a miracle occurs and your problem suddenly doesn't exist. Now, you're waking up tomorrow, not knowing that the miracle happened yet—what would be the first signs that the problem is gone?*

You're much more likely to overcome your mistakes faster if you focus on what you're doing right, not on what you're doing wrong. The medical model is to focus on what is wrong: What are the symptoms? How can we fix it? All too often, this leads to an overwhelmed feeling and frustration at the litany of issues needing attention. Instead, the goal of this booster is to have a snowball effect as you concentrate on all that is *right* with you. As a therapist I realized that this directly affects resilience. If we transform negative feelings caused by the judgment of others into a positive outlook on the things we're doing well, we equip ourselves to push through the hard times that everyone goes through.

There will always be people who will focus on what's wrong with you, but it's much more productive to focus on what's right with you. You don't need to be your own worst critic; the world will do that for you.

ASK

How has having a positive outlook helped you push through hard times in the past?

TASK

Think over the events of your day. Instead of dwelling on the things you did wrong, take a mental note of all the things you did right. When you wake up tomorrow, make a conscious effort to repeat these positive behaviors and add a few more.

LOOK FEAR IN THE EYE
STREET RESILIENCE BOOSTER #5

Fear is a part of life from the day we're born until the day we die. From the fear of separation from our caregiver as babies, to social and rejection fears in adolescence and adulthood, to fears of aging and death, fear is constantly with us. Fear is also a constant of life on the streets—a result of discrimination, disrespect, mistakes, uncertainty, and loneliness. If you're going to survive on the streets, you have to learn to look fear in the eye. You have to decide to use that fear as fuel rather than as an excuse to shut down. The same applies to all of us, whether we're on the pavement or in a penthouse. When we learn to channel our fear into positive outcomes, we're giving our Street Resilience a boost.

Fear can be created when someone disrespects you or puts you down. We can fear the consequences when we make mistakes. Sometimes when we are disrespected or discriminated against, we shut down and the fear increases. Sometimes we don't speak up out of fear. Channeling our fears and accessing Street Resilience means that when fear shows up in our lives, we refuse to back down. It means pushing forward and using the fear as fuel. Looking fear in the eye and doing it anyway is a Street Resilience mentality.

I still struggle with facing my fears on a daily basis. In fact, for most of my life I've been devoted to running away from them. One example is the fear of focusing on challenges in my immediate family, which I typically avoid by traveling for work (over the past ten years, I have traveled a total of six years of my life and over two million miles!). Banishing fear by simply checking out can be tempting, and for me, sometimes it's too easy.

But that travel itself also comes with fear, which I also tend to carefully avoid. Years ago, when I first started speaking across the United States, I was very scared of traveling because I couldn't read a map. I've always struggled with maps because of my learning differences, and whether rational or not, I was intensely afraid I would get so lost on a trip that I would never get back home. I avoided facing it by becoming an expert at negotiating with taxi drivers and begging them to drive me way out of their normal travel boundaries. I will never forget one time listening to a taxi driver telling his base that he had a man in his cab in an emergency situation who would die if he didn't drive me over eighty miles away to a very important speech.

Although I still struggle with these fears, I have had to learn to look this fear in the eye and do it anyway. It's hard to look a fear in the eye and continue to move forward and not let it stop you, but it's like lifting weights: You get stronger with every repetition or exposure. It's not fun in the middle of the workout, but the results can be great! Once I realized that confronting fear was a gateway to resilience, I worked on not using travel as an escape. And I've latched on to amazing tools—like the portable GPS unit—to help me confront my fear of travel and maps in manageable doses.

Because I have chosen to face my fears, I have been able to provide for my family. I've grown a business from the ground up. I've been able to help a lot of people with WhyTry, a program I believe in. And I've gained a whole new sense of myself and what I can do. I've realized that fear is a powerful teacher in life, one we need to respect and listen to. This teacher can warn us and protect us from danger, and it can motivate and inspire us. It is what gives us instant energy for fight or flight.

The ability to be resilient in the face of fear has nothing to do with how physically strong you are, how smart you are, how tough you can act, or even how emotionally stable you are. The most resilient people understand that exposure to fear is often the cure for fear's negative effects. It often comes down to your willingness to stand in the thunderstorm of your biggest fears with no umbrella or protection, and allow yourself to get drenched from the exposure. Fear thrives in the darkness of confusion and the unknown. The more you run from your fears, the more power they have. Everything is less scary when there is a spotlight shining on it.

Please realize, however, that too much exposure without protection or preparation may leave you feeling like you'll drown in the fierceness of the storm. Strategically handling your exposure to fear is more likely to create success. Let's see what that looks like in practice.

GUIDED MASTERY

Brad Anderson, a friend and collaborator on this book, had lunch a few years ago as part of an interview team with Dr. Albert Bandura, the fourth most frequently cited psychologist of all time, behind the likes of Skinner and Freud. Still working at Stanford in his late eighties, Bandura spent years studying phobias and developed a brilliant methodology for working people through their fears. We're not talking about little, easily managed fears here. During their lunch, Bandura told Brad about a woman in Santa Barbara who had a phobia of snakes. She'd read a story in the paper about a woman in San Francisco who had a snake crawl up through the sewer and into her toilet. The woman in Santa Barbara was now so paralyzed by her fear of snakes that she couldn't go to the bathroom. Bandura works with people like her to desensitize them from this fear. During the course of the lunch he went on to explain this process—typically it would start with him saying, "There's a snake in the next room. We're going to go in there." In the beginning the person would shudder and retort, "Oh no we're not!" But Bandura leads them through a step-by-step process: First they look at the snake through a two-way mirror. Then they stand in the doorway of the room where the snake is. Eventually they wear a leather glove and touch the snake. By the conclusion, people with a life-long fear of snakes would end up holding the snake in their lap, saying, "Look how beautiful it is!"[34]

Bandura calls this process "guided mastery," and it has applications beyond fear of snakes. David Kelley—founder and chair of the design firm IDEO (mentioned earlier in this section) and creator of the "d.school" at Stanford, where students study creative collaboration and problem solving in everything from business to medicine—spoke about Bandura's guided mastery in a speech on creative confidence. He explained that what Bandura does when working with phobics is similar to what he does with his business clients, taking them through a "series of small successes" that allow them to work through their fears. "People who went through this process with snakes had less anxiety about other things in their lives," says Kelley. "They tried harder, they persevered longer, and they were more resilient in the face of failure. Bandura calls that confidence 'self-efficacy'—the sense that you can change the world and that you can attain what you set out to do."[35]

Dr. Bandura didn't just throw a snake at them and yell, "Catch!"—he taught his clients a strategy to help them overcome fear through small doses of exposure to it. The work of other experts in this field backs up this approach. Although snake phobia isn't something most of us deal with, social anxiety is surprisingly common. Joseph LeDoux is a professor of neural science at New York University and has done extensive research and testing on social anxiety. He explains that avoidance, the opposite of exposure, frequently becomes an unhealthy coping mechanism. "People with social anxiety often cope with their problem by avoiding social situations altogether," says LeDoux. "This is not practical or beneficial. But neither is forcing oneself to show up at parties and just try to ride out the anxiety. A more effective treatment approach might be to combine anxiety-producing exposure with strategies that allow one to gain control over the anxiety trigger cues." For example, when someone with social anxiety goes to a party, they should identify strategies for "temporary escape and avoidance" in advance, such as going into the bathroom or stepping outside to make a call. After each successful social event, the amount of anxiety can be reduced. "People who learn to control anxiety triggers in this way . . . do much better than those who don't."[36]

Like the person overcoming the fear of snakes, you don't have to overcome a fear in a day; it often takes a significant amount of time and effort. You must learn strategies that give you a bit of control over your environment to overcome a fear. Combined with predetermined coping techniques, such as my use of the GPS device when I travel, sometimes it's best to slowly desensitize yourself to the fear. Other times you might just have to deal with it by jumping off the high dive and immersing yourself in it. Since I have so many fears and anxieties I often have to just jump in. And when I am brave and go for it, I'm constantly surprised at how often I land exactly where I need to.

THE BIG SIX

There are six big fears that, if we let them, can instantly stop us from accessing resilience. However, if we don't allow the fears to paralyze us, we can utilize them in a positive way—as fuel to *increase* our resilience. Although there are thousands of fears that can impact us, I chose the six that I believe are most prevalent and have the most impact on resilience.

Fear of Failure

Resilient people see failure as a reason to be humble and to continue to work harder. They know that failure is a human condition everybody struggles with, something that is normal, even expected. They see failure as key to their future success. It's only through the knowledge and experience gained through failing that they learn how to succeed. When you see failure as an opportunity to make adjustments and improve your life, fear of failure is less powerful.

When I started writing this book, I worried I would spend years working on it and then no one would want to read it. Then someone close to me who knew my flaws well said incredulously, "What? *You* can't write a book!" He confirmed out loud what the voice inside my head was telling me—that someone with my background doesn't write a book. As a special-ed student, I was behind every grade level in reading and writing. How could *I* write a book? But then I'd remind myself that a book is about thought and content. I've never struggled with that, and I knew I had worthwhile ideas. While I might be challenged with the technical side of writing, I could look my fear in the eye. I could enlist the help of people who had the writing skills I lacked, share my ideas with them, and move forward from there. The mere fact that you're reading this book right now makes facing this fear worth it. But even if some copies of this book sit for years gathering dust on bookstore shelves, it's been worth the effort it took to write it. My children will know everything their dad understood about not shutting down. Plus, I have a solid belief that the material in this book will help someone. This belief in and commitment to what I'm doing has helped me face my fear of failure. Even if I fail in the short term, it's worth it, because success may come in the long term. This helps put the fear of failure into perspective.

If you don't look your fear of failure in the eye, you become frozen, unwilling to take risks. Opportunities don't show up. Doors don't open. And sometimes, the opportunity you miss if you *don't* go for it can affect the whole course of your life.

Fear of Embarrassment

It's so much fun being around people who know they aren't perfect. I'm drawn to people who own their flaws and aren't afraid to show their imperfections. These resilient people mess up, and when others laugh at them, they're okay. They don't waste energy on being embarrassed. The ability to laugh at your own flaws and to let others laugh with you (or even at you) is a powerful resilience skill. Because I am a highly flawed individual, if I were unable to laugh at myself, I'd be in a world of hurt! Once I was on a crowded shuttle bus with a lot of business travelers going to the airport. I turned to my business partner and said, "Hey, I'm curious, what does the *e* in email stand for anyhow?" I was serious—my extremely technically challenged self didn't know what it stood for. All these business types just roared—fifteen guys in suits doubled over, laughing at me. I just laughed with them.

If you can roll with things like that, you give yourself a resilience edge. If you can't, negative emotions like resentment, anger, and self-loathing tend to dominate. You'll end up beating the hell out of yourself! I have some friends who never share their vulnerabilities or flaws. They have to always one-up you. So many people want to look like they're on top of things. They work hard to save face, no matter the cost. It is so much more enjoyable to be around someone who allows him- or herself to be vulnerable.

Fear of Death or Loss

We will all experience the pain that comes from death and loss, and many of us push others away because we fear this eventuality. But resilient people are able to create loving relationships in their life, all while knowing that mortality means they will experience loss again. Years ago, my older brother Billy was killed in a car accident. He was a Fairfax County, Virginia, police officer and the father of five children, and was well known and beloved by his community. Thousands attended his funeral, and in an extremely rare gesture of honor and respect, police officials closed Inter-state 95, which runs into the beltway surrounding the nation's capital, to allow the five-mile-long funeral procession uninterrupted passage. Billy was one of those rare people who made everyone around him a little bit better for having known him. He was cheerful and constantly helping others—in fact, when he died he was on his way to help a relative reroof his house. As a police officer he worked with some of the worst in soci-ety but treated them all like they were the very best. At his funeral, many people told me that he was their very best friend.

Billy is one of my heroes. He always fought for the underdog and for the disenfranchised. For example, he once found a homeless man living in the woods and helped him find a job. When Billy died, I decided that I was going to try to manifest those qualities and attributes in my life as a way to remember him. Although his death was a huge loss for me, I have strived to use his example as fuel to be a better person. Fear of loss is just another fuel source, one we can use to help us build relationships and cherish them while they last.

Fear of Rejection

All modesty aside, I am an expert in rejection. No, really I am. I started gaining this expertise early on in life, but one rejection in particular stands out. In fifth grade I fell madly in love with this beautiful, totally amazing girl. Aisha was a small but feisty twelve-year-old and I just knew I'd found the love of my life. I wrote her this beautiful love letter. You know the kind—I declared my undying devotion to her on a page of lined note-book paper, ending with two checkboxes—"Yes" or "No"—and "Will you be my girlfriend?" written in dull number-two pencil.

She hastily returned the note, and to my complete devastation she had checked "No." How could she possibly not want to be my girlfriend? Being someone with perseverance (and with many sisters, so I was not afraid of girls), I went busting in on her and all of her girlfriends at lunch.

Now I shouldn't have even been there—in fifth grade we self-segregated by gender, and there were no boys on this side of the room—but I didn't care! I just knew this girl should be spending her time with me!

It's all still crystal clear. I was wearing my favorite Izod shirt that I had begged my mom to get me. It was crisp white, with the little green alligator identifying it as *the* shirt to have, and I had taken great care to make sure my white shirt stayed stain free. I was so proud to wear it. So I sat across from Aisha in my awesome shirt, ignoring her giggling friends as I put my tray down. "Aisha, I'm really hurt. Why did you mark no on the box?"

This girl, the love of my fifth-grade life, looked me straight in the eyes. "Christian. You don't get it. Let me help you get it." And with lots of sassy-girl attitude, she took her tray, which, I should mention, was filled with spaghetti noodles soaking in soggy marinara, and threw the entire plate right in my face, just to make sure I understood that she had absolutely *no* interest in Christian Moore. The noodles and bright red sauce slopped all over me, dripping down my hair and face and staining my beloved shirt.

I thought I was going to die. Tears welled up in my eyes and streamed down my face. She and all the students in the lunchroom were laughing at me. It was literally every young boy's worst nightmare. Thinking about it, I still get mad today. This publicly humiliating experience with rejection impacted my relationships for years. It literally changed how I interacted with women for the next two decades. I took no risks—the only girls I'd spend time with were girls I knew without a doubt liked me. For a long time this event paralyzed me from reaching out to another human being. It was especially hard because during those years I was facing rejection on multiple levels and in various areas of my life. I felt rejected by my teachers as I struggled in my special-ed classes. I was terrible at sports and didn't fit in there. And when I went out for school choir, the director told me—no joke—to mouth the songs. I told you I'm an expert at the fear of rejection!

Gratefully, I have been able to work through this fear, thanks in part to a kind and patient wife. Rejection has become a great source of fuel for me. Some of the most resilient people I've ever met have also experienced much rejection in their lives. They use rejection as fuel to work extremely hard. Instead of becoming angry and bitter, they decide to be forgiving and move past the rejection. (Okay, so I'm still a little bitter about my failed fifth-grade love, but I'm working to move past it! I'm a work in progress.)

Fear of Loneliness

Some of the most resilient people are those who are able to live with loneliness and not give up. I'm inspired by people who don't have a lot of social contact, such as those elderly people who sit companionless for years, and yet continue to be kind and smile when someone finally shows up. Because of my own battles with this fear, loneliness is one of my favorite things to help someone overcome.

Over the years I have experienced some of my most hopeless moments alone in hotel rooms in cities where I don't know a single person. Intense loneliness is one of the most awful feelings you can have on this Earth. It's a major resilience killer, and I wouldn't wish it on my worst enemy. The extent that we'll go to fill the gap of loneliness is pretty extreme. The vices we can turn to for escape and self-soothing when we are lonely are seriously harmful. We allow ourselves to participate in destructive behaviors in order to get rid of the pain. This is why we should not try to power through loneliness alone! Instead, face the fear of isolation and being alone. Let it propel you to seek out connections, to reach out to someone.

Resilient people understand the paralyzing power of loneliness and constantly work at having multiple interests that open doors to potential support systems. They also use their own pain as a reason to go out of their way to help others not experience loneliness, which in turn lessens their own struggle with it. Human engagement on any level is the answer. There have been times during my travels where I've been the only person staying in a hotel. That's a really lonely feeling! Being alone in a big place magnifies the loneliness. Even walking by the desk clerk or someone in the hall and nodding at them makes me feel better. Humans are social beings. When loneliness threatens, try to find ways to connect with others rather than simply pushing away your fear. Even minimal connections can make a big difference. Just like many forms of pain, overcoming loneliness can make you stronger.

Fear of Pain

During our lives we experience both physical and emotional pain. I often see people who deal with long-term physical pain who decide to fight it by going through the motions each day. They complain little and will often help others who are stronger than they themselves are. This can be a way to take their minds off their own pain. As they fight for needed relief, they obtain resilience.

Sometimes relief is right around the corner. I have a pretty extreme fear of going to the dentist, and this fear has kept me from going there even when I have a toothache. In fact, I had a toothache for eight years straight, because my anxiety about the pain the dentist would possibly inflict on me was worse than the physical pain I was enduring. I was willing to sit with the pain for years. When I finally went to the dentist, I couldn't figure out why it had taken me so long to go! I certainly would have been more resilient had I sought treatment for the pain earlier.

Luckily we live in a time where we can usually find treatment for physical pain. Emotional pain, however, may be harder to treat. When dealing with emotional pain, we need to closely monitor it and find healthy interventions. Part V of this book, "Rock Bottom Resilience," provides specific tools for dealing with emotional pain.

We've all heard the phrase "No pain no gain." A muscle gets bigger when we endure the pain of the workout. Pain is a gateway to strength. Enduring pain can make us stronger. Working through something with another person strengthens our relationships as well—we bond through pain and often say "I feel closer to you now" after we've shared a painful experience with someone. Of course, we know that too much pain, either emotional or physical, can break us. But when I'm channeling my fear of pain toward meaningful action, I can risk more, be more patient; I can thrive.

◆ ◆ ◆

Resilience is created when you face a fear. You don't have to master these "Big Six" fears to access resilience—being able to battle them and live without any one fear governing you is what's significant. Each time you convert one of these six fears into fuel, it's like you're building a muscle. It gets stronger and stronger. The strength that can be developed when we don't freeze up from these fears is amazing to me! The ability to use any of these fears as fuel is a higher level of resilience.

STAY IN THE FIGHT

I want to touch on an important subject that I believe can't be left out of a book about resilience. There are people in our lives who walk around each day with hopelessness and despair. Chances are we don't have any idea who they are—possibly the guy two cubicles down from yours at work, or the lady you sat by on the bus today, or even the seemingly popular, has-it-all-going-for-him high school senior who lives on your street.

I have worked with people who are suicidal yet choose to live. These are the people who really know what it means to look fear in the eye and live anyway. People who are truly rock bottom have to choose to breathe, then breathe again. They take one step and then another step. Forward motion and breathing can check fear and put it in its place. When the fear of living is greater than the fear of dying, people must have a hope that there is love in the future that they don't see today. They have to believe it is there, like a gift that can be opened later. People who look fear in the eye and choose to live often tell me that if they had known how much love was around that next corner they wouldn't have been suicidal. If you've ever had these feelings, I urge you to get help. Please talk to someone who can help you work through it and find hope on the other side. I promise that what you don't see today will manifest itself and bring love to you when you truly decide to use the pain as fuel and move forward with the fear anyway. That is when love has the chance to reintroduce itself and crush the fear. These resilient heroes that I have worked with have taught me what it really means to not hesitate to look fear in the eye. They are some of the bravest people I know, and I thank them for their lessons.

THE FEARS BETWEEN OUR EARS

So often fear is an illusion. Even when our worst fears happen, it's usually not the end of the world. The sun rises tomorrow. I have learned 90 percent of my worst fears never come true. Most of my toughest battles are fought between my ears. The majority of what I worry about is wasted energy. It would be much more productive to focus on what is really happening right in front of me, not the anxieties in my head.

> **Even if I'm not able to conquer my fear, the ability to not let it govern me creates resilience.**

Fear isn't always a bad thing. Fear creates movement and prompts action. It's an important ingredient in bringing about change. While too much fear is paralyzing, too little fear creates stagnancy. Like a contractor's level, we want the amount of fear in our lives to be right in the middle.

TOO MUCH—FROZEN		TOO LITTLE—NO ACTION

You don't want to do everything out of fear, but the right amount is helpful. You can channel fear in positive directions, and when you use fear as fuel, the fear often goes away and you feel satisfied. You feel empowered. Once you get past the fear, you are driven by the desire to achieve. Performance anxiety is a good example—too much of it can leave you frozen, where as the right amount helps you to actually perform better. Fear can transition from anxiety and worry into accomplishment and achievement. There is energy in fear.

When I started studying the impact that fear has on resilience, I was shocked to see how large a role it plays. For most of my life, I've viewed my many fears as personal failures or weaknesses. Today I realize that each fear battle I win, or each fear I am simply able to cope with better each day, helps me become more resilient. Even if I'm not able to conquer my fear, the ability to not let it govern me creates resilience. There are many fears I haven't overcome, but the good news is that no one fear is governing my daily life. When one of my old fears rears its head to attack me, it's like I'm seeing an old friend. I acknowledge it and then look it in the eye. Sometimes I even laugh at it. Our fears will be with us throughout life. We need to acknowledge fear's influence, but refuse to let it dominate. When we understand fear will always be there, but don't allow it to govern us, that's resilience.

LOVE KILLS FEAR

The number-one reason to look fear in the eye is to love and be loved. Relationships are one of the scariest things in life. They are risky because they come and go. The loss of connection with someone we deeply love, or experiencing rejection from someone we love, is one of the greatest sources of pain. However, the reality is that relationships are also the way to feel the greatest joy and contentment. It is worth the risk! Love is the underlying fuel we need to stare down fear and access long-term resilience.

Since almost every aspect of life can be affected by fear, there is a built-in counterbalance. This is the power of unconditional love. The greatest way for a parent to lessen children's fear is to love them. Even as a forty-three-year-old, the greatest way to lower my fears is through love, and I'll bet this will still be the case when I'm on my deathbed. Everything is less scary when there is one of it and ten of you. That is why help from others and support systems are so important to accessing resilience (remember Relational Resilience?). Also, the love of others can inspire us to be stronger in the face of our fears. If my kids are watching me, I'm much more likely to step up. It's easier to overcome our own fears for someone else's best interest. Every reason to be resilient is founded in love. Love of others, love of self, love of a cause or passion, love of peace, love of something bigger than you. Love is the sharpest sword you can use to slay the fear monster. Fear working in conjunction with love boosts resilience.

Hope and resilience come when you face a fear, have success, and know you can do it again. One of the best lessons fear has taught me is life can be finer—filled with more adventure, more aliveness—when you look fear in the eye, and do it anyway.

ASK

Which of the "Big Six" fears—fear of failure, fear of embarrassment, fear of death or loss, fear of rejection, fear of loneliness, or fear of pain—do you think about or worry about the most?

TASK

Take a moment to think of strategies that could help you cope with your fear the next time you encounter it. Think about small, incremental steps you could take to actually confront this fear. Recall how a person with a snake phobia must go through a series of small, guided steps to eventually overcome his or her fear of snakes. If there's a way to expose yourself to your fear in a small way in the next week, do so, practicing the coping strategies you came up with.

STREET RESILIENCE FUEL

Circle all the emotions and mindsets that you are currently experiencing. The more emotions and mindsets you circle, the greater your capacity to access Street Resilience. Just harness the energy from these emotions into resilience.

- Value (despite what others think)
- Disrespected
- Not defined by mistakes
- Misunderstood
- Labeled
- Betrayed
- Hurt
- Unafraid to go against the crowd
- Judged
- Learning from mistakes
- Angry
- Relentless
- Unwilling to accept "no"
- Discriminated against
- Overlooked
- Mad
- Unaccepting of others' reality
- Desiring to "prove them wrong"
- Vindication
- Self-respect
- Put in a box
- Unwanted
- "Mistakes are a tool"
- Focused on a cause
- Desiring to stand for justice
- Refusal to shut down
- Looked down on

PART IV

RESOURCE RESILIENCE

Tapping into your known and unknown reserves

WHAT IS RESOURCE RESILIENCE?

I don't tell this story very often. It is actually painful to recall, the memory of it humbling. Years ago, while I was an undergrad and before we had kids, my wife was laid off from her job. She was working while I went to school, and now we had no income. As our funds quickly dwindled, I started having panic attacks. There was no money for rent, no money for groceries. Wendy was frantically looking for another job, and I tried to figure out how I could help and still pass my classes. (You might remember what a complete miracle it was that I was even on a college campus, and that to get through a class, I had to study much more than the average student.) Adding to the problem was the fact that no one would hire me for even the most basic minimum-wage job. Although I was a college student, because of my learning differences I didn't know how to run a cash register or operate a computer. I felt like a complete failure.

I would lie in bed at night, filled with anxiety, trying to think of a solution. Feeling highly aware of my many inabilities, I tried to think of things I was good at. My greatest talent had always been art. I could draw and was especially good with watercolors. I wondered if there were some way I could use this skill to provide for my wife and me. One night it hit me: *I'll go where the money is!*

I asked my grandfather if I could borrow his camera, then went to a very wealthy area of the city, a gated community with beautiful, multi-million-dollar homes. I took pictures of some of the houses, returned to my apartment, and spent hours painting one of the homes on large water-color paper with a pencil and my watercolor paints. I'm a detailed artist, and I took great care to make sure that the picture captured the home exactly—I painted each daffodil blossom blooming in the yard and drew in the homeowner's name on the mailbox. It took three or four days of work to complete the first painting.

My grandmother, very artistic herself, helped me figure out how to mat and frame the painting. She knew how to make it look nice without costing much money. Then I took the framed picture and all the bravado I could muster and knocked on the door of the house it depicted. An older lady opened the door and gasped when she saw what I was holding. "Where did you get that?" she asked. I presented myself very profession-ally, as if I'd done this a thousand times. "Ma'am," I said, "I'm an artist. This is what I do. I paint beautiful homes. I saw your home and thought it was so beautiful I wanted to capture it." She oohed and aahed, obviously very pleased with the picture, and asked me how much I wanted for it.

I was hoping to get $200 out of the painting, so I bravely answered, "Three hundred dollars," leaving room to negotiate. She immediately wrote me a check for $600. I couldn't believe it! I remember going home, so proud of myself, and more than a little amazed at what had just hap-pened. It was such a traumatic time in my life that I can still remember exactly what my bills were, and I calculated that this one sale would cover all of my meager college-student expenses, plus rent and our car payment. And we could buy groceries!

I was so excited I did four more paintings. Everyone who opened their door bought them from me, and three of them paid more than I asked for. Each time, the homeowner would rave about the picture. This was a very emotional experience for me. There I was, standing on a strang-er's doorstep, hearing them tell me how great I am, when just the week before I couldn't even manage to buy food. Before I knocked on these doors, my self-esteem had been at an all-time low. I was broke, unable to provide for our basic needs, and unemployable. Now I had strangers, oblivious to my prior struggles, complimenting me and my work.

My crazy plan had worked. I'd found a way to access my talents and abilities to begin to solve a really big problem. It hadn't been a quick or painless fix, though. It required a real investment on my part and was a huge amount of effort, on top of my schoolwork. I felt tremendous pressure to create something that couldn't be refused, under conditions that were very different than that of a commissioned artist. I put many hours into each picture, and there was no guarantee of payment. I just hoped someone would be willing to buy. It worked, because I had used my greatest talent—my ability in art—to my advantage, combining it with the communication skills I'd been honing my whole life. I'd drawn on my strongest attributes, and this made me resilient during a really difficult time in my life. I had shown what I call **Resource Resilience**.

When you have Resource Resilience, you recognize that your resilience can be increased by tapping into the resources you currently possess or could potentially possess. Not only do you maximize your talents, mindset, abilities, relationships, money, physical assets, and personality traits, you also realize that you have undeveloped talents and untapped capabilities that you can also use or develop. And as you proactively acquire and build upon your resources, you become increasingly resilient.

When I was choosing my life's work, I drew on all the resources available to me, which allowed me to access additional resilience. Some of those resources were my innate strengths and abilities. All my life, I was good at art, and I've always been able to talk nonstop, for hours and hours. When I decided to become a social worker, I found I was good at that, too. But the world told me that I'd barely survive on those wages. So I combined all three of those talents—art and talking and social work—into the development of the WhyTry curriculum. As I started my business, I drew resilience, too, from external resources, such as my relationships. In the areas where I knew I was weak—such as business management—I utilized people who had those skills and abilities. Recognizing that I wasn't a businessman, I brought in people who were skilled in business.

Everybody has resources, whether they're aware of them or not—talents, skills, and abilities, or strong relationships, or even financial resources. Some people are blessed with an abundance of resources while others have to fight for every resource they have. Whether you have loads of resources at your disposal or you're down on your luck and feeling "resource deficient," you can utilize Resource Resilience. You just have to recognize and begin accessing the resources all around you.

A HOMELESS ALCOHOLIC TAPS INTO RESOURCE RESILIENCE

In *7 Tools to Beat Addiction*, Dr. Stanton Peele, an internationally recognized expert on addiction, writes about Chet, a homeless alcoholic who found himself living in a shelter in an old school building where there was a basketball court. Although years before he had been an outstanding player in high school, and was even offered an athletic scholarship before getting sidetracked from college, Chet hadn't played any ball in decades. One day he picked up a ball and started shooting baskets, remembering his long-forgotten ability and love of the game. A social worker saw him and quickly gathered a group of kids to play with him. Chet began teaching them the ins and outs of basketball. This was the beginning of a journey that ended with Chet achieving sobriety and becoming a coach in a local athletic league.

Playing basketball reminded him of his long-dormant abilities and skills and ignited a spark within him that he forgot had existed. "I've been in treatment maybe a dozen times over the last decade and a half," he said. "Each time they asked me about my arrests, divorces, previous treatment, etc. All that did was remind me of what a failure I was. They really didn't need to do all that to determine that I was an alcoholic—I spent all day drinking from a bottle in a brown paper bag." In all those times in treatment, no one had discovered that he had been an excellent basketball player. This was ultimately the resource that became the foundation of Chet's recovery.

Peele tells Chet's story as a way of illustrating that overcoming any addiction requires you to evaluate your strengths and weaknesses. "First," he says, "you need to assess what resources you already have and what resources you currently lack. Then you need to develop the skills that will allow you to expand your resources." Of course, as I said before, *resources* doesn't just refer to the financial kind. Dr. Peele's research shows that simply being able to afford a fancy treatment center is no guarantee of overcoming drug or alcohol addiction. In fact, he even says that wealthy people have more opportunities to develop addictive behaviors.

"Nonetheless," Peele writes, "research shows that the more resources people have and develop, the more likely they are to recover from addiction." According to Peele, key resources include things like intimacy and supportive relationships, employment and work skills, hobbies and interests, and coping mechanisms such as social skills and the ability to deal with stress. "These personal assets are a better predictor of recovery than wealth," says Peele. Although he is referring to those struggling with addiction, this is equally applicable to resilience. In fact, I would argue that overcoming an addiction is resilience in action at the highest level.

For Chet, reconnecting with his athletic abilities opened the door for him to realize additional strengths. For example, he discovered he was very good at working with young people. He believed in himself for the first time in possibly his whole adult life. Peele says, "Identifying the resources that you already possess is a big part of the recovery process. The resources you command include not only your abilities, but also the confidence you have gained from your past accomplishments."[37] Rediscovering his ability and love for basketball gave Chet access to a confidence and resilience he hadn't had before.

Recognizing the things you are good at and maximizing those talents, strengths, and abilities gives you a huge resilience edge. In order to identify your own strengths, think of successes you have had in your life. Even seemingly minor abilities shouldn't be taken for granted. This can include things like "I am good at home repairs," "I am well organized," "People like how friendly I am," or "I have always held a job." Each of these is a resource in its own right and can lead to the discovery of further resources. Someone who knows their raw abilities has a resilience edge over people lacking this awareness.

Inventory your strengths by asking yourself what your greatest accomplishments are. What are you doing when you are feeling most fulfilled? What do people like about you? It might be helpful to ask others who know you well what they perceive your strengths to be—after all, your relationships are another resource for you to draw upon. Use the resources around you—people familiar enough with you to know—to strengthen your Resource Resilience.

WHEN YOU DON'T HAVE RESOURCES, YOU BECOME RESOURCEFUL

I was fascinated to discover that personal lessons on resilience can be learned from an entire country. Taiwan, an island that frequently experiences typhoons and is completely without any natural resources to live off, has the fourth-largest financial reserves in the world. Pulitzer Prize–winning author Thomas Friedman recently wrote about this phenomenon. "Rather than digging in the ground and mining whatever comes up, Taiwan has mined its 23 million people, their talent, energy and intelligence," he writes. Because this small country has no oil, no diamonds or gold or forests, they have focused on developing people's skills.

Friedman describes a study by the Organization for Economic Cooperation and Development (OECD), which maps how well a country's high school kids do on math compared with how much oil the country pumps or diamonds they dig. The results? There was "a significant negative relationship between the money countries extract from national resources and the knowledge and skills of their high school population," says Andreas Schleicher of the OECD. This pattern held across sixty-five countries that took part in the study. "That's why the foreign countries with the most companies listed on the NASDAQ (stock exchange) are Israel, China/Hong Kong, Taiwan, India, South Korea, and Singapore—none of which can live off natural resources," says Friedman.[38]

This global study validates something I strongly believe—that when you don't have resources, you are forced to become resourceful. I used to look at people I thought had it all—plenty of money, opportunities galore, good looks—and think they had it made. They had it easy. But I've reached the point in my life where I can look back and see that because I had to really work hard, because I had to really dig deep to access strengths that have gotten me through, I've become much stronger. I've developed abilities that I never would have if my life had been easy. And I'm much more resilient for it.

ASK

What skills, talents, and resources do you currently possess that you're not fully utilizing? What have others told you you're good at? Are you currently pursuing those skills or talents? If not, why? What would it take for you to get reconnected with this resource?

What talent have you dreamed of acquiring but haven't yet exerted the time and effort to pursue? Is now the time to take action? What are some initial steps you could take to get you moving in this direction?

TASK

Reflect on the times you felt the most personally or professionally fulfilled. If you're not currently engaged in these activities, set aside time to regularly reengage with them.

Sometimes, instead of passively trying to think of what you're good at, you need to put yourself in situations where you can see yourself in action in order to access potential resources.

Exposure to a range of new situations can help us understand what our strengths are; our strengths tend to surface during the experiences we have. Recognizing the things you are good at and maximizing your strengths gives you a huge resilience edge.

RESOURCE RESILIENCE
BOOSTERS

Imagine a scrawny ten-year-old as he stands at the plate, awaiting his first pitch during a game of Little League baseball. He's been watching from the dugout as, one after another, his teammates strike out. The pitcher seems twice his size, and the ball is nothing but a momentary blur when it leaves his fingers and whizzes past his ear.

He's frozen by fear, sure that public shame awaits him. At this point his only goal is to not get hit by that very hard ball being pitched very fast by a very large and intimidating opponent. This thought is so horrifying it overrides any thought of actually swinging the bat and attempting to connect with the ball.

His coach, sensing the emotional state of his small player, calls out, "Good things happen when you hit the ball!" Suddenly the boy realizes that not swinging almost certainly guarantees failure, and trying to hit the ball might be a gamble worth taking.

That sweet moment where ball connects with bat is what it's about. Swinging the bat doesn't guarantee he'll hit the ball, but it greatly increases his chances. The important thing is that he's made a hit *possible*.

I'd like you to keep this image in mind as you read the following Resource Resilience boosters. There are resources all around us. You might have to walk a few miles to access them, and some may help you more than others. But if you don't access these resources—if you don't try to hit the ball—you're guaranteed to not benefit!

Most my life I've been too intimidated to access resources described in the following boosters. I've felt I'm not worthy, or that "those people" deserve it more than I do, or that they'll do it better than I could. How you see the world is going to determine what resources are available to you. Every day I have to choose to see my talents, abilities, and strengths, and the strengths of others that can help me. It's an everyday battle. But the resources are always there for the taking. Remember: Good things happen when you swing at the ball. Go for it!

The following Resource Resilience boosters each give you a different way to swing at that ball and open doors to unforeseen options. Even when help seems beyond your reach, there are ways to access resources that can boost your resilience.

CULTIVATE A WORTHY MINDSET

RESOURCE RESILIENCE BOOSTER #1

If you're going to tap into the resilience resources all around you, you have to first decide that you're actually worthy of the effort. But my years of counseling others, and my own personal experiences, have taught me that many of us struggle to feel worthy of the good things in life. When we don't feel worthy, we self-sabotage. We let our strengths and talents go unused and pass up the strength we could draw from the people in our lives. Feeling unworthy of something you desire—whether it's a relationship, a job, a house, an education— is one of the worst feelings in the world. When we tell ourselves, *I'm not good enough for that, I don't deserve that*, or *They're better than me because . . .* , we are denying ourselves important resources that allow us to be resilient.

I have had dark times in my life when I really struggled with this. I didn't feel worthy of going to the dentist. I didn't feel worthy enough of becoming a father and having kids. I didn't even feel worthy of accessing healthy food. The first couple of years I traveled intensely for work, I'd only eat fast food. This was partly because I wanted to save my company money, but when I really admitted it to myself, I realized I didn't think it mattered if I ate vegetables. I wasn't worthy of a fresh apple or carrots and celery. A former business partner of mine realized what I was doing and had a heart-to-heart conversation with me. "Christian," he said, "spend a little more money. Eat a piece of fish. Eat a salad. It's okay." There I was, an adult having to convince myself that I was worthy of eating better than fast food.

I don't think I'm the only person who's struggled with this. I think it's an epidemic and that many of us battle with feeling unworthy of good things, whether we're outwardly successful or not. I recently noticed a friend's post on Facebook. She's an accomplished, outgoing high achiever, but her post stated, "I'm sick of never feeling good enough." The world is eager enough to pounce on our every weakness. It doesn't help that we often beat ourselves up on top of it.

In my social-work practice I counseled a lot of people who felt like they weren't worthy of receiving mental-health services. As a young social worker, I'd sit with homeless clients and say, "I've got a job for you. It's all arranged. I've talked with the organization, and they're willing to train you and help you get back on your feet." But often, no matter how hard I tried, I couldn't talk the homeless person into accessing employment. He didn't feel worthy, and in many cases mental-health issues made it even more difficult. It reminds me of *The Soloist*, starring Robert Downey Jr. and Jamie Foxx, which depicted a similar situation. The film is based on the true story of a journalist who befriends Nathaniel Ayers, a homeless man whom he found playing beautiful music on a broken, two-stringed violin on LA's skid row. The two develop a friendship and the journalist works to change Ayers's situation, ultimately arranging housing for him. The journalist doesn't understand when Ayers, no matter how much he wants to, is unable to stay in the apartment. He is just too uncomfortable there. On top of the mental illness at play, Ayers didn't feel worthy.

Although our situations were obviously different, I could relate to Ayers's struggles. When it was time for me to buy a home, I had the money in the bank. I had a good job. But I couldn't even wrap my head around actually owning a house. I hadn't grown up with the expectation of being a homeowner. So once again, I had to have someone sit me down and tell me I was worthy. My business partner Hans said, "Christian, you've got the resources, the money is here, you're worthy. You can buy a home; it's okay."

I needed someone to remind me that I had done the hard work. I'd paid the price. The resources—in this case, financial resources—were at my disposal, and I didn't need to bow my head or feel guilty for accessing them. For a lot of my life, I had resources: money, connections, relationships, abilities. But I didn't access them because I didn't feel worthy. In my case, I think I struggled with survivor's guilt. I had made it out of the neighborhood—but I'd left others behind. Even when I went to college, I really had to battle with myself and let myself believe that maybe, just maybe, it could happen—and that I was worthy of it.

I won that battle, but as I explained in the introduction, I struggled to feel worthy the whole time I was on a college campus. I kept thinking that someone was going to come over, tap me on the shoulder, and say, "We figured out who you are! Get out!" And something that happened right at the beginning of my college career solidified my already strong feelings of unworthiness.

When I first transferred to the university, I went to my academic counselor to review the prerequisites I needed to get into the school of social work. She was very young, just a few years older than I was, and probably fresh out of college herself. As she listed the rigorous requirements, I was honest and told her my concerns. I told her I didn't know how I was going to survive the intense math classes in particular, since I didn't know the answer to nine times six or how to read the clock on her wall. She thought I was joking. But once I finally convinced her I wasn't trying to be funny, she was completely shocked. She looked at me with what seemed like contempt, obviously blown away by my admission, and blurted, "You shouldn't be here. You'll never cut it on this campus."

I was devastated. I had approached her as an ally, thinking she was an advocate for me and would help me reach my academic goals. Now

I knew it wasn't just me who thought I was unworthy. A powerful person in my life was validating my invalidation of myself. I left her office feeling incredibly stupid and as low as I'd ever been. But I had done the hard work to get myself to that college campus. I had to remind myself of that. And although I made sure I never admitted my struggles so candidly to anyone there again, I worked hard to stay there. I didn't give up. Because of my efforts to be resilient, a whole new world of resources opened up to me.

YOU'RE WORTHY BECAUSE . . .

When I've had those times where I struggle, I purposefully try to create a worthy mindset. I practice containing my negative thoughts, which is challenging. It's human nature to dwell on the negative. Behavioral researchers tell us that as much as 77 percent of the thoughts we have are negative and counterproductive. "Bad emotions, bad parents, and bad feedback have more impact than good ones, and bad information is processed more thoroughly than good,"[39] say the authors of the article "Bad Is Stronger Than Good." This means, basically, that we zero in on the unpleasant, and it takes deliberate effort to focus on the positive. To do this I remind myself of some truths about the human condition:

- I'm worthy because I'm part of the human family.
- I'm worthy because I'm no different than anyone else. I have a heart, a mind, and emotions, the same as everyone else, and we're all deserving.
- I'm worthy because I have the same needs that other people have.
- I'm worthy because I've done all I could. I tried my best.
- I'm worthy because if I access this resource, I can use it to do good and to help other people.

DON'T LET LITTLE THINGS
BECOME BIG THINGS

If you don't feel like you're worthy to obtain something, even the smallest things are going to derail you. A few years back, when I was working as a therapist, one of my clients was a young man who was struggling with substance abuse and depression. I helped him enroll in the local community college and he was on track to make some real progress in his life. The college was having some parking issues and there was a bunch of construction in the parking lot. You had to pick up a shuttle to get to class. So he started telling me he was going to drop out of college because he couldn't find parking. I could relate to this frustration when I was in school. I also knew that this parking problem, which should be relatively small in the scheme of things, was something that he could allow to completely derail him from his goal of going to college. Because he didn't feel he was worthy to be on that college campus, a little thing like taking the shuttle could easily get in the way of him accessing that important resource. So I took the young man and I went out there and rode the shuttle with him. We worked through it. He learned how to work the parking system. And he stayed in school. I hope this experience helped him realize that when he is facing a resilience challenge, he can't let little things be the reason for defeat.

People who access resources feel in their hearts that they deserve them. We don't access something that we don't believe is possible. If I hadn't had a seed of hope that one day I could become a clinical social worker, that I would be able to help others have a better life, there is no way I would have ever even started the journey to become one. I could never have foreseen that one day I'd own a successful company. Someone else had to paint that picture for me, and I'm thankful someone was patient and took the time to plant that seed of hope, believing for me until I believed for myself.

If you can find even a speck of hope, and believe for a minute or two that you're worthy of better things, you have to take a risk and go for it! Go for it with every part of your heart, and don't look back. To create this access, you usually have to sacrifice something. You have to have determination, hard work, and perseverance. And you have to be willing to take a risk. You have to be willing to risk failure and rejection and look your fear in the eye. It's been my experience that when I do this, options open up to me, and I have access to resources I had no idea even existed.

ASK

Is there a goal or activity you feel unworthy of in your life? Where do you think these feelings of unworthiness came from? Are they logical? What have you given up or forfeited because of these feelings?

TASK

Now shift your mindset. Think of all the reasons you *are* worthy. Finish your list with the items we've looked at so far:

- I'm worthy because I'm part of the human family.
- I'm worthy because I'm no different than anyone else. I have a heart, a mind, and emotions, the same as everyone else, and we're all deserving.
- I'm worthy because I have the same needs that other people have.
- I'm worthy because I've done all I could. I tried my best.
- I'm worthy because if I access this resource, I can use it to do good and to help other people.

TAP INTO THE POWER OF PEOPLE
RESOURCE RESILIENCE BOOSTER #2

We are all surrounded by an almost limitless resource—other people. In my life, the people around me have helped me be resilient through seemingly impossible obstacles. I'm a people person, so this came naturally to me; however, even if you're not an especially outgoing person, you can access Resource Resilience by turning to the people in your life for support.

I start this booster with a warning, however. *I'm not advising you to manipulate others into doing things for you.* This is absolutely *not* a "how to use other people" guide. Be forewarned that if you do attempt to tap into the power of people without sincerely caring about them, these suggestions will not work—and may even backfire! I know I can tell when someone is trying schmooze me because they want something from me. And so can most people.

In their popular book *The Start-up of You*, LinkedIn founder Reid Hoffman and Ben Casnocha criticize traditional networking for this very reason. They argue that it's no longer effective (if it ever was) to be a "transactional" networker, overanxiously handing out hundreds of business cards while urging everyone you meet to call you. "They pursue relationships thinking only about what other people can do for them," Hoffman and Casnocha explain. "And they'll only network with people when they need something, like a job or new clients. Relationship build-ers, on the other hand, try to help other people first. *They don't keep score.* They're aware that many good deeds get reciprocated, but they're not cal-culated about it. And they think about their relationships all the time, not just when they need something." This reciprocity is absolutely key when accessing people as a resource. If you use your network to look out for others and connect people who can help each other, you'll boost others' Resource Resilience even as you boost your own.

The support of the people in our lives is absolutely integral to achieving success. No one will ever convince me that any one person's success is his or hers alone. There are always others involved. *The Start-up of You* says it well: "It's easier to tell stories that neglect the surrounding cast. . . . Indeed, if you study the life of any notable person, you'll find that the main character operates within a web of support."[40] Although one individual may receive all the glory, I'm convinced it takes a team to achieve any significant success.

IT TOOK A VILLAGE . . .
TO START MY COMPANY

When I had the crazy idea to start a business, I knew I had material that could help others. That was an important piece of the puzzle, but it wasn't the only piece. If I hoped to fight through the adversity every entrepre-neur faces, I'd need the power of people on my side.

It started with my business partner Hans, who had more business experience than I did and knew how to create a training program for our clients. We then aligned ourselves with other talented people who each brought a new talent to the table. All the pieces came together to create a better whole. I never could have done it on my own. When I try to go at something alone, my own limitations and faults stare me in the face and shut me down. But when I understand it's the combination of my resources coming together with others' attributes and talents, all of our resources are magnified. It takes the weight of the world off my shoulders. I become more motivated to be resilient in the hard times.

The opportunities I've had with my business never happened in a vacuum. One of the things I say when I'm speaking is, "You can't see this right now, but there's an army of kids behind me—thousands of kids who have participated in my WhyTry Program and have helped me to create the best product possible. You don't see this, but there are thousands of school counselors, teachers, mental-health workers, and corrections officers standing behind me, giving me feedback and helping me improve my program. I'm the one who gets to go around the country getting the credit, but I have an army standing behind me that has helped make it possible."

If you want to become good at something, or if you want to develop a certain skill or character trait, surround yourself with people who are already the way you want to be. Hoffman and Casnocha say, "Relationships matter because the people you spend time with shape who you are and who you become. The fastest way to change yourself is to hang out with people who are already the way you want to be."[41]

You might be thinking, *Oh sure! Easy for you to say. Who am I supposed to hang out with?* Connecting with these people most likely won't happen by accident, but you can make it happen. Take a look around you. Who do you know that is strong where you're weak? Society won't facilitate this for us; we have to actively seek out and utilize the resources that are there.

It hit me one day when I was in school—wouldn't it make sense for me, with my severe learning differences, to hang out with the very smartest people? It was a revelation. Isn't it more logical to take people like me, who struggle the most, and put them with the people who do the best? After I realized this, I started hanging out with my professors. I believe with all my heart that the reason I'm not making minimum wage right now is because I surrounded myself with really smart people. It made me see the world differently. It opened my mind to new and exciting ideas.

Other students didn't seem to do this much, and they weren't as awed by it as I was. I had never had this kind of access before. These brilliant people actually let me hang out with them! I could go into their offices and have enlightening conversations with them. It changed who I was and how I thought.

This applies to job situations as well. It might not always be possible, but try to find ways to spend time at work with other employees or managers you admire or who have skills you'd like to develop. The more positive changes you make, the more you will attract positive friends, so it becomes a great cycle. When you choose to access the awesome potential in human beings, you give yourself a huge Resource Resilience edge.

ASK

Who has recently served as a resource for you? How did you connect with this person?

Who else do you know that could serve as a resource? Who do you know that is what you aspire to become?

TASK

Write a letter of gratitude to the person who helped you in the past, then make a list of all the people in your life who could serve as valuable resources. For the next week, make a sincere effort to reach out to at least one of these people each day. Write an email, meet for lunch, or give them a call. Show sincere gratitude and follow through with any suggestions or advice they're willing to share, doing more than what they expected. On the flip side, do whatever you can to assist others in connecting with people, finding potential jobs, and developing their talents.

ACTION, ACTION, ACTION!
RESOURCE RESILIENCE BOOSTER #3

As we've seen, there's an abundance of resilience resources available to you, and they include your own strengths and abilities and the people in your life. But if you want to access these resources effectively, you have to *take action.* Taking action generates more resources than simply thinking or planning. There is power in preparation and goal setting, but it's a place we can get stuck. Especially when we're facing a setback, it's a safer, easier place to be than actually out there doing what you're thinking about. We can become so immersed in planning that we end up with a beautiful plan instead of results that come from launching into action. And that means that we're less resilient.

One of my favorite examples of taking action happened during one of the most devastating natural disasters in the history of the United States: Hurricane Katrina. In late August of 2005, a hurricane as big as England—over 420 miles wide—struck the Gulf Coast with devastating force. More than 1,700 people died and hundreds of thousands became refugees as the 145-mile-an-hour winds viciously attacked Louisiana and Mississippi. When a section almost as long as a football field of a main levee broke, floodwaters submerged 80 percent of the city of New Orleans. The very poorest neighborhoods were hit the hardest as the water rose to the rooftops. Rescue workers could hear people pounding from inside buildings, where they were trapped. The lucky ones were able to cut holes in their roofs and escape to open air.

The situation was desperate. The photos of New Orleans taken during this time tell heart-wrenching stories of the unspeakable devastation; entire neighborhoods submerged in a stew of gasoline, floating garbage, and corpses; fathers holding sobbing infants above their heads to keep them out of the filthy water; once-towering structures flattened to the ground and once-sound highways broken into pieces. There was no food, no drinkable water, no power, and no authority in sight to curb the chaos that ensued as a result. At the center of the tragedy was the Superdome, a last-resort refuge for over twenty-five thousand people who waited, without provisions, for help to come.

The few hospitals left operating were without power or supplies and were forced to start stacking dead bodies in the stairwells. They kept trying to reach FEMA, the federal agency in charge of relief, but all they would get was a busy signal or voice mail. It was apparent that a system that was put in place to help and provide aid during a disaster simply didn't work.

Finally, on the sixth day of this unimaginable human suffering—caused by a wide range of factors, from incompetence to hesitation, finger pointing, and overall inaction—came Lieutenant General Russel Honoré (pronounced ah-NOR-ay). Virtually alone, this "John Wayne dude," as New Orleans mayor Ray Nagin called him, was assigned to command Joint Task Force Katrina. "He came off the doggone chopper," described Nagin, "and he started cussing and people started moving."[42]

Honoré was in the trenches from the second he got there. Although the looting and violence had made most rescue workers fearful, he didn't see the people stranded there as enemies but rather as human beings who needed to be rescued. While commanding the rescue effort on the streets, he noticed a young, dazed mother shuffling up the sidewalk, barely able to carry her twin babies in the terrible heat and humidity and struggling with each step. Honoré slipped the babies out of her exhausted arms and handed them to soldiers as she mumbled a weary thank-you. He helped get all three to a Coast Guard ship, where they were treated for exhaustion and dehydration. He remains beloved there to this day because of his remarkable leadership and his ability to go on offense.[43]

I was in a hotel room in Florida watching this happen on CNN. I remember seeing General Honoré on the news and being so excited that I was pumping my fist in the air, yelling, "Yes! Yes!" I knew this approach was going to make a difference.

Five years later, CNN interviewed the general about the BP oil disaster cleanup effort in the Gulf of Mexico. The interviewer asked him, "What is the first thing you would do immediately, within an hour, to change the way this cleanup has occurred?"

I loved Honoré's response. "I would go on the offense. I would go on the attack. We've been on defense for too long, waiting for the oil to come into the shoreline. We'd leave nothing on the table—whatever it takes."[44]

Hopefully, most of us won't have to take action of such magnitude during such treacherous circumstances. But every day finds us in situations where taking action is a choice we can make that helps us be resilient.

This can be done in small but effective ways. A colleague of mine told me about a manager he once worked with who was famous for taking action quickly. My friend and his coworkers noticed that even during times when action usually takes a backseat to talking or planning, such as during team meetings, his manager, Janice Parker, would immediately do what they were talking about. She'd say things like, "Well, let's get so-and-so on the phone and find out!" and she'd dial the number. Or she'd send an email right then instead of adding it to a list of things to do after the meeting. The employees took note of her proactivity and labeled it. To this day, my friend will say, "I'm going to 'do a Janice Parker,'" whenever he takes immediate, problem-solving action.

LET'S TAKE CONTROL OF
THE NEXT ONE SECOND

Long before I had heard of this idea, I was doing something similar with clients in therapy. Often therapy is very goal oriented, with lots of talk of reaching milestones. I did something that some may consider radical. I'd say, "We're not going to set a goal. You know what we're going to do? We're going to take control of the next one second of your life." Say I was working with someone who was dealing with an anger-management issue. I'd say, "Okay, right now in this moment you're not yelling at me. That's success. How can we do more of that? What is enabling you right now to not yell at me? How can we take that and use that when you're back with your wife and kids?" I found it to be much more productive to focus on the action—the next successful one second, and then another second, and another—than sitting around talking, planning, and thinking about it.

TAKING ACTION UNDER PRESSURE

Taking action works especially well during stressful times. It's easy to sit and worry or wallow in anxiety. We've all been there before. But if you can transform that anxiety into action, you'll uncover resilience resources you hadn't seen before.

When I was in graduate school I had a crisis situation. I needed work, but my program was so intense that we weren't allowed to hold a job outside of it. The only job available was that of research assistant assigned to a professor. Although it paid well, I was literally the most unqualified person ever to be a research assistant. Not only could I not type on a computer, but I could barely spell anything, either, and I didn't know how to use the overwhelming university library system. I couldn't have found *Three Little Pigs* in that library let alone dig for scientific research and studies. But I desperately needed the money and showed up to work the first day praying for a miracle.

Within the first five minutes on the job I was almost fired. The professor, my boss, asked me to type "psychological assessment" in a search engine on her computer. I couldn't spell either of those words and was trying to pick out the letters with one finger when she asked me to stop playing around and take the job more seriously. When she realized I wasn't joking, she started to tell me this might not be the right job for me. I tearfully begged her to give me a chance to do the actual research in the library. I apologized for my lack of ability to conduct academic research. Luckily she decided to give me another chance, and asked me to find some data she needed at the library.

As I walked into the library feeling extremely stupid and scared to death, I felt the urge to shut down. I wanted to go home, tell Wendy what had happened, and start thinking about what I'd do now that I'd lost this opportunity. But fortunately, I felt a competing impulse—to act. I had the idea to get help from the top. I remembered that we'd once had a guest lecture from the librarian in charge of the social-sciences section of the library. I thought he'd be the best place to start. Although I couldn't figure out the library computer system, I knew I could negotiate and effectively communicate what this professor needed. Lucky for me, Mr. Law was highly entertained by my plight and had compassion. I gave him the topic I needed to research and he printed out volumes of relevant information.

Each week I would meet with this library expert and get stacks of material for my boss. The professor loved the research, and I loved the feeling of doing an effective job in a situation where I had no expertise. By figuring out a way to take action instead of allowing stress and anxiety to incapacitate me, I discovered a rich resilience resource—Mr. Law—and was able to keep my job; plus, my professor got what she hired me to do. On the last day I worked there, she gave me a gift and thanked me. She said I was the most productive research assistant she had ever had.

I realize that it's highly unlikely you'll be in a situation exactly like this, but I know you have—and will—encounter circumstances that involve similar stress. You may be given a challenge at work that you honestly have no idea how to solve. Or you might need to help a family member going through something difficult, something you have no experience with. When these things happen, find ways to take action.

I believe some people think, *I could be successful if I didn't have this depression, these anxieties, this anger inside me*. But it's the human condition to have to deal with those things. The best solution I've found is action, action, action. Resilient people walk side by side with their anxieties and fears and continue to produce. Just keep doing something! Doing anything, even something small or seemingly futile, helps me remain in control and be more resilient. If I sit around, or delay getting out of bed because I don't want to face the day, it's harder to go into motion. If I act, unforeseen options open up, and resources present themselves.

> **Resilient people walk side by side with their anxieties and fears and continue to produce.**

ASK

What's a task you've been avoiding due to a lack of experience, motivation, or resources? Do you tend to procrastinate tackling the task, waiting for the ideal moment that never seems to come?

TASK

Take *immediate* action today by tackling one of the problems around you. You can start small: Maybe there's a lightbulb that you've been putting off changing or a colleague you've been needing to talk to about a project. Flip the Switch and just do it. Next time a more serious problem arises, dive in immediately, regardless of how giant, stressful, or outside of your realm of expertise it may appear.

FIGHT RESIGNATION
WITH SPONTANEITY
RESOURCE RESILIENCE BOOSTER #4

Back in college when I was scrambling to get by, I had a part-time job at a manufacturing plant. One of my very exciting duties was sweeping out a warehouse. The first few days I was extremely frustrated with how boring the job was and how much crap was constantly being thrown to the ground. The assembly-line workers used a very sticky adhesive and they threw big, goopy globs of it onto the floor. A broom didn't cut it. I'd crawl around with a putty knife, scraping it off the floor. I felt disrespected by the other workers on the line. They would yell at me if their area was getting too dirty, "Hey! You missed a spot over here!" They threw their McDonald's wrappers on the floor, even though there was a trash can nearby. The floors were atrocious. I was thankful for the work, but it was a far cry from anyone's idea of a dream job.

One day, after weeks of feeling put down and belittled, I just went a little crazy. I didn't realize it, but I was about to boost my Resource Resilience—with spontaneity. As I started sweeping, I loudly announced, "The sweeping man is in the house! Who needs my professional services first?" Then, as fast as I could, and with as much enthusiasm as I had, I would sweep and clean up. I danced around with the broom as I swept. I spontaneously sang and rapped funny songs. I asked the managers how

I could help them. I may have been just a lowly, entry-level sweeper, but I took an interest in them and over the next weeks tried to get to know them personally. I learned how long they had worked there, how many kids they had, what they liked to eat—the details of their lives. Over the next three months, all the managers in that plant wanted me to work in their departments. I ended up getting a large raise and worked in several divisions of the company. Whenever a department was slow or needed energy and passion, they put me in it. I ended up working as the director of quality control and had to approve and sign off on the work of the very same people who had disrespected me when I was sweeping up after them.

This job could have easily been a miserable experience for me. I could have simply resigned myself to showing up and putting my time in. I could have easily lapsed into a state of resignation and put up with a lousy situation. It didn't take a massive effort on my part to make a big difference at this job. In fact, I didn't plan what I did. I just did it on impulse. I was spontaneous. I was doing the same work; I simply changed how I approached it. I decided to go all in. This made it more fun for all of us, and—similar to what happened when I decided to take action—it resulted in opportunities and resources for me.

If you can find ways to be spontaneous and find the fun (even when there seems to be absolutely no fun around), everything becomes a bit more doable. Instead of being resigned and going through the motions, take a look around you. If you can find ways to improve your situation, even if they're small, chances are it will improve not only for you but for those around you as well, which sometimes results in additional opportunities and options for you. I have found that changing my approach in this way and readjusting my attitude when faced with any undesirable task makes me more resilient.

> ## I was doing the same work; I simply changed how I approached it.

ASK

Is there an assignment or task currently confronting you that's uninspiring or menial but yet has to get done?

TASK

With that task in mind, get creative! Use spontaneity to bring some life to this project. Make a game out of the process, rewarding yourself at various milestones along the way. And instead of going about the task halfheartedly, go all in! Give the job everything you've got until it's done. Find the humor (if there is any) in the pure boredom of it all. Make up a song about the job!

WRESTLE COMPLACENCY TO THE GROUND
RESOURCE RESILIENCE BOOSTER #5

Complacency is the enemy of resilience. The minute you say, "I'm satisfied," and sit back or take it easy, resources will run from you. The scary thing about complacency is that it's insidious. It creeps in and causes harm that you don't see. It sneaks up on you. It's inconspicuous and may seem harmless, but has hurtful effects. And it affects a lot of us. To fight complacency, and to access all the resources available to us, we must seek to educate and improve ourselves constantly.

Americans have typically been known as go-getters—a nation of movers and shakers—but research says that during the past thirty years, Americans, particularly young Americans, have become "risk averse" and "sedentary," which to me means we are sitting around, waiting for life to happen. The number of young adults living with their parents has doubled during that time period. Stranger still, the number of teens getting their drivers licenses by age eighteen has dropped to 65 percent. Here's an example that caught my eye: At the time of this writing, job seekers in Nevada are facing a 13 percent unemployment rate. For about $200, young Nevadans can catch a bus to North Dakota, where because of the booming oil industry they'll find a significantly lower 3.3 percent jobless rate. Why are more people not taking advantage? It might not always be feasible to pick up and move, but if your back's against the wall, sometimes you've got to do what you've got to do.

In their article "The Go-Nowhere Generation," authors Todd and Victoria Buchholz say this is something to worry about. "Generation Y has become Generation Why Bother," they say. The current challenging economy is certainly at least partially to blame: "Children raised during recessions ultimately take fewer risks with their investments and their jobs. Even when the recession passes, they don't strive as hard to find new jobs, and they hang on to lousy jobs longer." The most worrisome part? "Kids who grow up during tough economic times also tend to believe that luck plays a bigger role in their success, which breeds complacency."[45] If the current generation believes luck counts more than effort, how much effort will they be willing to expend? A complacent generation is not likely to thrive. They're more likely to pass up the chance to learn and grow—and to pass up important resilience resources.

COMPLACENCY AND THE CRASH
OF THE AMERICAN AUTO INDUSTRY

In the 1960s, General Motors was far and away the world's largest car company. Its US market share was seven times that of Toyota. Japan was producing cars of woeful quality and was desperate to learn from American automakers. That led hundreds of Japanese productivity teams to come to America to study its factories. They were amazed at the eagerness with which the Americans shared information with them, a generosity made possible only by the Americans' condescending arrogance and complacency. The Japanese were also surprised by the Americans' complete lack of interest in exporting their products to Japan or customizing their products to be used by the Japanese factories. In his book *The Reckoning*, David Halberstam shares the recollections of Masami Muramatsu, an interpreter who accompanied many of these teams: "There was an unusual pride to the Americans then, Muramatsu thought, a pride that was attractive in its generosity of spirit but flawed by self-satisfaction. The Americans were powerful, they were rich, they were helping their former adversaries [from World War II]; but they did not need to look beyond their own coasts, and they did not need to learn."[46]

Pride, defensiveness, and an attitude of "I've been the best, I've dominated the market, and you can't teach me anything," were the beginning of a sustained decline for American automakers. In the 1980s, while American car companies were steadily losing market share, Japanese carmakers were rapidly gaining ground, implementing the Japanese concept of *kaizen*—continuous improvement. Even after this market shift was completely impossible to ignore, American companies seemed to remain in denial. "We're Americans, we're supposed to be the best, most important country in the world, and we can't build a quality car. And these Japanese are doing it. And there was a sense of hurt pride,"[47] explained Jeffrey Liker, an author and industrial-engineering professor at the University of Michigan. No one seemed to be asking questions and trying to change things. American automakers seemed to be entrenched, defensive bureaucracies and weren't willing to recognize the problem or have a sense of urgency. GM's market share started to drop dramatically from its 1960s peak—and, at the time of this writing, it's still dropping, down from 60 percent to 17.5, the worst it has been since 1922. An interesting side note: Twenty years after the Japanese visited American factories, things came full circle—GM started sending groups of factory workers to Japan to learn from *their* streamlined factory processes and significantly lower rate of production defects.

> Pride, defensiveness, and an attitude of 'I've been the best, I've dominated the market, and you can't teach me anything,' were the beginning of a sustained decline for American automakers.

Liker, who has studied Japanese auto manufacturing since the 1980s, further explains that everyone had settled into comfortable roles within the current dysfunctional system and learned to live with it. Even with their market share in a "free fall," he says, "they were more apt to blame others than themselves. They all believed that there was somewhat of a myth of Japanese quality."

By the time the myth of Japanese quality was proven to be the new reality, it was too late. It's a tragic story, really. Many auto factories have shut down and thousands of Americans have lost much-needed jobs. The end of the story is the most tragic of all. In 2009, General Motors became the largest industrial bankruptcy in US history. And the American taxpayers got stuck with the bill, bailing them out for $50 billion.

This story could have ended much differently had the industry not been complacent, had it pushed to learn and grow. But they were satisfied with their success and felt no need to improve, change, or even expand. They chose to ignore the warning signs, a sure indicator of denial. Complacency is powerful in that it is sneaky and often not apparent, taking years to cause long-lasting damage.

FIGHT AN ATTITUDE OF ENTITLEMENT

Entitlement is a close cousin of complacency. It, too, will quickly kill Resource Resilience, and it's particularly dangerous in today's world.

Even if we once believed we were entitled to a decent career and stability, that is clearly no longer the case. Times have changed. Technology, automation, outsourcing, and a quickly changing world necessitate adaptation and constant reinvention. LinkedIn founder Reid Hoffman puts it this way: "The old paradigm of climbing up a stable career ladder is dead and gone. No career is a sure thing anymore. The uncertain, rapidly changing conditions in which entrepreneurs start companies is what it's now like for all of us fashioning a career." He adds, "You can't just say, 'I have a college degree, I have a right to a job, now someone else should figure out how to hire and train me.'"[48]

{ **"[An attitude of entitlement] will quickly kill Resource Resilience."** }

What all this means is that, as columnist Thomas Friedman, the commentator on Taiwan's resourcefulness, says, "You have to strengthen the muscles of resilience." I second his opinion and add this guarantee: An attitude of entitlement will actually repulse resources. The opposite is equally true—someone who is willing to really put in the necessary time and effort will attract resources. The online radio service Pandora serves as a great example of this. In the early days the founder pitched his idea more than three hundred times to venture capitalists with no luck.[49] He never would have found that valuable resource (a VC willing to fund his idea) had he felt he was entitled to it. He had to act—over three hundred times!

None of us is entitled to anything. If we believe everything should simply be handed to us, we're not going to be out there seeking and striving—and our resilience will drop. But if we put in all our faculties, energies, abilities, and talents, the chances of succeeding are hugely increased. We begin to attract the resources that make us extra resilient.

THE ANTIDOTE TO COMPLACENCY: LEARN SOMETHING!

Learning is a great way to fight complacency; in fact, it's the antithesis of complacency. By now I'm sure you're well aware of the value I place on a college education, but self-learning has incredible value, too. When you're actively seeking out knowledge, you find resources that boost your resilience.

Whether you've had the chance to obtain higher education or not, you always have the opportunity to learn. There are plenty of incredibly successful people who don't have a college degree, and those who do must continue to learn well past the years spent on a campus. Charles D. Hayes, founder of the Autodidactic Press, says, "Millions of people pay a king's ransom for college tuition to learn what is free for the taking when motivated by a compelling desire to learn. In *Good Will Hunting*, Will (played by Matt Damon) chides an arrogant Ivy League student for paying a fortune for an education that would be free but for the price of a library card."[50]

Not to mention the things you can learn on the Internet—there is a world of information at your fingertips. It's astounding, actually—iTunes U has free content from many universities, and online courses are easily accessible via companies like Udacity and Coursera. TED.com, with its short videos from experts with big ideas, is a goldmine for self-learners. EdX, a partnership between Harvard and MIT, features content from a variety of universities. And there is a never-ending array of podcasts available for download on every topic imaginable.

Today, you can learn anything you want. And according to Hayes, people who are committed to lifelong learning have a higher quality of life, make smarter career choices, and see ways to better our society. Self-learners are able to take control of their lives. Learning is the antidote to complacency.

{ Learning is the antidote to complacency. }

There are countless examples of successful self-learners—from Florence Nightingale and Abraham Lincoln, both with less than a year of formal education, to Ralph Lauren and Bill Gates, both college dropouts. Perhaps lesser known is Eric Hoffer, acclaimed author and recipient of the Presidential Medal of Freedom. Hoffer was born in 1902 in the Bronx to immigrants from eastern France. When he was five years old, his mother fell down a flight of stairs with Eric in her arms. She didn't recover and died two years later. Shortly after her death Eric went blind.

Inexplicably, his eyesight returned when he was fifteen. Fearing he would go blind again, he seized the opportunity to read as much as he possibly could and remained a voracious reader throughout his life. In 1920 he caught a bus to Los Angeles and lived on Skid Row, reading, writing, and doing odd jobs. He eventually became a migrant worker, following the harvests along California and collecting library cards for each town where he lived.[51]

This self-taught migrant worker was nobody's ideal of a public intellectual, but he earned multiple honors for his writing, and today, the Eric Hoffer Award recognizes outstanding books and short prose each year. His masterpiece, *The True Believer*, is widely recognized as a classic by both scholars and lay readers. Hoffer overcame incredible adversity in his life, finding resilience through his quest for constant education and self-improvement.

Today, more than we could learn in a lifetime is literally at our fingertips. It's never been easier in the history of the world to learn. The best way I know of to fight complacency and entitlement is through continual learning—and when we do this, we're opening the door to the resources that will help us stay resilient.

ASK

Have you fallen prey to the "complacency epidemic" in your personal or professional life? Are you telling yourself you're satisfied with areas of your life that could actually use improvement? Have you allowed yourself to become smug or self-satisfied, taking for granted successes you may have enjoyed?

TASK

In the next twenty-four hours, do one thing to fight complacency in your life. Instead of kicking back to watch TV, try spending thirty minutes developing a skill, reconnecting with an old friend, registering for a free online course, or researching things that will help you move forward.

GET SOME PRODUCTION THERAPY

RESOURCE RESILIENCE BOOSTER #6

When I was fourteen, I spray-painted my name in big red letters on the water tower near my house and was then shipped to the western United States to live with my grandparents. Up to that point in my life, I had never been grounded, given a chore, had a curfew, or been accountable for anything at all. Needless to say, my old-school grandfather had his work cut out for him when I arrived on his doorstep, and he immediately threw me into his world of structure, rules, and hard work. Talk about culture shock!

It was winter, and the storms were fierce that year. My grandpa told me it was my job to keep the walks shoveled. He owned a snow blower, and I asked him to get it out for me, but he said, "No, Christian, you need to learn to work." So every day, I spent a couple of hours shoveling those walks. How I hated it! When the weather was good, Grandpa would have me doing other jobs like scrubbing down his truck and meticulously mowing the lawn. He sat me down a hundred different times and would say, "Christian, the greatest privilege, the greatest opportunity, the thing that will bring you the most happiness is the ability to work. Work is a gift." Repeatedly, he'd try to get it through my thick skull that the ability to work at something, to produce something, is the greatest happiness and gift available to me.

Needless to say, it was a lesson that took me a while to learn. I'd whine and complain and be rude to my grandpa, but he was amazingly patient with me. He'd say, "Okay, Christian, we're going to go fishing, but first we've got to rip up this tree stump." And since I wanted to go fishing, I'd agree. Fishing didn't happen, however, since it was dark by the time we hauled that stump out, eight hours later. As difficult as it was, I believe with all my heart that those years with my grandparents saved me. It was there I learned, for the first time ever, that being productive boosted my resilience.

My grandfather's philosophy was reflected in these words from Teddy Roosevelt: "Far and away the best prize life has to offer is the chance to work hard at work worth doing." I also love the words of advice from a judge who frequently dealt with youth offenders in the 1950s: "Hang the storm windows, paint the woodwork . . . Visit the sick, assist the poor, study your lessons. And then when you are through . . . read a book. The world does not owe you a living . . . you owe the world something. You owe it your time and your energy and your talents."[52] Although aimed at youth, these wise words are applicable to all of us.

One of the best ways I know of to increase my resilience is to get and stay productive. The opposite of this is what I call a stagnant state. Being stagnant is a resilience killer. When I'm bored, apathetic, focus on what's wrong, or am highly judgmental, I am more susceptible to negativity. I'm worried about what other people are doing, I'm more insecure, and I'm definitely less resilient.

> One of the best ways I know of to increase my resilience is to get and stay productive.

Being highly engaged in activities that aren't hurtful to yourself or others working hard, producing something—is what I have dubbed "production therapy." I use the word *therapy* because I believe productivity creates healing. It works because it's impossible to be productive and stagnant at the same time. When we allow ourselves to be stagnant, we become like a car that sits unused in the driveway—slowly disintegrating as it rusts and erodes. But if we work, if we produce, we banish stagnation. We polish our strongest attributes, attract resources, and become more resilient.

In a production state, we're contributors rather than consumers. When I was doing therapy with clients, I always told them that the best way to find long-term happiness was to work hard at something. It doesn't have to necessarily be work as in a job. It could be working at a relationship, or being artistic and creating something, or overcoming a personal obstacle—essentially, *anything that produces something positive*.

When you're producing, you have a sense of accomplishment. You also experience what Dr. Csikszentmihalyi calls "flow"—the feeling of being "in the zone."[53] You feel relief from anxiety, depression, and negativity; you enjoy yourself more; others are more likely to want to be around you; and you often learn something new. All of this adds up to more resources and more long-term resilience.

ASK

What is an activity you enjoy doing that creates a feeling of "flow," or being "in the zone"? On the flip side, is there a task you've been avoiding because it seems overwhelming or tedious? On an average day, how much time are you spending engaged in productive tasks or activities? What may be keeping you from being more productive and less stagnant?

TASK

Give yourself some production therapy. Start by replacing one stagnant habit with one productive activity today. *Production* therapy means we produce something of value. It could be sharing something new with a child, temporarily inconveniencing ourselves by meeting another's needs, or making something in a physical or creative sense.

DON'T ACCEPT NO

RESOURCE RESILIENCE BOOSTER #7

I have a "secret sauce," and I'm giving out the recipe! This is what has made all the difference for me throughout my life. Are you ready for it? Here it is: *I don't accept the word* no. If I accepted no as an absolute answer, you would not be reading this book right now. I love the word *no*, because it has been my fuel to succeed countless times in my life. Being told no is usually the motivation I need to become even more resilient.

You might recall that during high school I was told that I couldn't go to college—that I shouldn't even bother taking the SAT. Then, in college, only a few classes away from graduating, a professor told me that the institution's PhDs would be worth less if someone like me, with severe learning differences, could graduate. As hard as that was to hear, that was just the fuel I needed to make sure I got that diploma.

After I finished graduate school I was told someone like me would never make it in the business world. I was told I'd never be able to write a book. "No, you can't" are words I've heard over and over, and they are some of the most frustrating and painful words I've ever heard. But they are also three of the most motivational words.

Each time you get a no, potential resources are being pulled away from you. But when you stand up to the word *no*, more resources show up. Thus, when you fight past a no and get a yes, you're giving yourself the resilience edge.

The new field of workforce sciences has yielded startling findings that support my "don't accept no" approach—particularly research by Kenexa, a recruiting, hiring, and training company recently purchased by IBM. Tim Geisert, Kenexa's chief marketing officer, observed that an outgoing personality is often assumed to be the defining trait of successful salespeople. But the company's research, based on millions of worker surveys and manager assessments, has found that the most important characteristic for sales success is emotional courage and the persistence to keep going even after initially being told no. That is exactly the kind of person I attempt to hire in my company. I want a resilient team that can handle rejection and that doesn't easily accept the word *no*.

Understanding the reasons people tell you no can help you turn a no into a yes. For one, their negativity might not be personal. The naysayer may have an agenda that doesn't even involve you; perhaps they're just trying to show their power and importance. At other times, people may say no because they're trying to protect you. Parents often fit into this category, but even well-intentioned parents aren't always right. Here are some other common reasons someone may tell you no:

- Some people are paid to tell you no. These people can be some of the easiest to convert into a yes because there is no passion or conviction behind their no.
- Saying no might make them feel superior or one-up.
- Often people say no because saying yes will cause them to have to work harder to help you.
- It may simply be a habit for someone to say no first.
- If someone feels threatened or fears you, they will likely tell you no.

- They may say no as a way to screen your level of interest. They may want to see how badly you want it.
- People often say no because there is no glory or payback for them.
- Sometimes people say no because they aren't as knowledgeable on the subject as you are, so saying no quickly saves face.
- They had a bad day. So they say no.
- A very common reason for no is that they don't know you or trust you. No is also the response if they don't feel you care about them personally.
- They may say no if they feel you don't understand their perspective and situation.
- And, every once in a while, people will tell you no just to hurt you.

HOW TO TURN A NO INTO A YES

When I am working hard to turn a no into a yes in order to access resources, it is my job to understand the reason I'm being told no. There *are* times when no means no, and you have to use common sense. The goal isn't to create enemies or burn bridges, so pick the battles worth fighting. Nevertheless, the most resilient and effective leaders in the world know how to communicate and negotiate to get around no. *The ability to hear no and walk away and not argue is also a trait of the resilient.*

It's interesting that the people who have told me no over and over again have over time become some of my greatest friends and advocates. Once someone tells you no and you persist, one of two things happens. They might detest you and not want anything to do with you, or your persistence and dedication sends a message that you are committed and that their investment in yes is worth it. In return, they get behind you and open many, many resources for you.

One of my favorite stories of not accepting no is when Steve Jobs, as a stinky, long-haired college dropout (literally stinky—at the time he didn't believe in regular use of deodorant or showers) didn't accept no. After seeing an ad for a job in 1974 at video game manufacturer Atari, Jobs walked into their headquarters and stated he wouldn't leave until they gave him a job. Luckily for him, Atari's founder and chief engineer were unique visionaries who appreciated his passion and, instead of calling the police, brought him in. He became one of the first fifty employees at Atari, working alongside engineers and technicians and earning not only five dollars an hour but also a fantastic hands-on education that contributed to his career. This experience had lasting impact on Jobs and helped determine the kind of entrepreneur he would be.[54]

With that in mind, let's look at four tips for transforming a yes into a no.

1. **Always remember, people feel better inside when they say yes.** If I'm able to turn another person's no into a yes, it doesn't just help me—I'll help make their day better, too, because people like saying yes. When someone tells you no, sometimes it just means you didn't lower their anxiety enough to say yes. This is easiest to do face-to-face, so you can look them in the eye as you politely and sensitively educate them on why they should say yes. If you want resources, whether it's someone's time, an investment in you, or an opportunity, you need to show people through your hard work and integrity that you deserve support and a yes. Earn it. Ask them what would turn their no into a yes. Or, after they say no, be respectful, but act as if you didn't hear the no. Give them options if possible.

2. **Reevaluate whether you need their yes to proceed.** A single no isn't always an impassable roadblock, especially when you're dealing with a system or an organization. If one person says no, you can usually find someone else to say yes, though you may have to ask for the manager or insist to speak with the decision maker. I have to do this all the time with the airlines. I don't look like the typical million-mile flyer. There's a look.

I fly . . . well, let's just say I fly incognito. And this means that the agent behind the counter tells me no more often. When I get that no, I simply ask to speak with someone who is empowered to tell me yes—much more effective than arguing with the original person.

3. **Use humor whenever possible.** Humor is one of the greatest tools for getting a yes. Be careful with this one, though—trying to be too funny crosses the line and cements a no. But combining a bit of humor with humility can relax the other person and work in your favor. I do this all the time with rental-car companies when I'm trying to get a better rate. I'll say, "I know you're telling me no. And I know you have every reason to tell me no. But if you could find it in the deepest cells of your heart to let me get that other rental car, it would make my stay in your lovely city so much easier. I live on the road, ma'am. You can see how often I rent cars. I know I'm making your job harder, and you've probably had a long day, but I'd be so grateful for whatever you can do." I'm constantly negotiating things like that. I do it with a smile, and usually both the employee and I leave happier for the result. I try to show them that I know they are sacrificing the world to tell me yes, even if it's a small thing they're doing for me. Everybody wants to feel good about themselves, and if you use humor, you have a better chance of getting a yes even as you make them feel special for giving it to you.

4. **Make sure your mission and motives are truly in the best interests of others.** Selfishness creates nos, and service creates yeses. If your cause is noble enough, and especially if it benefits children or the elderly or anyone who is discriminated against, pull out all the stops. If I'm trying to help someone else and people see me as weak or desperate when I don't accept no, it doesn't really matter much. If I know I've picked a battle that's worth the yes—because it's for the good of others, not just me—I'll do whatever it takes. Be brave! When the "why" is strong enough, the "what" doesn't matter. Your perseverance and dedication may even inspire the person who gave you the no.

STUNNED AS I TOOK THE STAGE

Last year I was asked to speak to a large group of school counselors and school social workers. A few minutes before I was to go on stage, the director of the event turned to me and said, "I don't think you should be here."

Thinking that perhaps I'd misheard her, I stammered, "What?"

"You shouldn't be here," she continued. "You make too much money."

I was completely dumbfounded. Her words shocked me. Feeling completely awful, I thought I was letting down the organization that had asked me there to speak. After a long pause, I stammered, "Well, I can see how it would look that way. But you need to know I don't pocket this fee. It goes to my company. There are a lot of costs involved in doing what we do."

Unswayed and still obviously angry, she didn't let up: "We're paying you an exorbitant amount of money."

"So, you don't think what I'm going to do up there for the next hour is worth what you're paying me?" It was apparent she had wanted a different keynote speaker—somebody cheaper—but her colleagues had picked me.

"Absolutely not." She was furious.

I was now sweaty with anxiety and very shaken by her attack, but I continued to try to win her over. "I can understand that it seems like a lot of money—this is a room full of educators who don't make a lot. But here's a question for you. . . ." I tried to give her some perspective. "How many kids do you work with?"

"About a hundred and thirty."

"Ma'am, with all due respect, I work with over a million. For me to reach a million kids, it costs a lot of money. It takes a team of people helping me, plus the cost of producing materials, and travel expenses, as I live on the road. I'll happily show you my tax return, because hardly any of what you're going to pay me goes into my pocket. Sometimes I don't see any of it."

She continued to glare at me, her arms folded defensively.

This was a moment of truth for me. It was almost my turn to address the audience. And here she was telling me I wasn't good enough, that I shouldn't be there. I had to decide right then, in that instant, whether I would accept her no. I could've said to myself, *She's right. I don't deserve to even be here, let alone charge a fee.* I could've turned her words into a self-fulfilling prophecy, believed her criticism, and bombed my speech. I had to decide right then. So I took a deep breath and said, "Listen, I'll tell you what. When I'm done speaking, you can pay me what you think I'm worth. It can be the amount you hired me for, or you can pay me five dollars. It's up to you." I then walked on the stage and gave that speech absolutely everything I had. I went completely on offense. Instead of allowing her attack to make me doubt my worthiness to be there, I took action. I looked fear in the eye and tried my best to turn her no into a yes. I gave one of the best speeches I've ever given because of her confrontation. I used her challenge as the fuel to access every resource I could muster.

After I finished speaking I walked over to her. Now there was only a sly smile on her face. "Oh, you are *good,*" she said. "You were talking to me up there, weren't you?" she asked, referring to key parts of my speech that, I'll admit, I had hoped she would hear and understand. When she paid me the original amount we had agreed upon, I told her it would be used to help a lot of people.

Like the story I shared about selling art door to door, this isn't one I tell very often; in fact, I wasn't sure I wanted to include it in this book. Even though it ended well, it remains an emotional memory for me and isn't something I like to dwell on. I share it because it helped me learn a lesson that has influenced me every day since. When someone tells you no, it can be a self-fulfilling prophecy if you let it deflate and depress you. Unfortunately there are always going to be haters out there. There will always be someone who is anxious to block your path. Use it as your fuel! Let it motivate you to go on offense, take action, and refuse to accept no. Let it propel you toward maximizing your full potential as you acquire and build your resources and your ability to be resilient.

THE MAN WHO DOESN'T ACCEPT NO

In the early days of my company, I was commonly introduced as a keynote speaker like this: "I was sitting at my desk at four thirty in the afternoon, exhausted, and ready to go home. I got a phone call from the person who is about to speak to us. His name is Christian Moore. I started speaking with Mr. Moore at four thirty. At seven thirty, after multiple texts from my husband and kids, I was still on the phone with Mr. Moore. We had fifty other people who were more qualified to be the keynote speaker at this conference, but because this gentleman was willing to sit on the phone with me for three hours and explain why his message today is so important, I really believe he can impact our organization. That's why I'd like to introduce Mr. Moore, the man who does not accept no."

It's happened dozens of times. When I first started speaking as a consultant, I leapfrogged over hundreds of other more experienced and well-known speakers because of hours spent on the phone, working to turn a no into a yes. And these people who initially told me no have become my best friends. They've had me back to the conference several years in a row. I've been to their homes for dinner, and they'll introduce me to their family by saying, "Remember when I didn't come home till seven thirty at night because I was on the phone with that crazy guy? This is him!"

If you were to ask me how I have accessed resources throughout my life, I would say it's because I don't accept no. This is why I'm resilient.

> If you were to ask me how I have accessed resources throughout my life, I would say it's because I don't accept no. This is why I'm resilient.

ASK

What was your response the last time you were told no? Looking back at the list of common reasons people say no, which one do you think may apply most to your situation? What could you have done or said differently to get a yes?

TASK

The next time you're told no and decide it's worth the effort to turn the no into a yes, make a sincere attempt to understand the reason behind the no. Using the four tips for turning a no into a yes, see if you can turn the situation around.

RESOURCE RESILIENCE FUEL

Circle all the emotions and mindsets that you are currently experiencing. The more emotions and mindsets you circle, the greater your capacity to access Resource Resilience. Just harness the energy from these emotions into resilience.

- Productive
- Fighting feelings of entitlement
- Unworthy
- Desiring to learn
- Useful
- Confident in my abilities
- Appreciated
- Deficient
- Hopeful/ optimistic
- Able to influence the future

- "You don't know me yet" ("Wait and see what I can do")
- Plugged in to other resources (others' skills, opportunities)
- Bettering myself
- Reaching out to gain access
- Gratitude
- "I can fix it!"
- Humility
- Willing to ask for help

- Self-efficacious
- Wanted
- "I have gifts"
- Desiring to accomplish/ achieve
- Being of service to others
- Worthy
- Giving back
- "My effort leads to opportunity and unforeseen options"
- Desiring to make a difference

PART V

ROCK BOTTOM RESILIENCE

Accessing hope when hope seems lost

WHAT IS ROCK BOTTOM
RESILIENCE?

Back when I was a social worker, I had a client who slept on the grass in front of my office. When it was time for his appointment, he would stand up, brush the grass off, and come inside. This guy literally had nothing. His life was a complete mess. He had no reason to keep getting up each day, yet he did. He was at total rock bottom, but he continued to meet with me in an effort to get out. Watching him brush the grass from his front-yard bed off of his wrinkled and dirty clothes, it hit me that I could help my clients more if I could teach them the value of resilience by studying the lives of people like him—people who, given the reality of their current resources, were at an extreme disadvantage, yet somehow found the resilience to keep going. It was a huge breakthrough: I could learn a ton about resilience from people who were in the worst of situations. Studying a guy who walks around picking up bottles all day for a few dollars and then goes to sleep underneath a bridge at night could be just as effective—or more so—than studying millionaire motivational speakers. That millionaire has resources and support systems that help him be resilient. But the guy who, day after day, picks up bottles for a few bucks? Now that's resilience, when you look at the reality of his situation.

What I find impressive is the guy who has none of the support that many successful people do, who finds himself at a low point in his life, and yet finds it in him to get up every day and collect bottles, or just fights the fight by putting one foot in front of the other. What about the people who fight the fight through addictions, without friends or family, who are homeless? What impresses me is the single mom living out of her car, trying to provide for her three kids. If you want to understand resilience, I would recommend studying those peoples' lives.

After I had this breakthrough, I started to really pay attention. And I noticed something interesting. Everyone has a personal rock bottom. In spite of where you are right now, it is inevitable that we all, sometime in our lives, will experience this. We all crash. It's part of the human condition.

{ **Everyone has a personal rock bottom.** }

When we hear "rock bottom," we often think of the drug addict or the homeless person—someone whose circumstances feel far away from our own. As a social worker, I thought I was going to spend my career working with these people, people who obviously needed help. But one of the most fascinating things in my career is that I haven't spent most of my time with drug addicts, homeless people, or criminals. I've spent most of my time working with highly successful people who hit their own personal rock bottom. This included local business leaders, church and civic leaders, PTA presidents, and stay-at-home moms. Their rock bottom might be a divorce, a failed business, or a closeted addiction. Or perhaps their rock bottom is the fact that they live in a $2.5 million home and covet their neighbor's $4 million home and feel like a failure. These are people you'd look at and think they have it all. These people are players in the community. But they've all had times when they hit rock bottom.

Let me explain what I mean when I say "rock bottom." To me, rock bottom is when you feel you don't have the motivation to continue to try or go on in life. You lose the desire to fight on or to put effort into daily challenges and tasks. Rock bottom is twofold: It can be when you hit absolute rock bottom, the very lowest point in your life. I call this actual rock bottom. But it can also be what I refer to as "emotional rock bottom"—those times when you're simply burned out, exhausted, and overwhelmed, or even in mental-shutdown mode. You lack any joy in life. You're just going through the motions. You're numb to the world.

> **ACTUAL ROCK BOTTOM:** You've hit the lowest point in your life and feel hopeless about your future.

> **EMOTIONAL ROCK BOTTOM:** It's all you can do to just go through the motions to get through the day. You're simply trying to survive, and it's not a good place to be. I also call this dead man walking. The opposite of emotional rock bottom would be complete engagement in life.

Emotional rock bottom isn't necessarily the single, defining lowest point of your life so far. It might occur hourly, daily, weekly, monthly, or yearly. And you can hit emotional rock bottom in one area of your life when whole other areas are thriving. Your business may be doing great, but you and your teenage son aren't speaking. Or maybe you've put on a lot of weight as you've become so busy and it's impacting your health, even though other areas of your life are fine. Or maybe it's something completely out of your control, such as your spouse being diagnosed with cancer, and it's thrown your otherwise fairly stable world into complete upheaval. When any area of your life—physical, mental, social/emotional, or spiritual (any connection to a higher power)—falls into disarray or spins out of control, you can be thrust into rock-bottom moments. It's important not to judge others while they're in their own personal pain and dealing with their own rock-bottom situations. It happens to everyone, even your seemingly perfect neighbor. (You know the one—you grit your teeth and smile and wave every time he's outside watering his flawless lawn.)

One of the greatest rushes in life is when we learn how to handle or overcome the obstacles that led us to rock bottom. In fact, rock-bottom moments are powerful resilience sources, just like the three others we've looked at so far (relationships, "street" emotions, and resources). Because these times are so difficult, they're also particularly powerful as fuel.

Whether you're at the actual worst moment in your life or are simply bottoming out in one aspect of it, you can learn to access **Rock Bottom Resilience**—the ability to Flip the Switch when you're at your lowest point. Rock Bottom Resilience allows you to believe in your ability to change your circumstances, combat hopelessness, and fight on. It helps you believe in potential unforeseen options even during your most difficult times. And it makes you increasingly aware that losing in the past does not equal losing in the future.

WE ARE ALL ALWAYS TWO STEPS AWAY FROM ROCK BOTTOM

Some of you might be reading this and think, *This source of resilience doesn't apply to me. I've never been at rock bottom!* or *Everything is going pretty good for me right now—rock bottom seems pretty far away.* If that's where you're at in your life at this moment, I am happy for you. I hope your life continues on just as it is for a long time. I've also lived enough life to know that even if all is well for you at this moment, you're probably close to someone who has been or currently is at rock bottom. And life is full of curveballs. You never know what's around the corner. Life doesn't tend to remain easy or stable or predictable for very long.

Consider the following cases:

- You come home from work to your husband, a school psychologist at the local elementary school, who seems really, really down. You find out that he has just been transferred to a school in a depressed area of town, and instead of having a nice, sunny office, he will now work with students in a dark, converted broom closet in the middle of a crowded hallway. Although he knows he is lucky to still have a job during a tough economy, he just can't shake his despondency at leaving a good situation and colleagues he has worked with for years, as well as his complete lack of control or even input on the decision to move him.

- You are a passionate and committed musician and spend your whole life dedicated to your music. You know you're talented and have real potential, yet now, in your midthirties, after years and years of trying, you haven't caught a break. You're still playing small local gigs and aren't able to support yourself. You worry about your future and feel helpless as you become more and more depressed, unable to let go of your dreams that refuse to come to fruition.

- You're the parent of a teenage girl who by nature is fun loving and cheerful. As her senior year approaches, she starts to become withdrawn and moody, coming home past curfew without explanation and lashing out when you confront her about it. When she gets caught stealing prescription painkillers from a neighbor's house, your suspicions are confirmed. You insist on finding a rehabilitation service to help her fight her addiction, but your daughter responds violently, screaming that she doesn't have a problem and refusing to get help.

- You are a hardworking, extremely active person who felt a sudden and intense pain while running last week. The doctor tells you your back needs emergency surgery. Recovery is painful and lengthy—it is weeks before you can walk again and months before you can be active at all. You are on strong pain meds that make you nauseated, you aren't able to work, and worst of all, you are stuck indoors and dependent on others for your care. The days are long and you don't know how you're going to make it without losing your mind.

- You're stuck in a job you don't enjoy. Your boss is controlling and unfair and seems to criticize everything you do. Just mustering up the energy to go to work is draining, and you dread having to deal with him day in and day out. The work-week is painfully long and every day it's the same old grind. You continually search for new jobs and frequently send out resumes, but given the tight job market there isn't much available. There doesn't appear to be any way out.

These people all come from different environments and varied circumstances. But what they all have in common is that they found themselves somewhere they didn't want or expect to be. Anyone, no matter their circumstances, can find themselves at rock bottom.

When I'm working with a homeless person or a convict, if I really take a good look at that person, I know they're no different from me. We are the same. We are human beings battling to make it. Sometimes people think that the world of rock bottom is a thousand miles away from them. Truth is, rock bottom is always only about two steps away. There's no security in this world. Security is a lie, a delusion. Absolutely everything can be temporary. But believe it or not, there are benefits to this two-steps-away existence. If rock bottom feels far away from me, it is easier to be less human. Knowing that everything in this world is temporary, and that rock-bottom moments are inevitable, can increase your compassion and your patience. Your desire to share and connect in real ways with others can increase. The reality is, no matter how close or far away you feel from rock bottom, we're all closer than we realize. Anybody can lose financial security. Anyone can get cancer. Anyone can lose their job. Anyone can be ripped off. The advantage of knowing that we are mere steps away from rock bottom is that it helps us put our problems into perspective. This quote from Dr. Theodore Rubin, a renowned psychiatrist, helps do that for me: "The problem is not that there are problems. The problem is expecting otherwise, and thinking that having problems is a problem."[55]

> The problem is not that there are problems. The problem is expecting otherwise, and thinking that having problems is a problem.
> —Dr. Theodore Rubin

Uncontrollable external events aren't the only way to hit rock bottom, either. Planted in all of us are addictive tendencies that can lead us to places of despair. Obviously, some are more prone to addiction than others, but Dr. Gabor Maté, a physician and author who has dedicated his life to caring for hardcore drug addicts, believes that "there is one addiction process, whether it is manifested in the lethal substance dependencies of my Downtown Eastside patients; the frantic self-soothing of overeaters or shopaholics; the obsessions of gamblers, sexaholics, and compulsive Internet users; or the socially acceptable and even admired behaviors of the workaholic." In other words, we all struggle in similar ways, not just "those people," not just alcoholics, not just drug addicts.

The title of Maté's book, *In the Realm of Hungry Ghosts*, references a phrase used in Buddhist psychology, one that describes the impulses in all of us that can lead to rock bottom. "In the hungry ghost realm," writes Maté, "the creatures in it are depicted as people with large empty bellies, small mouths, and scrawny, thin necks. They can never get enough satisfaction. They can never fill their bellies. They're always hungry, always empty, always seeking it from the outside. . . . Most of us are in that realm some of the time. And my point really is, there's no clear distinction between the identified addict and the rest of us. There's just a continuum in which we all may be found."[56]

Because addiction of any sort can eventually drive a person to rock bottom, I feel like it deserves a special emphasis. "Addictions," says Maté, "even as they resemble normal human yearnings, are more about desire than attainment. In the addicted mode, the emotional charge is in the pursuit and the *acquisition* of the desired object, not in the possession and enjoyment of it."[57] This is a good explanation for why the ghosts are always hungry—it is a constant state of craving. As Dr. Vincent Felitti said, "It's hard to get enough of something that almost works."[58]

"A sense of deficient emptiness pervades our entire culture," explains Maté. While he is writing about addicts, he connects this void to all of us engaged in the universal dilemmas brought about by our experiencing the human condition. He continues: "The rest of us find other ways of suppressing our fear of emptiness or of distracting ourselves from it. When we have nothing to occupy our minds, bad memories, troubling anxieties, unease, or the nagging mental stupor we call boredom can arise." Maté goes on to point out that those of us who soothe our anxieties, fears, and discontents in other, more socially acceptable ways like workaholism are also responding to this "terror of the void."[59] Addiction is always a poor substitute for love and tends to flourish when there is a lack of human connection. To understand how to reconnect, revisit "Part II: Relational Resilience" in this book.

> Addiction is always a poor substitute for love.

Because it is so important for those struggling with addiction to get a handle on this behavior in order to escape rock bottom, we have to be able to distinguish between a passion and an addiction. To help yourself determine if your behavior is healthy, or edging into something unhealthy or harmful, ask yourself the following questions:

- Who is in charge, me or my behavior?
- Do I continue to engage in the behavior even though I know it harms myself or others?

- If any harm is caused, am I willing to stop? Am I able to stop?
- Are you closer to those you love after you engage in the behavior, or do you feel more isolated?

If your answers to any of these questions trouble you, I hope you are willing to seek help and get back to a healthy place. If you're struggling with an addiction, or fear you might be slipping into one, I urge you to take the steps necessary to begin your recovery process.

> There is honor in pressing through even the worst of circumstances.

THE UPSIDE OF ROCK BOTTOM

When things are going along smoothly, I don't tend to reflect or have deep thoughts about my life. It's the times that are challenging, when life throws obstacles at me that I have to figure out how to overcome, that define me. These are the times that have made me who I am and continue to shape me. These are the times that, as human beings, we celebrate, the ones that Hollywood makes movies about. Those are the things they'll talk about at my funeral. We all want the "smooth sailing" times, but an easy life can create complacency, selfishness, laziness, and a lack of compassion. Overcoming obstacles creates strength, hope, dignity, and self-respect, and that's what Rock Bottom Resilience is all about.

I feel so strongly about this that I'm going to repeat something I said in the introduction: This book isn't about success. It's about resilience. And resilience is being able to endure pain. It's being relentless in the face of adversity. It's facing our trials head-on, even if this means simply mustering the strength to get up today. There is honor in pressing through even the worst of circumstances.

When you have Rock Bottom Resilience, you're able to reframe your worst problems and situations, seeing them not as insurmountable setbacks but as the best kind of fuel. If we are able to reframe how we see things—shift our point of view, interpret something differently—our challenges can become fuel and we can respond more resiliently. There are limitless opportunities to practice reframing.

One of my mentors is Dr. Mark Katz, a clinical and consulting psychologist whom I referenced in the Relational Resilience section. He has spent years working with people who've learned to be resilient in the face of childhood adversities. Katz quotes Dr. Steven J. Wolin, a professor of psychiatry, and Sybil Wolin, a developmental psychologist, who discuss reframing: "While you cannot change the past, you can change the way you understand it. . . . You can frame your story around themes of your resilience or themes of your damage. You can find reasons to be proud in some of your worst memories, or you can let yourself be overwhelmed by the harm of it all. . . . Anybody can be a reframer. It's not something that only happens in therapy. The promise of sympathy that comes with a victim's status is enticing bait. But if you take it, you will be helplessly hooked to your pain."[60]

If we are able to reframe how we see things when we're at a rock bottom—if we can shift our point of view, interpret something differently—our challenges can become fuel and we can respond more resiliently.

POSTTRAUMATIC GROWTH?

There is such a thing as posttraumatic growth. We don't hear about it much. We usually hear about post-traumatic stress disorder, which is very real. But it's unfortunate that we hear so much more about the possible negative side effects of experiencing trauma, when in actuality, there can be positive outcomes to stressful events. Dr. Richard Tedeschi, a psychology professor at the University of North Carolina, coined the term posttraumatic growth (PTG) and says in his book, *Posttraumatic Growth*,

"Although there is still much to be learned about recoveries from trauma, we seek to explore the experiences of people who not only bounce back from trauma, but use it as a springboard to further individual development or growth."[61] To me, this is a very hopeful idea, that trauma can produce personal growth, and I consider PTG to be synonymous with Rock Bottom Resilience.

This means that experiencing rock bottom can make us more resilient in the future! Even NASA agrees. Dr. Carol Dweck, whom I introduced in the beginning of this book, described how NASA screens potential astronauts. "They rejected people with pure histories of success and instead selected people who had had significant failures and bounced back from them."[62] They knew survivors of this sort were the kind of people they wished to hire. I love this! And this is only one of many examples. There are so many paths to rock bottom. Some of them are trails we forge on our own, recklessly exploring in treacherous territory, but many are places in which we suddenly find ourselves due to circumstances far beyond our control. Nobody wants to hit rock bottom. No one wishes for life events that completely knock the wind out of them. But rock-bottom experiences are sources of resilience that can strengthen us. We can feel stronger, more empowered, less fearful, have more self-respect and dignity and more purpose in our lives after we've overcome something really hard. We can feel closer to our friends and family and understand ourselves better after we've had to figure out how to climb our way out of rock-bottom circumstances. As hard as it can sometimes be, it provides a tremendous source of resilience.

ASK

What's helped you combat hopelessness and fight on during times when you've felt you're at rock bottom? Are there any areas of your life where hope currently seems lost? Is this situation in or out of your control? How can the strategies you used in the past help you again?

TASK

Make a list of the ways in which your challenge could be transformed into something positive. This can be difficult, so don't be afraid to really think outside the box. Use your list to initiate action and regain hope, believing that positive, productive, unforeseen options will show up as you fight your way out of your personal rock bottom. Try to avoid the temptation to shut down. Moving forward just by showing up gives hope and the possibility that better days lie ahead.

ROCK BOTTOM
RESILIENCE BOOSTERS

The following Rock Bottom Resilience boosters will equip you with tools to help you be resilient and not check out of life when you hit emotional rock bottom (or actual rock bottom). Even at rock bottom, there are things we can do to increase our chances of finding hope, of discovering options and helping ourselves to get out. Whether I am struggling a little or I've had a complete down-and-out crash, utilizing even one of these boosters really helps me. Each of them is actually a way to reframe your situation and find hope, and resilience, even during rock-bottom times. The ability to have hope even during your lowest moments gives you a huge resilience edge.

RADICALLY ACCEPT
YOUR CIRCUMSTANCE
ROCK BOTTOM RESILIENCE BOOSTER #1

I know just about as well as anyone that Denial is a lovely place to live. It's great—I can swing in a hammock of no accountability and swim in a sea of no responsibility and tell myself that I'm just fine. Except that I'm not fine, and all the people around me whose lives are affected by mine aren't fine, either. And the hard truth is that I'm killing resilience if I sweep reality under the rug. Denial is a terrific way to spiral down, fast, to rock bottom—and stay there.

At age eighteen Marsha Linehan was committed to a psychiatric clinic for extreme social withdrawal. At risk for suicide, she was placed in the seclusion room, where there was nothing she could use to hurt herself, so she repeatedly banged her head, hard, on the walls and floor. It was the early 1960s, and at the time very little was understood about mental illness. Treatment practices were used that in many cases were actually harmful to the patient. The methodologies were crude, even barbaric, by today's standards. Electroshock therapy harshly administered in multiple rounds, very strong drugs, and a diagnosis of schizophrenia did not help Linehan. When she left the clinic twenty-six months later, she vowed to return and help others to get out.

Linehan is now a psychology professor at the University of Washington and founder of Behavioral Tech, LLC, an organization that trains mental-health care providers and treatment teams, but it took years before she shared the difficult personal story of her time in the clinic with anyone, doing so only after one of her patients told her that if Linehan were "like us" it would give everyone so much hope.[63] While earning her PhD, on her way to becoming a successful therapist who treats severely suicidal people, she developed the basis for a treatment program founded on acceptance of life as it is, not as we think it is supposed to be. She calls this *radical acceptance*—and it's a powerful Rock Bottom Resilience booster.

"There may be an infinite number of really painful things that can happen to you," Linehan explains. "But there are not an infinite number of responses you can make to pain. . . . Suffering, agony, are pain plus nonacceptance. Radical acceptance transforms suffering into ordinary pain."[64]

Linehan uses the word *radical* to mean "absolute." "It's when you accept something from the depths of your soul. When you accept it in your mind, in your heart, and even with your body. It's total and complete." When you've radically accepted something, you're not fighting it anymore. I love this idea, but I also know it's much easier to talk about radically accepting something than to actually radically accept it!

So let's break it down a bit. Linehan explains that there are three parts to this wholehearted embrace of reality. First, we have to accept that our reality is what it is. Think about your life. Is there a reality that you might be denying? Are there any circumstances in your life that you are not accepting for what they are?

Second, and hugely important, is to accept that the painful event or situation has a cause. Linehan explains, "Accepting that every event has a cause is the opposite of saying 'why me.'" Saying that something "should not be" is nonacceptance. There are things that cause things to be the way they are, even if the cause isn't clear to us. We may not know what the cause is, ever. But even if we don't know what it is, we have to know that there *is* a cause. We can't get hung up on constantly asking ourselves why. The universe is not out to get you, even when that's what it feels like.

The third facet of radical acceptance is accepting that life can be worth living even with painful events in it. To go from unendurable agony to endurable pain, you have to believe that you can build a life. Let me be clear, though—acceptance does not equal approval. Sometimes we think that if we radically accept something, it means we are condoning it. We think acceptance means we're being passive or we're resigned. That we're not standing up for ourselves. But that's not it at all. This third aspect is about realizing that there are positive things in your life, even in the bad times, that make it worth fighting through problems and staying resilient. (Warning: Radical acceptance doesn't mean allowing damaging or dangerous circumstances to continue. If you find yourself in one, do everything in your power to get out.)

So here's the deal—if you want to change something, you have to accept it first. Denial or anger or resistance won't effect any sort of change. It'll actually make you physically sick and tense. Acceptance followed by action is how you make effective changes in your life.

Alcoholics Anonymous has known this since its inception in the 1930s. You've probably heard of the Serenity Prayer, recited at the close of each meeting by all members: "God grant me the serenity to accept the things I cannot change; courage to change the things I can; and wisdom to know the difference." Also consider step 1 of AA: "We admitted [or radically accepted] we were powerless over our addiction—that our lives had become unmanageable."[65] AA doesn't use the same terminology, but the twelve-step program encourages its members to practice radical acceptance.

Finally, it's important to realize that we must practice radical acceptance every single day. "This is not one of those things you're going to get perfect at," says Linehan. "There's not going to be a day when you can say, 'Alright, I've got it; I can radically accept.'" She advises that in the beginning, when accepting is still really hard, to find small things on which to practice first. Then, every day, we have to consciously remind ourselves to practice accepting our circumstances.

Radical acceptance when you're at rock bottom can be tough. Really tough. It's super tempting to want to escape reality, and the more intense the pain, the harder it is to accept, the more tempting it is to seek relief in actions or substances that, while offering temporary comfort, ultimately increase the pain. But acceptance is the first step toward change and resilience; it's the first foothold in your climb out of rock bottom.

ASK

Do you have a tendency to ask *Why me?* or *How could this happen?* when confronted with painful or difficult circumstances?

TASK

In the next week, work on breaking free of denial and accepting the reality of your situation. Abandon the "why me?" philosophy. Accept the truth that your suffering has a cause, even though it may not be obvious. Adopt the belief that in spite of the circumstance you're facing, life can be worth living—unendurable agony can be converted to endurable pain, and a meaningful, satisfying life can result. This is a big assignment, so start by radically accepting small things in your life. Put a note on your mirror or on another prominent place that says "Radically accept!" so you remember to practice this principle on a daily basis.

DON'T MAKE THINGS WORSE
ROCK BOTTOM RESILIENCE BOOSTER #2

Years ago, in an AA meeting that my friend attended, a man recounted a brief but powerful story. "Growing up, things in my house were bad," he said. "My mom was an alcoholic, my dad was often out of work, and I had a handicapped brother. I was struggling with alcoholism myself and had started attending meetings. During these obviously very difficult times, my dad said, 'Son, your job is to not make things worse.'"

This idea—of not making things worse—stayed with me. So many times our reaction to an adverse situation makes that situation bigger and harder. When your life goes terribly wrong, or even slightly awry, it's your reaction that counts. So if you want to be resilient, even at rock bottom, your first job is damage control—making sure you don't get into the crisis any deeper.

Say you've learned that your spouse cheated on you. You're devastated and feel utterly betrayed—an emotional rock bottom for sure. What you do now matters greatly. Will you allow yourself to become enraged, to threaten aggressive acts? Will you give in to the temptation to call your spouse out on social media? If you did, many would certainly understand your reaction, but you'd only make a bad situation worse, perhaps even jeopardizing any chance of healing the relationship. Far better an option is to take the pain of betrayal and use it as fuel to start making things better. When emotions are on edge and maybe even boiling over, if you can engage in damage control, you can prevent a terrible situation from getting worse and give healing a chance to begin.

DON'T BUY A DAMMIT DOLL

Ever heard of a Dammit Doll? This stuffed little fellow can be "thrown, jabbed, stomped, and even strangled till all the frustration leaves you." A little poem comes with the Dammit Doll:

> When you want to kick the desk or throw the phone and shout
> Here's a little dammit doll you cannot do without.
> Just grasp it firmly by the legs, and find a place to slam it.
> And as you whack its stuffing out, yell, "dammit, dammit, dammit!"

Sounds like a good idea, right? I mean, we've been taught for years about the catharsis of venting our anger in "safe" ways and not letting it fester, about how expressing anger gets rid of anger, and about how we'll feel better if we let it out. So wouldn't it be a good idea to let loose with our frustration when we're at rock bottom? Well, the problem is that research disproves this idea. In the book *Mistakes Were Made (But Not by Me)* authors Carol Tavris and Elliot Aronson explain the findings. "When people vent their feelings aggressively they often feel worse, pump up their blood pressure, and make themselves even angrier."[66] In other words, venting backfires.

Venting can be even more harmful if it involves an aggressive act toward another. Once this happens, a powerful new factor is involved— our need to justify the aggressive act. We try to convince ourselves that the recipient of our actions was truly deserving of them. This justification is preparation for more aggression, and so the cycle begins.

The experiments that prove venting to be unhealthy shocked the scientific community, who expected opposite results. But it's true: Using a Dammit Doll turns out to be a misguided attempt at damage control. In our effort to cope with the damage, we tell ourselves that if we just take out all our negative emotions on something "safe," we'll feel better. In reality, we're just digging ourselves deeper. So before you vent—whether it be verbally by attacking someone online or physically by beating on a Dammit Doll—ask yourself, *Is this going to cause anyone, including myself, any harm?* Because, at that moment, your job is to not make the situation worse.

In the work environment, we tend to rely on email for our venting, permanently recording our negativity in cyberspace. When you send one of those dreaded angry emails in the heat of the moment, you'll probably have "email regret" later, when it's too late to take it back—and you will have lessened your chances of bouncing back from the situation. Jack Lampl, president of the A. K. Rice Institute for the Study of Social Systems, says that venting through an angry email "serves as a relief valve, but tends to inflame conflict. It takes a very corrosive role in the workplace, for gossiping and undermining others."[67] To avoid regretting an email, wait twenty-four hours until you've calmed down and then send it. You will likely be able to express yourself in a softer, less inflammatory way, which in turn will do less damage.

However, suppressing anger or pushing things under the rug isn't the healthiest tactic, either. Once we've ensured that we're not making things worse, we can get on the path to making them better by being honest and communicative. Dr. Sylvia LaFair, president of Creative Energy Options, has some effective suggestions: We should tell the truth about problems and frustrations, but keep our voices measured and calm. Use short, seven- to twelve-word sentences that state the problem and begin with "I" ("I hear what you're saying but I disagree," for example). Instead of yelling, lower your voice and speak slowly. This dials down the overall volume and emotion in the room, and allows us to initiate damage control in a difficult situation.[68]

AVOID EXTREME RELAPSE

"Extreme relapse" is another way we tend to make things worse when we're already at rock bottom; it's the complete opposite of damage control, and if you want to boost your Rock Bottom Resilience, you'll need to learn to get around it. I sometimes have extreme relapses with sugar. Every time I try to reduce or eliminate my sugar consumption (and this has happened many, many times), I do pretty well for a while. I might even last a month or two. But then, inevitably, I have a bad day. I mess up. And I feel like such a failure that I throw my hands in the air, tell myself it's no use, and go on a complete sugar binge until I am in a prediabetic coma. I undo any good I did or any progress I made over the past weeks in one single day! I relapse to the extreme.

This happens in all sorts of areas of our lives, and it kills our resilience. We have a bad day and we tell ourselves we are failures, again. We're angry at ourselves, depressed, and frustrated that we let ourselves down, again. And usually the vices we are trying to overcome but turn to in our moment of weakness are coping mechanisms. They tend to fill a need. So for a little bit it soothes us and we feel better. But the self-loathing we feel afterward is killer. It's like we've fallen in a hole, and, well, we might as well maximize being in the hole. Once I eat too much sugar, I'm mad at myself for doing it, so I eat more sugar. Everything snowballs out of control.

Most of my time as a social worker was spent trying to prevent people from having extreme relapses. This can happen with everything—in dealing with anger management, trying to control any type of addiction, or how you handle relationships, to name a few. Relapse is a normal part of the process—it's going to happen—so we have to be prepared when it does. Think of the difference: When I have a bad day (because I know I *am* going to have a bad day or two), instead of throwing all the good days away with an episode of extreme relapse, what if I just said, "Well, that was a crappy day. Good thing I can do better tomorrow," and recommit quickly and get back on the wagon? If (and when) you do relapse, it's key that you practice acceptance. Accept that it happened, accept responsibility for it, and move on.

When I recommit quickly when I mess up, there is much less time for the damage to occur. If I already know that relapses occur, and that I might mess up, but then I'm going to recommit quickly, I'll be much more resilient. The secret to this is speed. I need to recommit as quickly as possible. Then I can control the damage. Life is basically a series of recommitments, and I believe the most resilient people recommit at a faster pace than people who aren't as resilient. And that's the idea of not making things worse—to set the stage for resilience by doing no more harm as quickly as possible.

ASK

Can you think of a time when your reaction to a rock-bottom situation improved the situation rather than making it worse? (Maybe you calmly confronted the person responsible, reacted sincerely rather than aggressively, or were quick to forgive.) Is this your usual response to such situations? Can this reaction be repeated in other potentially damaging situations?

TASK

By the end of today, do two specific things to apply damage control even if no crisis exists. For example, if you find yourself having negative thoughts, commit to spending one hour when you are around others not saying or doing anything negative.

GO FOR A SMALL WIN
ROCK BOTTOM RESILIENCE BOOSTER #3

My colleagues in the mental-health industry sometimes mock the idea of "baby steps," primarily because it reminds them of the very funny film *What About Bob?* In that movie, highly dependent, multiphobic Bob Wiley gets some very quotable advice from his arrogant psychiatrist, Dr. Leo Marvin, who is pushing his book, *Baby Steps*. If you've seen the movie you'll remember the scene. Clutching his doctor's newly published book, Bob quickly latches on to the idea. "Baby steps through the office. Baby steps out the door. It works! All I have to do is take one little step at a time and I can do anything! Baby steps out of the office . . . baby steps to the hall . . . baby steps to the elevator . . . baby steps into the elevator," he says, before the doors close and you can hear him screaming throughout the building. But in spite of its presence in a zany spoof on the mental-health industry, the concept of baby steps can be invaluable in boosting Rock Bottom Resilience.

For our purposes, we'll call these baby steps "small wins." Sometimes all it takes is one of them—a tiny, seemingly insignificant victory—to create some momentum and hope. Organizational theorist Karl Weick argues for the importance of small wins in our lives. Instead of tackling a large, overwhelming problem, Weick says small wins can help to create an environment where change seems more possible and is more likely to happen. He defines small wins as a "a series of controllable opportunities of modest size that produce visible results." He also says, "By itself, one small win may seem unimportant. A series of wins at small but significant tasks, however, reveals a pattern that may attract allies, deter opponents, and lower resistance to subsequent proposals. Once a small win has been accomplished, forces are set in motion that favor another small win."[69]

As a therapist I see great value in the idea of small wins, and I've always tried to help my clients reach, recognize, and celebrate even the smallest of victories—especially when they're languishing at rock bottom. About twelve years ago I worked with Chad, a thirty-year-old man who for most of his life had been a functional person—outgoing, financially successful, married. Then, at age twenty-eight, he made a bad business decision, lost his business, and had to declare bankruptcy. After he lost everything, there was some kind of emotional break. Chad became reclusive and dysfunctional. He totally stopped trying. His wife couldn't take it and left.

When I worked with him he was living with his father in a trailer in a small town. Before his dad took him in he'd been homeless for a while. Now he just lay in bed all day. He refused to leave his room, so I had to go to the tiny trailer for our therapy sessions.

My assignment was to get this guy out of his bedroom. Chad's aging dad would sit in an old recliner in the living room and just shake his head, looking at me like, "Good luck—I've been trying to get this kid out of his room for six months." We started slow. I thought, *Well, if I can't get him out of his bed, I'll try to get him to sit up.* I told him that the past has happened— he'd lost in the past—but if he didn't walk out of his bedroom door there wouldn't be a future.

Three or four sessions later I got him to stand up (small win). It probably took me ten more visits before I could get him to stand in the doorway of his bedroom (another small win). Finally I got him to come out to the kitchen and have a Coke with me at the table. That went on for a couple of weeks. Then he progressed to the living room, and then to the front door. I think it took a month to get him to come out on the porch. Every little step of progress was a small win that we celebrated.

While we sat in the kitchen with our Cokes, I helped him set a goal. I asked, "Where's your favorite place to eat?"

Chad replied, "I used to go to Fuddruckers. I loved it—it was my favorite hamburger place." So we set a goal to sit together in Fuddruckers and eat a hamburger. It took three months, but he sat in that chair and enjoyed a burger. When I saw him flirt with the waitress, I knew we'd had a breakthrough. At that moment I grinned with satisfaction and happiness for his success.

This guy had been at rock bottom for two years, with very little to live for. But that day in Fuddruckers, we celebrated a pretty big win that came after months of small wins. After that victory I was able to help him get his own apartment and an entry-level job. Chad never went back to his father's trailer. By embracing gradual, incremental wins, he'd successfully boosted his resilience and begun his climb up from rock bottom.

SMALL WINS AT WORK

This idea of small wins is equally applicable in a business setting. In a blog post on the site of *Harvard Business Review*, titled "Hey Boss—Enough with the Big, Hairy Goals,"[70] Robert Sutton (whom we first met in "Part III: Street Resilience") explains why the idea of small wins is important at work. For years, he says, it was believed that high-performance organizations had to be made up of leaders who set ambitious goals, like the BHAGs (big, hairy, audacious goals)[71] advocated by *Good to Great* author Jim Collins. While not denying that big goals are essential to motivation, Sutton emphasizes that a really large goal does not provide daily guidance or satisfaction, and can also be too daunting, causing individuals to freeze up or freak out from the pressure of it.[72]

Sutton shares the story of a CEO who set such a goal for his organization. Not only was the goal itself seemingly unattainable, but the business was facing some dire circumstances—the corporate version of rock bottom. They had lost some key accounts and were facing large-scale layoffs. The employees were uninspired by the huge goal, and many fears were expressed that it was simply unattainable. But instead of simply repeating the goal to his employees in do-or-die mode, the CEO led a discussion of what steps it would realistically take to make it a success.

"Before long," says Sutton, "the list of 'to do's' had stretched to over 100 tasks, causing even more doubts to be vocalized. The turning point came when the CEO asked the group to sort that list into 'hard' and 'easy' tasks. When a task was declared easy, he asked who could do it and by what date. Within fifteen minutes, the group realized that they could accomplish over half the tasks in just a few days. The anxiety level dropped, and the stage was set for a succession of small wins." The result? The company ran the most successful sales campaign in its history at the height of the recession. With increased confidence and a similar small-wins strategy, the following year was even more successful.

Any person—or organization—that is facing rock bottom will likely be overwhelmed with a large number of issues. Under all that pressure, our resilience can diminish. But when we break the problem down into more manageable pieces and allow ourselves to enjoy small wins along the way, we increase our chances of fighting our way out of a bad situation.

In a separate post, "12 Things Good Bosses Believe," third on his list is "Having ambitious and well-defined goals is important, but it is useless to think about them much. My job (as boss) is to focus on the small wins that enable my people to make a little progress every day."[73] Another Sutton gem: "Devoting relentless attention to doing one good thing after another—however small—is the only path I know to becoming and remaining a great boss."[74]

I wholeheartedly agree that a boss who applies this piece of wisdom from Sutton will create a more resilient work team.

ASK

Is there a problem in your work or personal life that seems too oppressive to overcome? Would achieving a small victory lift your spirits?

TASK

Use the approach that Bob Sutton shared in his story of the CEO. Break the task down into as many smaller "to-do's" as you can think of, then sort the list into "easy" and "hard" tasks. Make a timeline for when each task will be accomplished, beginning today with the easiest.

FIX A BROKEN WINDOW

ROCK BOTTOM RESILIENCE BOOSTER #4

In the late 1970s a friend of mine visited New York City for the first time. He was fairly well traveled and had been to a number of large cities, but he still vividly remembers being shocked at the filth in the streets and gutters and the brazenness he encountered on the sidewalks. He didn't return to New York until the 1990s, and once again he was shocked, this time because of the stark difference he found. The streets weren't dirty and trashy. He wasn't approached by strangers asking him to visit any peepshows. It seemed the whole city had been cleaned up.

Downtown New York had indeed received an overhaul. The late James Q. Wilson, a social scientist who taught government at Harvard for over two decades, came up with the theory that became the cornerstone of the "quality of life" crime-reduction program used by Mayor Rudy Giuliani and his first police commissioner, William J. Bratton, in the 1990s in New York. Wilson's theory is based on a metaphor of broken windows. "When a window is broken and someone fixes it, that is a sign that disorder will be not tolerated. But one unrepaired broken window is a signal that no one cares, and so breaking more windows costs nothing," said George Kelling, a criminologist who worked with Wilson on the theory.[75]

In simple terms, the broken-windows theory means that if an environment is well kept (the broken windows are quickly repaired), it is perceived to be inviting and safe. Even the appearance of a safe and tidy neighborhood helps to eliminate crime. So Giuliani went about cleaning up New York using this approach, and as he did so, violent felonies plummeted. When Bratton left New York to become commissioner in Los Angeles, crimes decreased there as well. Although there were other factors involved, the broken-windows theory is seen as a key component in the improvements made to the quality of life both in New York and Los Angeles.

I like to apply the broken-windows theory to people when they're at rock bottom, too. If there are areas of my life that are in chaos, then I am well served to try and get them under control and in better order. We all have broken windows in our worlds—at home, in the workplace, or even within our physical self. When you have a metaphorical broken window in your life, are you quick to repair it? Or do you think, *That window doesn't matter much. I'm not going to worry about that for a while*? If you allow the disarray in your life to remain, it affects not only others' perceptions of you, but also, inevitably, how you feel about yourself. And just as with any job, the larger the mess, the more overwhelming it is to clean up. For example, let's say I have inadvertently offended someone I work with. I know they are hurt and I need to make amends, but I keep putting it off. The longer I procrastinate mending the situation, the worse it can potentially become, the more distance can grow between us, and the less likely I am to fix the other broken windows in my life.

This idea applies to organizations as well. Fast responses and fixing issues in work settings quickly can mean avoiding big, and often costly, problems at work. Look for areas of opportunity where you can be proactive and fix a small problem before it gains momentum. Also, something doesn't have to necessarily be broken to be fixed. We can look for ways to beautify and improve as well.

Quickly instituting a fix whenever something gets broken in your life heads off entropy (that fancy word for the natural progression of disorder). Maintaining is certainly much easier than gutting and redoing, but if you're at rock bottom and a complete overhaul is necessary, fixing a window is still a great place to start.

Fixing broken windows also means supporting our resilience by making sure that we keep our surroundings reasonably organized and treat our bodies with respect. If you look around and see clutter and chaos, or if you feel unhealthy and tired all the time, it's going to be harder to fight through tough situations. It's not that there's a direct, causal relationship between cleanliness, health, and resilience, but as we saw with the broken-windows theory, there is a correlation; broken windows didn't cause the crime, but fixing them seemed to help curb it. At rock bottom, it can be tempting to let everything fall into shambles, but you'll be better poised to haul yourself up if you pay attention to mending the broken windows in your life.

ASK

View yourself from the perspective of an outside observer: How do you and your physical and emotional circumstances appear to others? Place yourself in another's shoes and view yourself objectively. What about you, including your environment, could use some touching up?

What areas of your life could be in better order or more in control?

TASK

Think over the physical and emotional areas of your life that could use some repair. Stop putting off the repair process! If your problem is in your control, set aside a specific time to tackle it. If your problem has spun out of control, research ways you can get help. If it involves another person, formulate a plan to "fix a broken window" between you.

TEAR OFF LABELS
ROCK BOTTOM RESILIENCE BOOSTER #5

I've been writing this book with my colleague, Kristin McQuivey. While we were working on Rock Bottom Resilience material, I shared a story with her that really struck a nerve, as she had a son the same age as the boy in the story. I asked her to retell that story from her point of view.

I am the mother of a fourteen-year-old boy. The middle school years are tough! This year, my usually fun, happy-go-lucky son suddenly became a sullen, silent, and grouchy teenager who spends the great majority of his time in the basement playing Halo. Suddenly he is incredibly sensitive and his normal swagger has turned to insecurity. Eighth grade is a dog-eat-dog world, and I don't think anyone escapes unscathed.

When I heard Christian tell the story of another fourteen-year-old boy he had worked with as a therapist, it really affected the way I try to reach my own son. Christian had been assigned an especially tough case. This boy had been assaulting kids at school and was really angry. He was expressing suicidal thoughts and was on round-the-clock watch to keep him from hurting himself. His mother was beside herself. I can only imagine how hard it was for her to watch her struggling son do things that were ruining his life through his eighth grade year.

During one of their first meetings, Christian sat down with him and walked him through an exercise called "Tear Off Your Labels" from the WhyTry Program. He gave him a worksheet with illustrations of three soup cans. Two of the cans have negative words written on them, things like delinquent, liar, lazy, and attitude problem. He had the boy circle all the words that he thought applied to him. This boy just drew a big, fat circle around both cans and all the words.

But there's a third can on the page. The label at the top of this can says, "The Real Me." He told the boy that they were going to fill up the can with his strengths. Christian had noticed that the boy's backpack had some cool writing on it that looked like an Old English font. He thought maybe he could get the kid's attention if he wrote down the words on the can in the same way as the words on his backpack were written. So they started talking about things the boy was good at. They started out slowly (positive words are so much harder for a teenager to come up with than negative!) with things like "good skateboarder." But then they started getting somewhere—the boy loved his brother ("good brother" went on the can), and he worked hard when he wanted to ("determined"). They filled up the can with positive labels. At the end of the session, Christian noticed that the boy took the paper and carefully folded it, making sure that none of the artwork got caught in the fold.

That day, instead of coming straight home from school, the boy went to the hardware store. Then he came home and locked himself in his room. His mom kept anxiously knocking and talking to him, nervous that he was in there alone since he was supposed to be on twenty-four-hour suicide watch. But he kept yelling through the door, "I'm fine, Mom! Everything's cool." Finally, at around nine that night, he let her in. His mom burst into tears when she walked into the room. There on the wall behind his bed, he had painted a huge copy of the worksheet—the can with the title "The Real Me" and all the words in Old English font, just like Christian had drawn on the paper.

The mom called Christian the next morning. He got after her a bit for letting her son stay locked in his room like that, but then he asked her to take a picture of the wall and send it with her son for their next session. When he met with him for his counseling appointment, Christian asked him why he did it. As a mother, I was really moved by the boy's answer. "Mr. Moore," he said, "I wanted to see the real me first thing when I wake up in the morning and the real me before I go to bed at night." The answer got to Christian as well. He didn't want the boy to see him cry, so he hurried and changed the subject to football.

When the boy's mom called to check with Christian, he told her that having her son paint his bedroom wall without permission was a really, really good problem to have. That it was 'good graffiti.' This story makes me want to run downstairs with a can of paint and draw my son's strengths in big letters all over his room—words that describe the real him, not this sulky impersonator who's taken over his teenage self while he struggles to figure out his place in this precarious and often cutthroat world. That's the kind of graffiti I want to have around.

Although I don't have a teenage son yet, this is one of my favorite stories about the power of a label. We toss around labels as easily as we order a fast-food burger and fries. These labels have power. The words we hear other people say as they label us can become the words we believe and the characteristics we live up to—words like *loser, lazy, pushy, incompetent, ridiculous, controlling, perfectionist, uncooperative* . . . you know the kind of words I mean. For years I have tried to teach the youth I've worked with to break free of these labels—to tear them off and feel powerful enough to give themselves labels of their own choosing. It can be a life-changing lesson for them. And it's equally important for adults who fight society's labels, too. Living up to negative labels can be a surefire way to stay down at rock bottom, but when we learn to tear them off, we become more resilient.

DISABLED? I DON'T THINK SO

Aimee Mullins was born without fibula bones. As an infant she had to have both legs amputated below the knee and wears prosthetics in order to walk. Fortunately, she is a champion at tearing off labels. As an athlete, Aimee competed and medaled in the 1996 Paralympics. As a student, she landed a highly competitive and coveted internship at the Pentagon. And as a model, she has worked for the likes of British fashion designer Alexander McQueen. She has had to fight to tear off limiting labels her whole life. She talks about looking up the word *disabled* in her thesaurus and the shock she felt at what she found.

"Let me read you the entry," she says. "'Disabled, adjective: crippled, helpless, useless, wrecked, stalled, maimed, wounded, mangled, lame, mutilated, run-down, worn-out, weakened, impotent, castrated, paralyzed, handicapped, senile, decrepit, laid-up, done-up, done-for, done-in, cracked-up, counted-out; see also hurt, useless and weak. Antonyms: healthy, strong, capable.' I was reading this list out loud to a friend and at first was laughing, it was so ludicrous, but I'd just gotten past 'mangled' and my voice broke, and I had to stop and collect myself from the emotional shock and impact that the assault from these words unleashed."[76]

She thought that maybe her thesaurus was outdated, that perhaps a more recent printing wouldn't be so antiquated. But the updated version was equally unsettling. You might be saying to yourself, *But they're just words. Does it really matter?* Aimee argues that it does. "It's not just about the words," she explains. "It's what we believe about people when we name them with these words. It's about the values behind the words. . . . Our language affects our thinking and how we view the world and how we view other people." In fact, recent brain-imaging studies show that we feel emotional pain (the kind we feel when we hear something hurtful or feel rejection) in the same place in our brains as we feel physical pain. This means that words can hurt!

The words we have heard other people use as they label us make a difference. The words we choose to label ourselves with make an even bigger difference. Aimee Mullins made a conscious decision to not let the many labels her circumstances gave her hold her down. "By casually doing something as simple as name a person," she says, "we might be putting lids and casting shadows on their power. Wouldn't we want to open doors for them instead?"[77]

Negative labels undermine our ability to bounce back from adversity, and someone like Aimee could easily have a permanent address at rock bottom. Instead, thanks in large part to her ability to rip off the labels applied to her, she is the prosthetic-wearing embodiment of resilience.

ASK

Have you ever given yourself a negative label? What caused you to do so? Do you have an underlying belief that you should be perfect and never make mistakes? Are you aware of the potential negative effects of such a label? That you might live up (or down) to it? If you have a tendency to place negative labels on yourself, can you envision yourself making mistakes and avoiding self-condemnation?

TASK

Write down all the traits or labels others perceive in you or that you perceive in yourself. Don't just write down the negative—include positive things that others have said about you or that you see in yourself. Cross out all the labels that you don't want to live up to, and circle the ones that characterize who you really are and that you'd like others to see more of. From the moment you wake up tomorrow morning, choose one trait to radiate all day.

DISCOVER THE POWER OF A FUTURE PROMISE

ROCK BOTTOM RESILIENCE BOOSTER #6

Like most boys, I seemed to always be hungry when I was growing up. Because there were so many of us in my family, and money was really tight, we went through food really fast. I used to come home from school and open the fridge five hundred times, hoping that something would magically appear in there. I was a bear when I was hungry—fighting with my siblings, screaming at my mom, and sometimes even punching a hole in the wall.

In an effort to stave off these attacks, my mom would sneak me into the laundry room where the other kids couldn't see us before school. She would give me three or four dollars out of her little zipper purse and tell me to walk to the Dairy Queen after school for a foot-long hot dog. I don't think she was giving the other kids money like that. But she knew I was more likely to not come home angry or violent or aggravated if I wasn't so hungry.

I'd go to school and sit in class all day, frustrated, struggling academically with my learning differences, feeling stupid and socially outcast, and all I could do was think about that hot dog at Dairy Queen. It was cooked perfectly, you know, with those beautiful grill lines, and I'd smother it with mustard and onions. It was the highlight of my day, and the thought of it literally got me through so many hard times. Just the idea of something as simple as that hot dog out there somewhere in the universe gave me something to look forward to. That hot dog gave me hope.

Finding something to look forward to, something that can give you a vision or the incentive to keep going, can make all the difference during a rock-bottom time in your life. It can be something small, something as simple as a hot dog, or it can be something bigger, like a vacation you're planning. If you can identify something to look forward to—anything that doesn't harm yourself or others—you'll be more apt to find the resilience to get through your rock-bottom circumstance.

ASK

Is there a project, goal, or circumstance in your life that is proving difficult or unpleasant? What do you usually look forward to (remember, it can't hurt yourself or others) when you're trying to push through such a circumstance? Could you use this reward or future promise as motivation to be resilient?

TASK

Do whatever it takes to push through on your project, goal, or circumstance, and reward yourself once you've followed through. You earned it!

BE ILLOGICAL

ROCK BOTTOM RESILIENCE BOOSTER #7

There are times in life when things really are as bad as they seem. There are situations where there seems to be no clear way out, and all you see is dead end after dead end. When your back's against the wall and you see no hope, when you don't see any logical options, there's always one other option—the illogical one.

There are times when, as crazy as it sounds, we simply have to let go of logic. Sometimes, if we map out on paper the reality we are faced with, there is no apparent solution. There's nothing we can do to solve our problem. For example, let's say you are hopelessly in debt and have been unemployed for months. All you can find are three minimum-wage jobs, and on paper, things will never work out. You can't possibly make enough from those jobs to cover your debts and your living expenses. At a time like this, reality makes you want to give up. What's the point of going to three low-paying jobs, working night and day, if it still doesn't solve your problem?

What you don't see, what your current reality can't show you, is that if you decide to be illogical, show up, and work hard, the unforeseen happens. Options open up for you that you couldn't possibly have seen. Something pans out with one of those jobs. It gives the chance for something good to happen. It was so illogical for me to go to college. If I had been completely logical, I never would have gone. I mean, come on! How could I pass statistics with my severely limited math abilities? It just didn't make sense. But I showed up, I worked really hard, and I ran into many people who opened doors for me.

Like many of the resilience boosters we've covered so far, this one applies in the business world as well. Entrepreneurs have to be at least a little illogical. Chances are a new business isn't going to make it. Eight out of ten new businesses fail within five years. Based on this statistic alone, why would anyone try? Most people who accomplish something great, in business or anywhere else, didn't limit themselves by only thinking logically. Most people have to defy logic to pull off something great, and defying logic could be the first step to getting out of rock bottom.

It's totally illogical to think that unforeseen options will show up if you keep pushing through an otherwise hopeless situation. It requires, if you will, a leap of faith, often defined as an "act of believing in or accepting something intangible or unprovable, or without empirical evidence." That's a great definition for what is sometimes, or maybe often, necessary to get out and stay out of rock bottom.

But don't forget, after being willing to think illogically, you have to *do* something. A slogan used in Alcoholics Anonymous is "You can act yourself into right thinking, but you can't think yourself into right acting." One AAer with twenty-eight years of sobriety puts it this way: "I can alter my attitude and my mind—not necessarily by thinking, but by acting. I can diminish fear, I can diminish anxiety, I can diminish neuroses simply by taking action."[78] Now obviously, I'm not anti-thinking; of course we have to think! Without thinking, everything we did would simply be the result of an impulse. But taking action based on what might seem like illogical thinking is sometimes the first step out of a rock-bottom situation. It creates unforeseen options—and leads to resilience.

ASK

Have you ever faced a difficult reality that had no apparent solution or logical way out? How did it get resolved? Was there an element of the illogical in the resolution?

TASK

Read this statement: Unforeseen options are more likely to take place if I don't give up. In other words, the next time you're in a rock-bottom situation that doesn't seem to have a way out, take a leap of faith. Believe that your plight will improve as you put forth effort. The effort can seem illogical, but at least you're putting yourself out there, giving yourself the opportunity for the unforeseen to show up.

FORGIVE—IT'S THE ONLY OPTION
ROCK BOTTOM RESILIENCE BOOSTER #8

I couldn't possibly write a list of Rock Bottom Resilience boosters and not include forgiveness. Forgiveness is absolutely essential if you have any desire at all to get out, and stay out, of rock bottom. Conversely, if you want to hang out in rock bottom, simply weigh yourself down with the heaviness that comes with carrying grudges or holding on to bitterness and resentment. Anger and resentment are surefire ways to block your progress. Forgiveness, letting go of these things, enables you to move on with your life.

Chances are we will have frequent opportunities to practice forgiving each other. We need to realize ahead of time that due to the simple reality of the human condition, someone may hurt us or let us down today. And we have to decide in advance that when that happens, we're going to have an attitude of forgiveness. If I predetermine that when someone lets me down, whether it's a family member, a coworker, a friend, or a complete stranger, I'm not going to let *myself* down by harboring anger and resentment, I'm going to be more resilient.

I'VE GOT SCIENCE!

There's even scientific research to back this up. Forgiveness, a concept that was typically considered to be spiritual or religious, has become a measurable action, engaging researchers from a wide variety of academic disciplines. Frederic Luskin is the director of the Stanford Forgiveness Project, the largest study to date on forgiveness. Results of his studies are striking. Participants who learned forgiveness techniques showed reductions in levels of stress, saw themselves as less angry, and felt a marked increase in confidence. Equally exciting were the documented improvements in physical health as well—the treated group showed significant decreases in symptoms like chest pain, back pain, nausea, headaches, sleep problems, and loss of appetite. When people forgave others, there were measurable, positive changes in participants' cardiovascular and nervous systems. As Luskin said, "If you feel good but want to feel even better, try forgiving someone."

Even those participants who weren't depressed or overly anxious improved their emotional and psychological functioning by learning to forgive. "This suggests that forgiveness may enable people who are functioning adequately to feel even better," says Luskin. Perhaps this is because grudges and unresolved distress sap the happiness from otherwise healthy people. "Forgiveness may be important not just as a religious practice but as a component of a comprehensive vision of health."[79]

> If you feel good but want to feel even better, try forgiving someone.
> —Frederic Luskin

SO WHY IS FORGIVENESS SO HARD?

Dr. Katz, my mentor whom I referenced earlier, refers to Dr. Roy Baumeister, a prominent social psychologist, who conducted a forgiveness study that found that there are a number of reasons we hesitate to forgive. People with a high sense of entitlement tend to perceive forgiving as risky and unfair. Another barrier is the belief that forgiving leaves you vulnerable to being hurt again.[80] But perhaps perception is the biggest problem.

Think about a time someone hurt you. Can you remember it well? Can you think of all the little details? Typically, we don't forget when someone really hurts or angers us. Now, think about a time that you hurt someone else. You might not be able to think of one right away, but maybe eventually something will come to you. The details might be a bit fuzzy. Or, maybe you think the person you hurt overreacted.

The Baumeister study shows that there is a "magnitude gap," which Katz describes as the "difference in how we perceive an event when we're in the victim or victimizer role."[81] He goes on to explain that when we think of a time someone hurt us, it often feels intentional, even malicious. But when we think of a time we hurt someone else, we feel they overreacted, because we know we did not intend to hurt them. It can all come down to our perception of intent. Baumeister's research shows that it can be harder to forgive when we believe someone's intent is malicious. Although there are clearly times when someone's motive is to hurt us, I don't believe this is always the case. I believe there are times people deserve the benefit of the doubt because they didn't intend to cause us pain through their actions. In fact, they may have no idea they did cause us pain. The next time you feel offended or hurt, question your assumptions about the person's intent. Is it possible they truly meant no harm? This may make it easier to forgive.

However, regardless of your perception of another's intent, forgiveness is imperative if you want to be resilient and give yourself the opportunity to thrive. It's the only way you can take back control and not be manipulated by the harm that's been done. Anything short of forgiveness enables the person who's done the damage to run your world.

This same study shows that if we are able to forgive, we may have increased persistence on tasks, as mental and emotional energy is freed up for use and helps us sustain good performance, even on tasks completely unrelated to the situation that required forgiveness in the first place.

One reason why forgiveness may be so beneficial to our physical health is that it has such a positive impact on our relationships. Think about the kind of people you want to be around. I know that I have to surround myself with forgiving people. Because I mess up! I want my children to be around forgiving people. We are drawn to those with compassion and empathy and mercy. Truly forgiving someone can strengthen and deepen a relationship. This doesn't mean we have to condone the behavior. Any type of behavior that hurts another human being, I condemn. We've got to learn how to condemn the behavior but forgive the human being.

I don't know a principle that is more powerful than that. There are always plenty of reasons to hate each other. Since man has been on this Earth, there have been hatred and violence. The only antidote is forgiveness. Seeking revenge when we have been wronged will not help. Revenge causes more harm. In our quest to increase resilience, we have to try to do no more harm, even when it seems justifiable. Of course, there is a difference between exacting revenge and getting out of a bad situation. There may be times you simply need to get yourself out and not allow yourself to remain in a position where you can be harmed.

Forgiveness enables resilience because a natural power comes to those who forgive. When we are able to let go of anger when someone hurts us, we become more productive. More energy is available to us. And we gain self-respect. There is no better feeling than the pride that comes from knowing that when someone hurts me, I didn't hurt them back. Plus, when I can forgive and love other people, knowing their flaws, I can forgive my own flaws and love myself better. I really believe that if you have a forgiving heart, people will be more likely to forgive you. I believe forgiveness is one of those universal truths that pays immediate as well as long-term benefits.

FORGIVE YOURSELF

Maybe most important of all is the need to forgive ourselves. If we are unable to forgive ourselves for our failures, mistakes, and weaknesses, our energy is drained. We feel unworthy of good things. We may turn to harmful behaviors. Shame is a resilience killer. There is a difference between shame and guilt. In our society, shame is introduced very early as a means of control—people use it to manipulate others. But forgiving yourself is how you overcome shame. It's okay to make a mistake; you just have to realize, *I made a mistake. I am not a mistake.*

I believe that not forgiving ourselves is a bigger resilience killer than the inability to forgive others. And forgiving ourselves may be much harder, because sometimes that's who we're the hardest on. But the truth is, we can't treat others with love, respect, and tolerance if we are intolerant and unkind to ourselves.

THE SKILLS OF FORGIVENESS

So now that we've spent some time on the whys of forgiving, let's talk about the how. Many of us grew up hearing about the moral reasons for forgiveness. But actually putting it into practice is far trickier than hearing about it in Sunday school.

I feel like somewhat of a hypocrite talking about this, as it has taken me a while to learn, and I'm not an expert in it. There are still people and situations in my life that I have to work at forgiving. But one thing I'm proud of is that I can honestly say that I don't look behind me and hate anyone. I don't usually walk around weighed down by the burden of anger and resentment.

I've learned two skills that are especially helpful with forgiveness: creating scenarios and writing it down.

Skill 1: Create Scenarios

As a counselor, I have worked with people who have done extremely horrible things to hurt themselves and others. I have learned that one of the greatest aspects of being a therapist is that you have the time to meet with someone and figure out why they are making the decisions—good and bad—that they make in their lives. I am able to sit down with clients and learn the "why" behind their bad choices. If we could all know the "why" behind someone's actions, we would feel much greater compassion and real empathy for them. If we all had this opportunity to see and understand the whole picture, it would be much easier to forgive.

Most of us don't have that luxury in our real lives. We can't sit down in a therapeutic setting and get the whole picture. It just doesn't work that way most of the time. We don't usually take the time to ask, "Why is this person hurting me?" It's much easier to say, "This person is a jerk!" If I can realize there is a cause underlying their hurtful behavior that I don't know or understand, it will be easier to let go and move on. Because we so rarely get to know someone's motivations, or what inner battles someone is fighting, I often choose to speculate and make up a reason for their actions. Maybe they had a terrible day at work, or perhaps they have a sick child and no health insurance and the huge stress of the situation is taking a toll. Just the other day somebody driving a BMW flipped me off on the road. I said to myself, *Hey, that's a lot of pressure to drive that BMW. It's a lot of pressure to make that car payment.* Instead of chasing him down, or even getting angry, I just kind of laughed to myself as I drove along in my ten-year-old, paid-for car. Even if I am wrong and I'm way off (let's face it—even though I think most people are inherently good, there are a few jerks out there), doing this allows me to let go and forgive them. Even malicious behavior is usually rooted in some type of pain, and I've learned that the only way to lighten my personal burdens is through forgiveness—of myself and others.

Skill 2: Write It Down

Science has shown that writing a letter can help you to forgive. For years I've heard about "cathartic writing," where the writer vents on paper but then doesn't send the letter. I think this is the same thing as a damaging Dammit Doll. Venting in this manner raises your blood pressure, makes you relive the situation, and might leave you even angrier as you dwell on it. However, if you are able to send a letter to the person who offended you, it may help facilitate forgiveness. It may also be an opportunity for you to really think (and filter!) as you confront them. You may be able to remain calmer and more objective than if you were to have a conversation with them. A word of caution, however: Please make sure you are safe. There are situations where any contact with someone who has hurt you may not be recommended.

And what if you're the offender? Forgiving yourself when you screw up is key to resilience, but when you've hurt someone else this can be difficult. It's especially hard to forgive yourself if you don't try, whenever possible, to make amends. Letter writing can be a part of this process as well. Write a letter of apology to the person you've offended. Use good judgment—sometimes it's okay to mail that letter to the person you've hurt, but sometimes it may cause more damage. If there is any chance that is the case, write the letter but then rip it up. Taking responsibility and restoring what you did if you can, resolving to never repeat the offense, and offering a sincere apology can make all the difference. Always try to make amends except where to do so would cause harm. When you can't personally say you're sorry, or it's not possible to fix whatever it was that you broke, learn from it and don't repeat the behavior again. If you're able to do that, that deserves some self-forgiveness, too.

Forgiveness is something that is easy to talk about but can be incredibly hard to do. There are people from my childhood that, twenty-five years later, I'm still trying to forgive. I understand all of this, and I've made a conscious decision to forgive. But sometimes it's a process. Even when I realize that it is hurting me when I don't forgive, there are times it doesn't come immediately and I continually have to work at it.

FORGIVENESS IS THE ONLY OPTION

On April 20, 1999, one of the deadliest school shootings in history took place at Columbine High School in Colorado. Two students went on a murderous rampage that killed twelve classmates and one teacher, injured twenty-one others, and ended in their joint suicides. Rachel Joy Scott, a seventeen-year-old girl known for her kind and happy nature, was shot four times and killed instantly. Rachel's younger brother Craig lay in the blood of his two good friends, who died that day, and survived by pretending that he too was dead. Rachel's funeral was broadcast on CNN and was at that point the most watched event ever on that network, surpassing even the funeral of Diana, Princess of Wales. Rachel is the inspiration for Rachel's Challenge, a nationwide school outreach program for the prevention of teen violence.

I have the great privilege of knowing and working with Rachel's father, Darrell Scott. Darrell has been a good friend to me, and his example of forgiveness has inspired me and millions of others as he travels the world with the message he believes his daughter would want the world to know. From a very young age, Rachel had expressed the desire to change the world. Her family has pictures she drew and ideas she wrote down that capture her heart and vision. On the third Christmas after her death, Rachel's sister found a picture that she had drawn on the back of her dresser years before when she was thirteen years old. It was an outline of Rachel's hands, and in the center of one hand she had written, "These hands belong to Rachel Joy Scott and will someday touch millions of people's hearts!" Darrell has dedicated his life to sharing the message he believes his daughter would like the world to hear with millions of people. I'd like to share some of his thoughts on forgiveness, as he shared with me in a recent interview.

My daughter Rachel was the first person to be killed in the Columbine tragedy in 1999. Our first instinct was to be angry and unforgiving and to want revenge, all of which are natural reactions. Fortunately, I had learned early in life that when a circumstance happens, you can either react, or you can respond. Most of the time we react first, and maybe later we respond. But our reactions are almost always wrong. When someone wrongs us, we turn around and wrong them back. So when we brought our family together to talk about what we were going to do, we talked about issues like forgiveness, and letting go, and about celebrating Rachel's life.

Looking back, that was a crucial point in time where we as a family could have chosen to go down a path that many families go down, a path of forever being angry or wanting some kind of revenge. And I can't blame those people; I mean, it's a natural reaction. Revenge is a reaction. Forgiveness, however, is not a reaction. It's a chosen response. We chose forgiveness and to celebrate Rachel's life. It wasn't easy at first, but you just keep choosing, and eventually it is easier, because it's part of your whole system. So your reaction is really a response.

There's a difference between pardon and forgiveness. I would never have pardoned them; that's a judicial decision. And I would have prosecuted if they had lived, to see that they could never do it again. But forgiveness is an issue of the heart. If we don't forgive, we become victimized over and over and over again. The person who has wronged you dominates your thinking and your life.

> ## If we don't forgive, we become victimized over and over and over again.
> ### —Darrell Scott

Because we had made early choices—and they were not emotional choices, they were commitments—we decided that we will be committed to this path. We will choose to forgive. We will choose to let go. And we have to keep choosing. It's amazing—there is a universal grace that comes when we choose. If we take one step, the universe takes a step with us. It doesn't matter how I feel about it. You're feeding on a feeling that gives you a certain amount of satisfaction—to be angry, to be unforgiving. But if I commit to forgive, eventually the feelings will follow. Sometimes we *have to go against our instincts, our normal reactions. But if you just grit your teeth and choose to forgive, the feelings will follow. Not immediately, but they will follow.*

It wasn't easy. My son Craig didn't immediately choose to forgive. He was very angry for two years. Craig's last memory of his sister was of getting in a fight with her that day. So Craig had to deal with dual for-giveness—forgiving himself, and forgiving the killers of his sister. It took him two years to come to that place where he made that step. We had a talk one day, and he said, "Dad, I'm choosing to forgive, I'm choosing to let go of the past, I'm choosing to celebrate Rachel's life like the rest of the family." He saw the difference it made for us, and it's made a huge difference in his life.

My daughter can never be replaced, so there's always going to be a certain amount of pain in my life from that. I miss her, I love her, I wish and would do anything to see her for five minutes. But I can't live there.

So what can I do? I can celebrate her life. I can share it with other people. Because of those choices to forgive, doors that we never dreamed of began to open. We didn't do it to make doors open, but that is what immediately began to happen. Millions and millions of people have been able to hear her story and have been challenged by her life. In the last two years, 453 suicides have been prevented because of her life and story. Seven school shootings that we know of have been prevented. And count-less numbers of people have forgiven each other. There are so many stories we will never hear, people that have been changed and touched. So there has been a huge harvest from the tragedy that we didn't ask for, that we didn't expect or look for at the time. But because we made the choices to be resilient from that tragedy, so many good things have happened. In my life, I took the deep, deep grief and the deep wound from losing a beau-tiful daughter, and it's been channeled toward helping other people, just like Rachel wanted. I'm honoring her by channeling it in that direction.

I believe there are places in our heart that can never be reached except through adversity. I just think there are chambers in our spirit that are never touched except through pain. And when they're touched we have an opportunity: We either retreat into those chambers and hide, or we open them up and discover the treasure that's there. I believe for every deep grief in our life there's an equal amount of joy that can only be there because we've reached that level of grief.

> # I believe there are places in our heart that can never be reached except through adversity.
> ## —Darrell Scott

I choose constantly to lay down my pain. And I think all of these things are part of resilience. You can't learn all these lessons after you lose a child—at least you can't learn them on the spot. Life throws us a lot of curves and we go through a lot of pain in this life; we experience a lot of loss. As we make those right choices, those difficult choices, purpose is there waiting for us like an opportunity. You don't make those choices for that reason, but if you do, good things happen. So the only thing we have the power to do is make the choice: I will not allow this to destroy my life; I will choose to forgive. It's the only option.

One day I was in a restaurant in Canada with Darrell and he shared with me what it was like that day, waiting to find out if his kids were okay. Parents waited for hours at a nearby elementary school for buses that came throughout the day bringing survivors, racing to embrace their child as he or she got off the bus. Each time a bus came, Darrell would run over and jump on the fence, frantically looking in the bus windows. When the last bus came and the last student got off, it wasn't Rachel. That's when he knew. It was one of the worst feelings Darrell has ever had. Yet he had the ability to forgive. He's an incredible example to me.

I thought I understood what forgiveness was, but I didn't really understand it until I learned it from him. My life changed when he told me this story.

I've been with Darrell on many occasions and I've seen the outpouring of response that he receives when he shares his story of tragedy and forgiveness with people. He is completely authentic and has amazing credibility. This response wouldn't happen if Darrell had been unable to forgive. But because he was able to forgive, people feel it. I've been a witness to it, and it's powerful. It has enabled Darrell to be resilient while going through something unimaginable, and to inspire millions of others to be more resilient as well.

ASK

Is there a person in your life whom you are struggling to forgive? Would it be beneficial for you to forgive this person?

Are you struggling to forgive yourself for a past mistake? Do you have a belief that "letting go" could eventually be possible?

TASK

Carrying the pain and anger of not forgiving is an unnecessary weight in your life. Use the two skills of forgiveness to get started. First, create scenarios. Consider the reasons behind this person's actions toward you. Understand that the person who caused your suffering may not have had malicious intent. They may have been incredibly selfish or stupid, but their motive may not have been to cause harm. Even if their intentions were evil, holding on to bitterness and resentment only hurts you and those closest to you. Second, write a letter to the person who offended you. Sort your thoughts out, and if it is possible and safe, have a conversation with this person. (Remember, however, that there is no guarantee your effort will be reciprocated. People are good at justifying their behavior!) As Darrell Scott explained, the desire for revenge is a natural reaction. Forgiveness, however, is a chosen response. Right now, choose to forgive. And each time the desire for revenge and feelings of bitterness begin to resurface, choose to forgive again.

If you're struggling to forgive yourself, write a letter to the person you've offended (if it's safe, appropriate, and won't cause harm to them or others). Do everything you can to make amends, then let go. Focus your energy on moving forward. It won't be an overnight process, but you can start the journey today.

ROCK BOTTOM RESILIENCE FUEL

Circle all the emotions and mindsets that you are currently experiencing. Do your best to harness the energy from those emotions into resilience. If you feel there is no way out of rock bottom, I strongly encourage you to seek professional help.

- Seeking redemption
- In "comeback mode"
- Determined
- "Why try?"
- Overwhelmed
- No place to go but up
- Down
- Anxious
- Going through the motions
- Seeking a small victory
- Pessimistic
- Humiliated
- Broken
- Letting others down
- Controlling the damage
- Guilty
- Still breathing
- Taking one step at a time
- Desiring forgiveness
- Apathetic
- Feeling desperate
- Keeping hope alive
- Angry
- Repairing a broken or damaged relationship
- Taken advantage of
- Desiring change
- Forgiving
- Powerless
- "Things can't get worse"
- Desiring to make things right

RESILIENCE BOOSTERS

Relational Resilience	Street Resilience
• Surrender the one-up relationship. • Engage emotionally. • Friendship—don't take it for granted. • Turn outward. • Put down that device! • Drop the facade. • Connect with something bigger than you.	• Get the whole picture. • Channel pain into a cause. • Reframe your limitations as potential strengths. • Focus on what you're doing right. • Look fear in the eye.
Resource Resilience	**Rock Bottom Resilience**
• Cultivate a worthy mindset. • Tap into the power of people. • Action, action, action! • Fight resignation with spontaneity. • Wrestle complacency to the ground. • Get some production therapy. • Don't accept no.	• Radically accept your circumstance. • Don't make things worse. • Go for a small win. • Fix a broken window. • Tear off labels. • Discover the power of a future promise. • Be illogical. • Forgive—it's the only option.

SELF-GRACE: THE FINAL KEY TO RESILIENCE

My nine-year-old son, Cooper, loved basketball. We've watched NBA games together on TV for years, and his blue eyes got big every time someone made a winning shot just in time or landed a sweet slam dunk. Cooper had already started picturing himself in an NBA team jersey and a $200 pair of Nikes, sprinting across a shiny court to the wild applause of thousands of fans. These were Cooper's dreams. And the reality is this: Cooper's parents are both five-foot-something, and the only slam dunk he'll probably ever make is into the child-size hoop we have installed in our basement. Nevertheless, Wendy and I try to encourage our children's passions, so we signed him up for a youth basketball league. Before his first game, he walked around the house holding his basketball, talking about how great the game was going to be. "Dad, should I go to college first or go right to the NBA?" he asked me. Sitting in the bleachers during that game, Wendy and I heaved sighs of relief as Cooper got possession of the ball, tossed it toward the hoop, and watched it bounce off the backboard and swish through the net. His teammates cheered and gave him high fives, and in that moment, Cooper's visions of being on ESPN's *SportsCenter* became even clearer. He could see his potential right there in his first two points.

During Cooper's second game, Wendy and I were crossing our fingers for another lucky shot. But as the game drew to an end, we could see it wasn't going to happen. After the game, Cooper dragged his feet across the court toward us. The look on his face told us he could see himself more likely to be selling popcorn in the arena than playing on the NBA court. His little shoulders were slumped, and I've never seen him looking so disappointed. On the ride home, he turned to me and said, "Dad, I suck. I didn't even make one basket. I just want to quit basketball." I used everything in my arsenal to convince him that he was still learning, that there was more to basketball than making baskets—like making assists and playing solid defense—but I couldn't get through to him. He threw his beloved basketball into a corner when we got home that day and let it sit there. He started to dread going to practice. He had beaten himself up until his drive to excel was completely gone. He was just focused on what he couldn't do, not what he could learn and improve. He was the very opposite of resilient.

Fear of failure is something we all struggle with. Like Cooper, we cripple ourselves with fears of all the horrible things that might happen if we take a risk and try. But even Michael Jordan, the greatest basketball player of all time, acknowledged the reality of failure when he said, "I've missed more than nine thousand shots in my career. I've lost almost three hundred games. Twenty-six times, I've been trusted to take the game-winning shot and missed. I've failed over and over and over again in my life. And that is why I succeed."[82]

When we do fail, we punish ourselves and feel no motivation to try again. We exert so much energy into fear of failure and then into beating ourselves up when it happens that we have no energy left to be resilient. I know this feeling all too well; I experienced it constantly for the first forty years of my life. I like to compare it to walking around with cement blocks on my feet. And it's almost impossible to go on offense and attack life when I feel that way.

> We exert so much energy into fear
> of failure and then beating our-
> selves up when it happens that we
> have no energy left to be resilient.

I still have not mastered the art of combating this fear of failing. But I'm ending this book with this principle so that it will be attached to me for the rest of my life. It will be a constant reminder to me, and hopefully it can serve as a guide for my children when they read this book ten or fifteen years from now. I don't want them to go their first forty years without this understanding. I also want you, the reader, to walk away from this book with that weight lifted. Instead of concrete blocks, I want you to feel barefoot. I want you to breathe easier, let go of that fear, and not let past mistakes hold you back. And the best way for that to happen is to give yourself what I call "self-grace."

The word *grace* has a couple of definitions: "unmerited divine assis-tance," or "an act or instance of kindness, courtesy, or clemency." What I'm asking you to do is apply the second definition and start giving your-self a little more kindness. I define *self-grace* as a recognition of the human condition. Instead of fearing failure, you embrace the idea that it's inevita-ble, and you're completely prepared to forgive yourself and keep moving forward when failure does happen. You realize that you'll never be perfect, but because you're constantly in the mindset of forgiving yourself, you don't get stuck in the resilience-killing rut of self-contempt. Your goal is to put failure in perspective so that when you fail, you can move on to a better use of energy and time. I have wasted hours of time beating myself up, when I could have put that energy into being more productive.

Grace is completely letting go of guilt and shame after doing every-thing possible to make amends. Self-grace is whole and complete. It means completely letting go of the mistake, letting go when you fall short, or letting go when you fail to complete something. "Grace" equals "gone." With grace, I stop looking for reasons to beat myself up. It's different from self-tolerance or self-forgiveness. It doesn't have conditions. The process of forgiving ourselves is important, but sometimes we get bogged down in the process. Self-grace eliminates the things we can get hung up on and allows us to simply let go. Grace is a higher level of forgiveness.

If we all walked around with an attitude of self-grace, a lot of the crippling anxiety that we humans experience would decrease. Businesses would be more likely to thrive, families would be happier, and individually we'd get a lot more accomplished. This is, of course, easier said than done. I struggle with this principle constantly. But it gets easier when I do seven things:

- Maintain a sense of humor.
- Have understanding and compassion for others.
- Accept the reality of being human.
- Start where I'm standing and move forward.
- Find positive channels for my weaknesses.
- Avoid comparing myself to others.
- Continue to use the Four Sources of Resilience.

Maintain a Sense of Humor

When I mess up, humor is what keeps me from falling into a downward spiral of negativity. It's the antidote to anger, depression, and lashing out, and it often determines the way others respond to your mistakes. Sometimes, when I've been on the road for a long time, I'll stand before an audience in Detroit and shout, "It's so good to be here with you in New York!" The audience will groan, and I'll realize that I just made a mistake. At that point, I could walk off the stage in shame (which I nearly did the first time this happened!) or laugh it off and say, "I'm sorry, I have no idea where I am. I've been on the road for ten days straight and averaged four hours of sleep every night." My ability to laugh at my mistake helps the audience ease up and judge me less harshly—and helps *me* judge myself less harshly, too.

This same principle applies when we make bigger mistakes. Sometimes all I can do is laugh and say, "Wow, I'm very human. Here's proof."

Have Understanding and Compassion for Others

When I have compassion and understanding toward myself, I'm more likely to give it to other people. When I show compassion and understanding toward others when they mess up, I'm more likely to give it to myself. It's a beautiful cycle.

Accept the Reality of Being Human

During the past forty years, I have tried to master many things—my insecurities, my physical health, the demands of family and running a business, to name a few. I try to maintain healthy relationships, to stay mentally and emotionally healthy, and be all things to all people. Like all of us, I'm trying to juggle all these balls—including the roles of a husband, son, brother, and father—and they all seem important. I might juggle well for a while, but eventually I always drop one. Or two. Or five. Society tells us we should be good at keeping all the balls in the air. Billion-dollar industries exist because we keep buying books and systems and products that promise to help us lose weight, or be more productive, or master whatever our weaknesses are. But when I try to master something and don't reach my desired destination, my resilience wanes. The older I get, the more I realize that the concept of perfect mastery is just marketing.

We're being hustled on this every day. The marketing industry does not allow for much self-grace. We're constantly being told that we have to have the perfect family, job, body, and image. Just try to *avoid* being exposed to these messages for a day and you'll realize how often you see them. This marketing machine tells you if you don't have the exact right everything, you're a failure. Think how much money is spent on this, on frontin'—appearing as if everything is how it's expected to be.

A recent NPR piece about the tendency we have to feel overwhelmed asks, "Is life overwhelming us more now than ever before? . . . Is this a particular malaise of our times? It sure looks like it. One culprit may be The New Perfectionism. Somehow, somewhere along the line, we got the idea that each of us is responsible for perfecting *every aspect* of our lives."[83] I see so many people who are trying to be perfect in every area of life, and when they fall short, their resilience crumbles. We should be striving for improvement. We should be the best we can. But the idea that we need perfection is a lie we're being sold. We need to accept the reality of being human; we can't master every area of our existence, and being imperfect is actually okay. Self-grace, combined with our best effort to recommit to a task or situation, is what long-term resilience looks like. You have permission to feel self-worth even when you fail or don't completely master something.

> **Self-grace, combined with our best effort to recommit to a task or situation, is what long-term resilience looks like.**

Start Where You're Standing and Move Forward

In his article "10 Steps to Forgiving Yourself," Dr. Rick Hanson says that the only purpose of guilt and remorse is learning, not punishment. "Anything past the point of learning is just needless suffering,"[84] he says. Shame is a resilience killer, something that society uses to manipulate and control you. That's why it's so important for us to simply learn from our mistakes, pick ourselves up, and start again from where we're standing.

John Newton, born in 1725 in London, is an example of someone who could have spent his life wallowing in shame. He was a rebellious youth, and his disobedience caused his father to enlist him into service in the Royal Navy. He did not last long, and after deserting the navy, Newton began a career in slave trading. While at sea, he had several disagreements with crewmates, which resulted in his being nearly starved to death, imprisoned, and ultimately enslaved on a plantation in Sierra Leone. His father intervened and sent a ship to bring him home. On this voyage, he became known as one of the most profane men the captain had ever met. During this journey Newton was almost killed by a violent storm, and thus began the process of picking himself up and learning to exercise self-grace. Newton eventually became a devoted clergyman in a small village. He started writing a poem or hymn for each prayer meeting. The famous Christian hymn "Amazing Grace" was one of them[85], and years later it remains a testament to the power of overcoming mistakes and weaknesses:

Amazing Grace, how sweet the sound, that saved a wretch like me.
I once was lost, but now I'm found, was blind, but now I see.

This song emphasizes that you can go to the depths of depravity and still find redemption and that we all are capable of forgiving ourselves and moving forward. I love the four words, "But now I see." When I give myself grace, I see my options and potential so much more clearly. My motivation to fight on increases.

I've had to do this myself on countless occasions when it comes to my greatest weakness: impulsivity—especially when it comes to food. I try really hard to have self-discipline, to eat less dessert, to cut out soda. But sometimes, especially when I'm traveling, I drop that ball big time. I'll spend an hour dining on a city's world-famous pizza; then I'll get in my car and drive to the restaurant that serves the city's world-famous steak. Other times I'll throw three desserts into the mix. I can't say my love of eating is something I'm particularly proud of, and in the past, mistakes like this completely threw off my resilience and destroyed all resolve to keep striving for self-discipline. Now, realizing that I am a human being who is prone to mistakes, I'll say, *Okay, I messed up. Tomorrow I will start the fight again.* And I will. I'll start where I stand and move forward. It's the best thing I can do, especially when my other option is to waste my energy on beating myself up.

A word of caution here: You might be tempted *before* making a big mistake to justify it with, *I'll just mess up now then move forward afterward.* This is *very* dangerous thinking and will actually kill your resilience. It will make self-grace and moving forward way more painful and difficult.

Find Positive Channels for Your Weaknesses

I've been given lots of labels in my life: "crazy," "misfit," "attitude problem," "troublemaker," or "a round peg in a square hole." Over time, I've come to realize that all of these attributes, though seemingly negative, have helped me to accomplish something. Even the impulsivity I just told you about has helped me take positive risks, be creative, strike up conversations with strangers, and make connections with people that others wouldn't connect to. I told you earlier how my ADHD, while difficult, is something I would never want taken away from me. Think about your own perceived weaknesses. As long as you aren't hurting yourself or others, channeling the "negative" can be a positive fuel source.

Resilient people understand and deal with the reality of their personality flaws and traits, and they thrive despite or *because* of their weaknesses. When my grandpa was a little boy, he drove his mother crazy. He had lots of attitude, didn't listen to his parents, and frequently ran away. Then, as a young man, he became a bombardier in the US Air Force during World War II. When he was shot down over Germany and held for months in a German prison camp, his mother said she never worried about him. She knew that the negative attributes—the stubbornness and attitude—that almost did her in when he was a little boy would be the same attributes that would keep him alive in that prison camp. The good news for me is that she was right.

It's easier to have self-grace when you recognize that the weaknesses causing you to make mistakes are the same ones you've identified as strengths in other areas of your life. As a human being, I realize that sometimes I can be selfish and sometimes I'm generous. Sometimes I'm ambitious and sometimes I'm lazy. Sometimes I'm brave and sometimes I'm scared. When I realized that being human causes me to have both of these extremes, I better understood the importance of self-grace.

Avoid Comparing Yourself to Others

Comparisons always invite a win-or-lose situation, and in today's world of unrelenting social media interaction, it's generally a lose. When I'm tempted to rate myself against others, I have to constantly remind myself that I never have the whole-picture view of anyone's life, especially when I'm just looking at their online presence. A social media acquaintance may post numerous photos of his garage full of classic cars, but what Facebook won't show me is a photo of his failing marriage. Someone else may envy a friend's perfect vacation to Europe, but they likely wouldn't envy the financial strain it may have put on their friend's family. Even the most successful, put-together-looking person does not have complete mastery over all areas of their life. As I mentioned earlier, perfection is a big facade, and when we try to compare ourselves against it, we'll always fall short. Someone once wisely said, "Comparison is the thief of joy." Even if you're happy with your lot, the moment you compare it to someone else's, your perspective changes and it doesn't look the same. Suddenly the good doesn't look as good anymore. If you have a mindset of self-grace, however, you'll be nice enough to yourself to avoid these comparisons—even when others try to force them upon you—and recognize that you're not a loser for not having the lifestyle you perceive others to have. When you do fall into the trap of comparison, however, you can still have self-grace. Forgive yourself for those self-berating feelings and move forward.

Continue to Use the Four Sources of Resilience

I hope by this point you have learned how to Flip the Switch in your own life and have started to internalize some of the ideas in the book. I hope you're asking yourself, *Am I using the messes in my life to become greater? Am I using the adversities I encounter as fuel to try harder?*

You've come this far, and I hope you'll keep Flipping the Switch and applying the Four Sources of Resilience in your own life. I hope you're using the boosters, especially the ones that you've found the most impactful and applicable to your own situation. I'm going to make you a promise that's opposite to the promise of the "marketing monster" (the one that promises perfection when you use a certain product or service): You'll mess up. You'll trip on boosters and they won't always work out perfectly. In a word, you'll fail. The good news is, we can all maintain a mindset of self-grace and never give up. The process of applying the booster is more important than the outcome the booster will produce. I can't promise you a dream career, permanent weight loss, a perfect relationship, or freedom from debt. I can't promise that the Four Sources of Resilience will help you channel your pain perfectly. I *can* promise that as you keep trying, you'll keep getting better, and your sincere effort will create long-term resilience.

KEEP THE COMEBACK SWITCH TURNED ON

I explained earlier that trying to master ten things at once is like a great juggle that inevitably ends with a dropped ball or two. Depression, anxiety, and fear are magnified when we beat ourselves up each time this happens, and that's why self-grace is so important. But there's a second step—one that becomes easier when we've given ourselves grace—and I call it "keeping the comeback switch turned on."

Keeping the comeback switch turned on is the process of picking up the balls as you drop them. Combining self-grace with the comeback is the healthiest thing you can do for yourself when you drop the ball. It doesn't mean you suddenly become perfect at juggling that ball; it means you make a real effort to improve and don't shut down. The comeback is not an end result. (Remember, perfection is a myth!) Long-term fulfillment and resilience take place in the *doing*.

> **Keeping the comeback switch turned on is the process of picking up the balls as you drop them.**

We all fall short. Maybe we swear too much, don't serve our neighbors enough, sleep in too often, or are impatient with our family members. I'd love to be the perfect husband, business leader, dad, and public speaker, but the reality is that, try as I might, I'll drop the ball in all of these roles at some point or another. It's okay to have demons—*if* you're constantly combining self-grace with the comeback. The process of the comeback is likely to include some painful lessons, but resilience is not the path of least resistance. It takes place in the striving, not the accomplishing. And it only dies the moment you give up.

> **Resilience takes place in the striving, not the accomplishing.**

I've learned that lifelong resilience is nothing more than a series of small and large comebacks—it's making the effort to pick up the ball *every single* time you drop it.

SELF-GRACE CREATES FLOW

A mindset of self-grace helps you prepare for the comeback instead of for the failure. You're not afraid to fail—in fact, you embrace the idea of failure as an opportunity to come back and become better.

When you approach any task—whether it's meeting a deadline at work or working on a personal project—a mindset of self-grace can actually help you perform better. If you have the "Cooper basketball mindset" and approach a project with thoughts of *I have to be perfect; I suck at this; I'm going to fail; I don't know why I'm doing this*, odds are you'll be tense and anxious and will lack the creativity, motivation, or energy that would make your project great. It will be like working with foggy glasses. The fact is, when you sit down to do anything, you have the potential to make a mistake. It's much better to embrace the idea that messing up is part of the creative process and throw yourself into your project. This positive mentality creates flow—that "in the zone" feeling written about so compellingly by Dr. Csikszentmihalyi. It allows you to be more focused, have a better attitude, and see more clearly, and you are more likely to create an environment where others are willing to help you.

The mentality of self-grace can benefit employers as well. In his book *Good Boss, Bad Boss*, Stanford University's Bob Sutton says, "The best bosses . . . learn to forgive people who lash out at them . . . and they learn to forgive themselves, too."[86] When we give each other grace, our own levels of anxiety, depression, and frustration decrease. When I don't grant my wife grace, my kids grace, my business partner grace, I'm the one who gets all worked up inside. I'm the one who feels bad. I am more resilient when I am able to give others grace. This isn't a message of total permissiveness, but if I'm going to err, I want to err on the side of grace.

When I started writing this book, I don't think I had fully internalized the idea of self-grace. There was a time in this book's production that I was running out of money to fund it and I wasn't sure if anyone would even read it. As in any major project, my collaborator, Brad Anderson, and I were running into challenges. I had wanted a smooth-flowing project with no bumps in the road, and it seemed like everything that could go wrong *was* going wrong. Then one day it hit us. We looked at each other and said, "We're writing a book on resilience!" And when you're writing a book on resilience, you cannot quit, no matter how many problems you face on the way.

Since then, we've developed the self-grace mindset. And we've certainly had to apply it. I've thrown out hundreds of ideas that, quite honestly, were too downright ridiculous to even put on paper. Some months, we've scrimped by on dwindling funds. We've made countless mistakes along the way. At this point, however, we don't fear the worst; we embrace it. We've felt the flow that comes from not stressing about failure. We recognize that the only way to make something meaningful is to dive in, fail, stumble through the process, and keep the comeback switch turned on for every time we need to pick ourselves up again.

As I've already mentioned, I spent the first forty years of my life not knowing how to forgive myself. The refreshing thing about the process of writing this book is that I've finally convinced myself of its necessity. Despite some things that went wrong during my workday yesterday, I drove home feeling lighter. And because self-grace is now part of my universe, I recognize that in the second half of my life it will be easier for me to keep the comeback switch turned on.

BACK TO THE BEGINNING

I started this book by telling you about the personal hell I experienced to get myself through college. Ironically, I was recently asked to return to my university fifteen years after graduation and speak to over three hundred students facing a variety of adversities—and to faculty, athletic directors, deans, and the university president—about the Four Sources of Resilience. I've been the featured keynote speaker at hundreds of events across the country, but this invitation hit closer to home than any speech I've ever given.

Years ago, I fought so hard to get on that campus because I thought that gaining knowledge and thriving academically was the key to thriving in life. Years later, as I came back to the campus I had staked my future on, I realized that the most important thing I learned during the time I was there didn't come from a lecture or a textbook. The years I spent developing resilience on that campus were more valuable than any degree I earned. I was struck with the thought that in actuality, I had what I really needed before I ever stepped foot on that campus. I was already equipped with one of the most powerful tools in the world: the ability to Flip the Switch and draw on resilience. The capacity to channel pain as fuel was something I had already started learning by the time I first walked on that campus, and that was what I needed—not only to survive there, but to survive everywhere else.

What I didn't realize then was that the most valuable truth I could learn was the knowledge that my problems could be my best friend, and I had plenty of chances to practice using them as fuel during those years! While in school I was around some of the greatest minds, and I was learning brilliant content. But, if I had to choose between all of that knowledge, all of that academic brilliance, and the ability to Flip the Switch, I'd choose Flipping the Switch! That ability, along with the resilience I'd been acquiring my entire life, had a far greater impact on me and my family and the people I've worked with and served in my life than anything I learned academically. Years ago I worked so hard for that university degree, but the greatest degree I could ever earn is an honorary, self-given PhD in resilience. To me, that's been worth more than any degree in any subject matter from any university on Earth.

I was thinking and reflecting about all of this that evening as I sat at the table next to the university president, watching as student after student was honored—many in wheelchairs with physical disabilities, but even more who had less obvious challenges more similar to mine. Years ago when I was a student there I had been one of the first to be accepted and graduate with severe learning disabilities. I could see that there has been great progress and doors have opened for other students, each with their own struggles, each fighting hard to earn their degree. It was very humbling and powerful to watch these students be honored before it was my turn to speak to them. Each one had overcome tremendous adversity. Each one of them had a story of resilience.

When it was my turn to take the podium, I couldn't stop myself from choking up as I told the students of my tremendous respect for their unyielding perseverance, heart, and passion. I told them that their ability to not give up was more important than their scholarly gifts; that if they continue to be relentless in the face of adversity, they will find success in life, no matter what their transcript says. Afterward, dozens of these students came up to share their own inspiring stories of learning to thrive in the face of adversity with me. I remained there with them long after the event was over, moved by their stories.

By all accounts, the night was a success. I had returned to the campus where years before I had seen some of my darkest moments to give a heartfelt and well-received keynote speech. But even if I had fallen on my face or mixed up all my words or not hit it off with the university president, I would have the tools to move forward and make a comeback. I still would have walked off that stage feeling lighter—feeling barefoot. My hope is that you can walk away from this book feeling the same.

If you don't get anything else from this book, I hope you can commit to pushing through when all hell breaks loose in your life. Predetermine that, come what may, you're going to Flip the Switch, draw on the Four Sources of Resilience, and give yourself grace, and you'll be equipped with resilience throughout your life.

WHAT'S YOUR SOURCE?
RESILIENCE SELF-ASSESSMENT

The purpose of the following assessment is to help you determine what sources of resilience you are strongest in and which sources could use some work. Using the scale at the top of each page, answer each question as honestly as possible. Don't worry if you score low in some areas. The goal of this book is to increase your understanding and help you strengthen the areas where you're currently weak. You can retake the assessment as many times as you'd like to keep track of the progress you're making.

Relational Resilience

	Never like me	Seldom like me	About half the time like me	Usually like me	Always like me
1. I can do multiple tasks and still pay attention to the people in front of me.	1	2	3	4	5
2. There are times when I feel a lack of connection with other people.	1	2	3	4	5
3. Others have told me I can become emotionally distant.	1	2	3	4	5
4. My circle of friends is increasing.	1	2	3	4	5
5. I go out of my way to acknowledge service workers.	1	2	3	4	5
6. I have important relationships where I feel unsafe expressing myself.	1	2	3	4	5
7. If I'm having to work at a relationship, there is something wrong with that relationship.	1	2	3	4	5
8. I am comfortable admitting my weaknesses.	1	2	3	4	5
9. I've been told I do a good job of being aware of the needs and concerns of others.	1	2	3	4	5
10. I've received feedback that I sometimes fail to think about how my choices would affect others.	1	2	3	4	5
11. I actively seek ways to help those who are less powerful feel needed and influential.	1	2	3	4	5
12. There are some personalities I can't handle being around.	1	2	3	4	5
13. I have friends who are there for me even when I have nothing to offer them in return.	1	2	3	4	5
14. I've been told I do an excellent job of reaching out to others.	1	2	3	4	5

Scoring Your Relational Resilience

Add up the scores from the following questions:

Question 4: _____

Question 5: _____

Question 8: _____

Question 9: _____

Question 11: _____

Question 13: _____

Question 14: _____

COLUMN A TOTAL: _____

Now add up the scores from the following questions.

Question 1: _____

Question 2: _____

Question 3: _____

Question 6: _____

Question 7: _____

Question 10: _____

Question 12: _____

COLUMN B TOTAL: _____

Subtract this number from your Column A total.
(COLUMN A – COLUMN B): _____

Relational Resilience Score
Finally, to calculate your Relational Resilience score, add 28
to the number above: _____ + 28 = _____

Street Resilience

	Never like me	Seldom like me	About half the time like me	Usually like me	Always like me
1. I react to rejection by giving up or decreasing the amount of effort I put forth.	1	2	3	4	5
2. Making a mistake just makes me want to try harder the next time.	1	2	3	4	5
3. When people aren't confident in my abilities, I tend to put forth less effort.	1	2	3	4	5
4. I have experienced or am likely to experience some discrimination in my life.	1	2	3	4	5
5. I believe innovation is possible without mistakes.	1	2	3	4	5
6. When I have a conflict with someone, it's usually because the other person lacks the relevant facts.	1	2	3	4	5
7. I sometimes fear exposing my ignorance.	1	2	3	4	5
8. I rarely step out of my comfort zone to experience something new.	1	2	3	4	5
9. I've been able to transform some of my limitations into strengths.	1	2	3	4	5
10. During a typical day, I tend to focus more on what I've done right than what I've done wrong.	1	2	3	4	5
11. Fear of failure doesn't deter me from taking action.	1	2	3	4	5
12. I use rejection to work harder to achieve my goals.	1	2	3	4	5
13. There are multiple people and interests in my life I can turn to during times of loneliness.	1	2	3	4	5
14. Fear of embarrassment keeps me from being my true self.	1	2	3	4	5

Scoring Your Street Resilience

Add up the scores from the following questions:

Question 2: _____

Question 4: _____

Question 9: _____

Question 10: _____

Question 11: _____

Question 12: _____

Question 13: _____

COLUMN A TOTAL: _____

Now add up the scores from the following questions.

Question 1: _____

Question 3: _____

Question 5: _____

Question 6: _____

Question 7: _____

Question 8: _____

Question 14: _____

COLUMN B TOTAL: _____

Subtract this number from your Column A total.
(COLUMN A – COLUMN B): _____

Street Resilience Score
Finally, to calculate your Street Resilience score, add 28
to the number above: _____ + 28 = _____

Resource Resilience	Never like me	Seldom like me	About half the time like me	Usually like me	Always like me
1. When I'm pursuing a goal, it's easy for me to become discouraged when small setbacks take place.	1	2	3	4	5
2. When I lack an ability or skill to perform a task, I reach out to ask for help.	1	2	3	4	5
3. I find myself saying things like, "I'm not good enough for that," or "They're better than me because . . .," or "I don't really deserve . . ."	1	2	3	4	5
4. I'm not hesitant to approach people who I perceive to be of a higher status than I am to ask for their opinion or help.	1	2	3	4	5
5. I often fall short in getting the most out of my talents and abilities.	1	2	3	4	5
6. When I make plans, I could do a better job following through.	1	2	3	4	5
7. When I'm uncertain how a job is to be done, I wait for others to tell me what to do rather than risk making a mistake.	1	2	3	4	5
8. When faced with a tedious or boring task, I become resigned to the situation, going through the motions in hopes that it will soon end.	1	2	3	4	5
9. When I've experienced success, I don't assume it will continue.	1	2	3	4	5
10. I surround myself with people who have different skill sets from my own.	1	2	3	4	5
11. I create learning opportunities for myself.	1	2	3	4	5
12. I stop making progress when I lack structure or goals.	1	2	3	4	5
13. When I'm told no, I seek ways to turn the no into a yes.	1	2	3	4	5
14. When resources appear to be out of reach, I don't hesitate attempting to access them.	1	2	3	4	5

Scoring Your Resource Resilience

Add up the scores from the following questions:

Question 2: _____

Question 4: _____

Question 9: _____

Question 10: _____

Question 11: _____

Question 13: _____

Question 14: _____

COLUMN A TOTAL: _____

Now add up the scores from the following questions.

Question 1: _____

Question 3: _____

Question 5: _____

Question 6: _____

Question 7: _____

Question 8: _____

Question 12: _____

COLUMN B TOTAL: _____

Subtract this number from your Column A total.
(COLUMN A – COLUMN B): _____

Resource Resilience Score
*Finally, to calculate your Resource Resilience score, add 28
to the number above:* _____ + 28 = _____

Rock Bottom Resilience

	Never like me	Seldom like me	About half the time like me	Usually like me	Always like me
1. I have been or am likely to be in a rock-bottom situation in my life.	1	2	3	4	5
2. When a setback occurs, my immediate actions usually make the situation worse.	1	2	3	4	5
3. I don't need things to make sense before I act.	1	2	3	4	5
4. During times I'm really struggling, making small accomplishments seems meaningless.	1	2	3	4	5
5. When going through a difficult time, I cope by finding something to look forward to.	1	2	3	4	5
6. It's easy for me to let go of resentment toward those who've harmed me in some way.	1	2	3	4	5
7. When dealing with adversity, I seek relief through excessive behaviors. These could include, but are not limited to, compulsive shopping, excessive exercise, television watching, video game playing, working, substance abuse, or sexually acting out.	1	2	3	4	5
8. After making a serious mistake, I immediately move on with my life, not dwelling on the error I committed.	1	2	3	4	5
9. When negative things happen, I tend to deny or downplay their reality.	1	2	3	4	5
10. During times of adversity, it's difficult to envision the possibility that better times lay ahead.	1	2	3	4	5
11. When I get angry, I don't vent my emotions.	1	2	3	4	5
12. I have asked "why me?" when enduring a painful event or situation.	1	2	3	4	5
13. When I make a mistake, I tend to procrastinate mending the situation.	1	2	3	4	5
14. I have decided in advance that when someone hurts me, I will choose to forgive him or her.	1	2	3	4	5

Scoring Your Rock Bottom Resilience

Add up the scores from the following questions:

Question 1: _____

Question 3: _____

Question 5: _____

Question 6: _____

Question 8: _____

Question 11: _____

Question 14: _____

COLUMN A TOTAL: _____

Now add up the scores from the following questions.

Question 2: _____

Question 4: _____

Question 7: _____

Question 9: _____

Question 10: _____

Question 12: _____

Question 13: _____

COLUMN B TOTAL: _____

Subtract this number from your Column A total.
(COLUMN A – COLUMN B): _____

Rock Bottom Resilience Score
*Finally, to calculate your Rock Bottom Resilience score, add 28
to the number above:* _____ + 28 = _____

ABOUT RESILIENCE
BREAKTHROUGH TRAINING

Resilience Breakthrough is an innovative corporate training company based on the principles contained in the book *The Resilience Breakthrough: 27 Tools for Turning Adversity into Action*. We specialize in enabling individuals, leaders, teams, and organizations to transform setbacks and challenges into resilience fuel to create increased innovation, opportunity, and change. Visit us at www.resilienceedge.com.

ABOUT WHYTRY

The WhyTry Program uses a multisensory approach to teach resilience to youth of every learning type. Over two million students have been taught with WhyTry in over sixteen thousand schools, making it one of the fastest-growing programs of its kind. WhyTry is implemented in all fifty states and in countries throughout the world, with over three hundred WhyTry training events held each year. WhyTry also recently received the Children and Adults with ADHD National Award. Studies have shown that students are three times more likely to graduate from high school with WhyTry than without it. For more information on the program, visit www.whytry.org.

ABOUT THE AUTHOR

CHRISTIAN MOORE, AUTHOR

Christian is a licensed clinical social worker (LCSW) and founder of the WhyTry Program, a resilience education curriculum for youth.

Coming from a blended family of twelve children, Christian spent most of his childhood years on the streets. In a neighborhood just outside of Washington, DC, he was exposed to a wide array of social problems, which opened his eyes to the many injustices that exist in our world today. These experiences, combined with severe learning disabilities and an inner-city volunteer experience as a youth, all contributed to Christian's eventual decision to become a social worker and help others who struggle with similar challenges. After fighting his way to receiving a master of social work (MSW) and working in education, corrections, and a homeless program, Christian recognized the need for a new approach and created WhyTry.

Thousands of school districts across the United States have had Christian consult on how to increase resilience, lower dropout, improve school climate, prevent bullying, lower the achievement gap, and improve academics through teaching social and emotional education to all students.

Christian lives in the Rocky Mountains with his wife, Wendy, and their two sons, Carson and Cooper.

BRAD ANDERSON, COLLABORATOR

Brad was a cofounder and vice president of the Covey Leadership Center (currently FranklinCovey) and produced *The Seven Habits of Highly Effective People* product line, including the *Seven Habits* course and *Seven Habits* facilitator training used by millions. He is an award-winning producer of films on leadership and resiliency and was director of trainer development at VitalSmarts, creators of *Crucial Conversations.* Brad worked closely with Christian in producing *The Resilience Breakthrough* and is the developer of *The Resilience Breakthrough* curriculum for the workplace. Brad is a proud grandparent.

KRISTIN MCQUIVEY, WRITER

As the lead writer of *The Resilience Breakthrough*, Kristin worked closely with Christian Moore to capture his unique voice and message. For over twenty years, she's been a writer, teacher, and organizational trainer, conducting corporate training throughout the United States and internationally. Kristin is a freelance journalist and a certified trainer of FranklinCovey's *The Seven Habits of Highly Effective People.* When she isn't writing, she is teaching college writing courses and developing course curriculum. Kristin lives in the Rocky Mountains with her husband and three children.

NOTES

Introduction: The Resilience Breakthrough

1 Brené Brown, "Brené Brown: The power of vulnerability," TED video, 20:16, filmed June 2010, posted December 2010, http://www.ted.com/talks/brene_brown_on_vulnerability.html.

2 Carol Dweck, *Mindset: The New Psychology of Success* (New York: Ballantine Books, 2006).

Part I: Core Principles of Resilience

3 Shawn Achor, *The Happiness Advantage: The Seven Principles of Positive Psychology That Fuel Success and Performance at Work* (New York: Random House, 2010).

4 Paul Tough, "What if the Secret to Success Is Failure?," *New York Times*, September 14, 2011.

Part II: Relational Resilience

5 Mark Katz, *On Playing a Poor Hand Well* (New York: WW Norton, 1997).

6 Bill Clegg, *Ninety Days: A Memoir of Recovery* (New York: Little, Brown, 2012).

7 Dave Packard, "Dave Packard's 11 Simple Rules," Hewlett-Packard Development Company, first presented by Dave Packard at HP's second annual management conference in 1958 in Sonoma, California, http://www.hp.com/retiree/history/founders/packard/11rules.html.

8 Michael S. Malone, *Bill & Dave: How Hewlett and Packard Built the World's Greatest Company* (New York: Penguin Group, 2007).

9 Bernard Golden, "David Packard and the HP Way," *CIO*, April 10, 2008, http://advice.cio.com/bernard_golden/david_packard_and_the_hp_way.

10 Robert I. Sutton, "Extraordinary Contempt and Defiance Beyond the Normal Call of Engineering Duty," *Bob Sutton Work Matters*, April 26, 2007, http://bobsutton.typepad.com/my-weblog/2007/04/extraordinary_c.html.

11 Mihaly Csikszentmihalyi, *Finding Flow: The Psychology of Engagement with Everyday Life* (New York: Basic Books, 1997).

12 John M. Gottman, *The Seven Principles for Making Marriage Work: A Practical Guide from the Country's Foremost Relationship Expert* (New York: Three Rivers Press, 1999).

13 Miller McPherson, Lynn Smith-Lovin, and Matthew E. Brashears, "Social Isolation in America: Changes in Core Discussion Networks over Two Decades," *American Sociological Review*, 71 (2006): 353–375.

14 John Rudolf, "Prison Visits Make Inmates Less Likely to Commit Crimes After Release, Study Finds," *HuffingtonPost.com*, December 7, 2011, http://www.huffingtonpost.com/2011/12/07/prison-visits-inmates_n_1135288.html.

15 Kelly McGonigal, "Kelly McGonigal: How to Make Stress Your Friend," TED video, 14:29, filmed June 2013, posted September 2013, http://www.ted.com/talks/kelly_mcgonigal_how_to_make_stress_your_friend.html.

16 Csikszentmihalyi, *Finding Flow*.

17 Pico Iyer, "The Joy of Quiet," *New York Times*, December 29, 2011.

18 Trevor Smith, "2010 Survey on Cell Phone Use While Performing Cardiopulmonary Bypass," presented at the 32nd Annual Seminar of the American Academy of Cardiovascular Perfusion, Reno, NV, January 27–30, 2011.

19 We are indebted to Dr. Gabor Maté for the idea of attunement and proximate separation.

20 Robin Rauzi, "Tapping Into the Power of Mindfulness," *Los Angeles Times*, February 23, 2013.

Part III: Street Resilience

21 Michael Gates Gill, *How Starbucks Saved My Life: A Son of Privilege Learns to Live Like Everyone Else* (New York: Gotham Books, 2007).

22 Ken Robinson, "Ken Robinson: How Schools Kill Creativity," TED video, 19:25, filmed February 2006, posted June 2006, http://www.ted.com/talks/ken_robinson_says_schools_kill_creativity.html.

23 Jeff Stibel, "Why I Hire People Who Fail," *Harvard Business Review*, December 9, 2011.

24 Robert I. Sutton, "Forgive and Remember: How a Good Boss Responds to Mistakes," *Harvard Business Review*, August 19, 2010.

25 Ibid.

26 Robert I. Sutton, *Weird Ideas That Work* (New York: Free Press, 2002).

27 Doris Kearns Goodwin, "Team of Rivals: The Political Genius of Abraham Lincoln," *Historian's on the Record: Podcasts from the Gilder Lehrman Institute*, 52:52, February 28, 2007, at the London School of Economics.

28 "Edgar Mitchell's Strange Voyage," *People*, April 8, 1974, http://www.people.com/people/archive/article/0,,20063934,00.html.

29 Michael Collins, *Carrying the Fire: An Astronaut's Journeys* (New York: Farrar, Strauss and Giroux, 1974).

30 *Eleanor Roosevelt*. Originally broadcast on PBS as a segment of *The American Experience* documentary series, a film by Ambrica Productions, Inc., written and directed by Sue Williams; WGBH-TV, Boston; WGBH Educational Foundation (Arlington, VA: PBS, 2005), DVD.

31 "Do You Know the Story of Gillian Lynne?" blog entry posted on November 16, 2010, www.peakexperienceparenting.com.

32 Specialist People Foundation, http://www.specialistpeople.com.

33 Insoo Kim Berg, "Solution Focused Therapy: The Miracle Question," http://key-hypnosis.com/Self-Help/Set-Your-Goals/Solution -Focused-Therapy-Miracle-Question.php (accessed November 2011).

34 Albert Bandura, "Cultivate Self-Efficacy for Personal and Organizational Effectiveness," in *Handbook of Principles of Organization Behavior*, ed. E.A. Locke (Oxford, UK: Blackwell, 2000), 120–136.

35 David Kelley, "David Kelley: How To Build Your Creative Confidence," TED video, 11:43, filmed March 2012, posted May 2012, http://www .ted.com/talks/david_kelley_how_to_build_your_creative_confidence .html.

36 Joseph LeDoux, "For the Anxious, Avoidance Can Have an Upside," *New York Times*, April 7, 2013.

Part IV: Resource Resilience

37 Stanton Peele, *7 Tools to Beat Addiction* (New York: Three Rivers Press, 2004).

38 Thomas L. Friedman, "Pass the Books. Hold the Oil," *New York Times*, March 10, 2012.

39 Roy Baumeister, Ellen Bratslavsky, Catrin Finkenauer, and Kathleen D. Vohs, "Bad is Stronger Than Good," *Review of General Psychology*, 5, no. 4 (2001): 323–370.

40 Reid Hoffman and Ben Casnocha, *The Start-up of You: Adapt to the Future, Invest in Yourself, and Transform Your Future* (New York: Crown Business, 2012).

41 Ibid.

42 "Lt. Gen. Honore a 'John Wayne Dude.'" *CNN*, September 3, 2005, http://www.cnn.com/2005/US/09/02/honore.profile/.

43 Center for Creative Leadership, "General Honoré: Leading the Response to Katrina," podcast audio, *Leading Effectively* series, http://www.ccl.org/leadership/podcast/transcriptLeadingResponse.aspx.

44 "CNN: Gen. Honore: 'Find this oil and kill it,'" YouTube video, 3:25, posted on June 14, 2010, http://www.youtube.com/watch?v=LeTV021O9Ls.

45 Todd G. Buchholz and Victoria Buchholz, "The Go-Nowhere Generation," *New York Times*, March 10, 2012.

46 David Halberstam, *The Reckoning* (New York: William Morrow, 1986).

47 "403: Nummi," Ira Glass (Host), *This American Life* from WBEZ podcast, 61:35, March 26, 2010, http://www.thisamericanlife.org/radio-archives/episode/403/nummi (accessed April 30, 2012).

48 Hoffman and Casnocha, *The Start-up of You.*

49 Henry Blodget, "How Pandora Survived More Than 300 VC Rejections and Running Out of Money," *Business Insider*, June 15, 2011.

50 Charles D. Hayes, "Autodidactic Hall of Fame: Self-Educated People Who've Made a Difference," Autodidactic Press website, retrieved 2013, http://www.autodidactic.com/profiles/profiles.htm#TOP.

51 "Eric Hoffer," Wikipedia, last modified April 17, 2012, http://en
    .wikipedia.org/wiki/Eric_Hoffer.

52 Sonia Mullally, "No Holds Barred Message to Teens," *Pierce County
    Tribune*, January 7, 2010, http://www.thepiercecountytribune.com/
    page/content.detail/id/501139/No-holds-barred-message-to-teens
    .html?nav=5011

53 Mihaly Csikszentmihalyi, *Flow: The Psychology of Optimal Experience*
    (New York: Harper & Row, 1990).

54 Walter Isaacson, *Steve Jobs* (New York: Simon & Schuster, 2011).

Part V: Rock Bottom Resilience

55 Theodore Rubin, quotes from Inspiration Peak website, http://www
    .inspirationpeak.com/cgi-bin/search.cgi?search=Theodore+Rubin.

56 Gabor Maté, *In the Realm of Hungry Ghosts: Close Encounters with
    Addiction* (Berkeley, CA: North Atlantic Books, 2010).

57 Ibid.

58 Vincent J. Felitti, "The Origins of Addiction: Evidence From the
    Adverse Childhood Experiences Study," (unpublished manuscript,
    February 16, 2004), http://www.acestudy.org/files/OriginsofAddiction
    .pdf.

59 Maté, *In the Realm of Hungry Ghosts.*

60 Mark Katz, *On Playing a Poor Hand Well* (New York: WW Norton,
    1997).

61 Richard G. Tedeschi, *Posttraumatic Growth: Positive Changes in the
    Aftermath of Crisis* (Mahwah, NJ: Lawrence Erlbaum, 1998).

62 Carol Dweck, *Mindset: The New Psychology of Success* (New York:
    Ballantine Books, 2006).

63 Marie Ann Potter, "Getting Out of Hell: A Suicide-Prevention Therapy That Saved My Life," *The Courant*, July 27, 2011.

64 "Marsha Linehan, Radical Acceptance Part 1," on Lisa Dietz's website *DBT Self Help*, 2003–2012, www.dbtsclfhelp.com/html/radical_acceptance_part_1.html (accessed March 2012).

65 *The Twelve Steps Illustrated*, pamphlet, (New York: Alcoholics Anonymous World Services, 1991), www.aa.org.

66 Carol Tavris and Elliot Aronson, *Mistakes Were Made (But Not By Me): Why We Justify Foolish Beliefs, Bad Decisions, and Hurtful Acts* (Orlando, FL: Harcourt, 2007).

67 Sue Shellenbarger, "When the Boss Is a Screamer," *Wall Street Journal*, August 15, 2012.

68 Ibid.

69 Michael McKinney, "The Nature of Small Wins," *Leadership Now*, December 23, 2009, http://www.leadershipnow.com/leadingblog/2009/12/the_nature_of_small_wins.html.

70 Robert I. Sutton, "Hey Boss—Enough with the Big, Hairy Goals," *Harvard Business Review*, June 5, 2010, http://blogs.hbr.org/sutton/2010/06/hey_boss_enough_with_the_big_h.html.

71 Jim Collins, *Good to Great: Why Some Companies Make the Leap . . . and Others Don't* (New York: HarperBusiness, 2001).

72 Robert I. Sutton, "Hey Boss—Enough with the Big, Hairy Goals."

73 Robert I. Sutton, "12 Things Good Bosses Believe," *Harvard Business Review*, May 28, 2010, http://blogs.hbr.org/Sutton/2010/05/12)_things_good_bosses_believe.html.

74 Ibid.

75 George L. Kelling and James Q. Wilson, "Broken Windows: The Police and Neighborhood Safety," *The Atlantic*, March 1, 1982.

76 Aimee Mullins, "Aimee Mullins: The Opportunity of Adversity," TED video, 21:55, filmed October 2009, posted February 2010, http://www .ted.com/talks/aimee_mullins_the_opportunity_of_adversity.html.

77 Ibid.

78 *The Twelve Steps Illustrated*, pamphlet, (New York: Alcoholics Anonymous World Services, 1991), www.aa.org.

79 Frederic Luskin, "The Art and Science of Forgiveness," *Stanford Medicine*, 16, 4 (1999).

80 Roy Baumeister, *Humility, Egotism, Forgiveness, and the Victim Role*, Florida State University, 2002, (research grant funded by the Templeton Foundation [$248,391] #5039), www.forgiving.org/Result _Summaries_2006/Roy_Baumeister.pdf.

81 Mark Katz, interview with Christian Moore, September 2012.

Conclusion

82 Robert Goldman and Robert Papson, *Nike Culture: The Sign of the Swoosh* (London: Sage, 1998).

83 Alva Noe, "Are You Overwhelmed? You Don't Have to Be," *NPR News*, 13.7 *Cosmos and Culture: Commentary on Science Society* blog, March 1, 2013, http://www.npr.org/blogs/13.7/2013/03/01/173216644/ are-you-overwhelmed-you-dont-have-to-be.

84 Rick Hanson, "10 Steps to Forgiving Yourself," *HuffingtonPost.com*, posted on August 31, 2011, http://www.huffingtonpost.com/rick -hanson-phd/forgive-yourself_b_906769.html.

85 Al Rogers, "Amazing Grace: The Story of John Newton," http://www .anointedlinks.com/amazing_grace.html.

86 Robert I. Sutton, *Good Boss, Bad Boss, How to Be the Best . . . And Learn From the Worst* (New York: Hachette, 2010).

INDEX